ADVANCES IN HUMAN RESOURCE MANAGEMENT IN ASIA

Also by Frank-Jürgen Richter

THE EAST ASIAN DEVELOPMENT MODEL

INTANGIBLES IN COMPETITION AND COOPERATION
(edited with Parthasarathi Banerjee)

MAXIMIZING HUMAN INTELLIGENCE DEPLOYMENT IN ASIAN BUSINESS
(edited with John B. Kidd and Xue Li)

Advances in Human Resource Management in Asia

Edited By
John B. Kidd

Xue Li

and

Frank-Jürgen Richter

Published by
PALGRAVE MACMILLAN
Houndmills, Basingstoke, Hampshire RG21 6XS and
175 Fifth Avenue, New York, N. Y. 10010
Companies and representatives throughout the world

PALGRAVE MACMILLAN is the global academic imprint of the Palgrave
Macmillan division of St. Martin's Press, LLC and of Palgrave Macmillan Ltd.
Macmillan® is a registered trademark in the United States, United Kingdom
and other countries. Palgrave is a registered trademark in the European
Union and other countries.

ISBN-13: 978-0-333-94815-6
ISBN-10: 0-333-94815-7

This book is printed on paper suitable for recycling and
made from fully managed and sustained forest sources.

A catalogue record for this book is available from the British Library.

Library of Congress Catalog Card Number: 2001021718

Printed and bound in Great Britain by
Antony Rowe Ltd, Chippenham and Eastbourne

Contents

List of Figures

List of Tables

Notes on the Contributors

Dieter Albrecht was educated in Germany, the Netherlands and the USA. Prior to living and working in China, he was Assistant Professor for Land Use Planning at the Technical University of Berlin (West), where he started research and teaching on problems of developing countries, mainly China, Yemen and Senegal. Since 1984, he has gained extensive management experience in development work through the reform and the opening period of the Chinese society and economy. Based on his intercultural experience, in the beginning often a painful learning by doing, he has traced back his successes and failures in management to a theoretical foundation of intercultural interaction. Together with Chinese colleagues, he established a joint Chinese–German venture, West-East Dragons®, for intercultural training and project management.

Neal Ashkanasy is Professor of Management in the University of Queensland Graduate School of Management. His PhD is in Psychology from the University of Queensland. He is an editorial Board member of the *Academy of Management Journal* and the *Journal of Management*, and currently Programme Chair for the Managerial and Organizational Cognitions Division of the Academy of Management. Dr Ashkanasy's chief research interests are in emotions, culture, leadership, and ethical behaviour, and he has published widely in journals such as *Accounting, Organizations and Society, Organizational Behavior* and *Human Decision Processes*, and the *Journal of Organizational Behavior*. He is the Australian Country Co-Investigator on the multinational GLOBE (Global Leadership and Organizational Behavior Effectiveness) programme, led by Professor Robert J. House. Dr Ashkanasy has travelled widely in Asia, including teaching in the GSM's Singapore programme.

Vinda Chainuvati received her BA in Economics from Thammasat University and her Masters in Business Administration from Chulalongkorn University in Thailand. She also completed an MA in Psychology at Claremont Graduate University, writing her thesis on careers of Thai women managers. Currently she is working toward her PhD in organizational behaviour at Claremont Graduate University. Prior to coming to the United States, she worked as a manager for Procter & Gamble (Thailand), and Berlin Pharmaceutical, and held an internship at Watson Wyatt Consulting. Her research interests include career management, the effects of national culture on organizational behaviour, and women in management.

Brigitte Charles-Pauvers was first educated in management (in a French Business School at Rouen) and she completed her formal education as a social psychologist (Universities of Rouen, and Nantes). Later she became head of the HRM department in the School of Management (Nantes). She has held consultancy posts in major organizations (electricity company, central administration, banks, automotive industry, etc.) and she was in charge of the development of human resource management in an educational organization. She was invited to join the Business Administration Institute as a senior lecturer in 1993, and submitted her PhD in 1996. She is currently director of the French–Chinese International Management Center and is responsible for the French–Chinese International Management MBA. Her research focuses on organizational behaviour related to human resource management topics in a French as well as cross-cultural perspective.

Philippe Debroux has strong European as well as Asian viewpoints. He was educated initially in Brussels University as an economist, and later took an MBA from INSEAD and then an MA in Asian Studies from Sophia University in Japan. Still later he read for a PhD once more at Brussels University. Now, having been Professor of Economics at Hiroshima University for some years, he is Professor of International Management at SOKA university (Tokyo) where he continues research on human resource management and labour organizations in East and South-east Asian countries. He had published widely, both in English and French, as well as in Japanese.

Niti Dubey-Villinger is a researcher who received her PhD in International Business and Management at the University of Cambridge (UK). In addition to graduate studies at the Universities of Chicago and Cambridge, she has lectured at Wolfson College (Cambridge) and worked for a number of companies in Germany (Siemens Public Communications Networks, Audi AG). Her research has focused on international management issues pertaining to cross-border investment strategies of Western multinationals in emerging markets.

Birgit Ensslinger studies Business Administration at the University of Erlangen-Nuremberg, specializing in International Management. She is a research assistant at the Chair of International Management (Prof. Dr B. N. Kumar) and has been reasearch assistant for the project 'German FDI in China' which is also the main topic of her thesis.

Susanne Esslinger studied Management Sciences and Foreign Relations in Erlangen-Nuremberg (Friedrich-Alexander Universität) and Glasgow (Glasgow Business School). Since 1997 she has been working as a research assistant and assistant to the Director at the Department of Business Administration and is a PhD-candidate. At the moment she is preparing for a further degree in Psychogerontology. Her fields of interest in research are Intercultural Management, Health Management and Social Skills.

Alexander Fliaster studied cybernetics and Japanese language in Moscow, Russia, and received his PhD in management at the German Armed Forces University, Munich. He is now an Assistant Professor at the Institute for Human Resource Management and Organization Studies at German Armed Forces University, Munich, where he teaches knowledge and innovation management, as well as human resource management. Fliaster is the author of many articles and book contributions that have appeared in Germany, Japan, Russia, and other countries. He is also a faculty member at the Munich Institute of Foreign Languages and Interpretation.

Cherlyn S. Granrose (Cherry) received her PhD from Rutgers University and has held tenured faculty positions at Temple University School of Management and Claremont Graduate University School of Organizational and Behavioural Sciences. Her current position is Professor of Management and Organizational Behaviour at Berry College, Mt Berry, Georgia. She is an active member of the International Division, and has served on the executive boards of the Gender and Diversity Division and the Careers Division of the Academy of Management. She has been the recipient of Fulbright awards to South Korea, Taiwan, Singapore and the People's Republic of China. Her previous books include *Work–Family Role Choices for Women in Their 20's and 30's*, co-authored with E. A. Kaplan (1996); *Careers of Business Managers in East Asia* (1997); and, co-edited with S. Oskamp, *Cross Cultural Work Groups* (1997). She has written extensively on Asian human resources management and on women's work and family decisions.

Trevor Grigg is Deputy Vice-Chancellor (International & Development) at the University of Queensland. He previously held the position of Pro-Vice-Chancellor (Academic) at the University of Queensland and has held academic positions as Dean of the Faculty of Business at the Queensland University of Technology (1995–7) and at the University of Queensland in the Graduate School of Management, of which he was Head from 1991 to 1994. He is a member of the Institution of Engineers Australia as well as a Fellow of the Australian Institute of Management. He holds several directorships of private and government corporations, but continues to have active research interests. These focus primarily on the management and performance of public utilities and on public infrastructure investment and finance.

John B. Kidd was educated in the UK and worked for several major UK organizations before returning to university scholarship. In the University of Birmingham and now Aston Business School his research focused on the development of IT use in SMEs; the management of projects; and the softer management issues which concern multinational joint ventures. At one time he was looking only at Japanese/European ventures, but now focuses on Asian/European ventures. He has held visiting professorships in several European Universities, and in the China Europe International Business School, Shanghai.

Brij Nino Kumar was formerly Professor and Chair of Business Economics and International Management at the University of Erlangen-Nürnberg, Germany. Previous Chairs were at the Munich and Hamburg Universities. He authored and co-authored over 100 publications (including 10 books) on international management in Germany, USA, UK, Japan and China. Besides his academic career, he was a consultant to several companies and ministries; and he was an active member of the editorial boards of various professional management journals. We (the editors) are sorry to announce that soon after receipt of the manuscripts Professor Kumar died suddenly. His wit and clarity will be missed by many.

Corinna T. de Leon is a psychologist and consultant based in Hong Kong. She received her doctoral degree in social psychology from Sussex University, UK. The research interests of Dr de Leon include cross-cultural management, business negotiations, and gender differentiation in Chinese culture. She has published widely in academic journals such as *Human Resource Management Journal, International Journal of Human Resource Management, Journal of Organizational Behavior*, and *The International Executive*. Her clients in executive development and training include International Orientation Resources, the Hospital Authority of Hong Kong, Nobel Industries, Singapore Airlines, Singapore Institute of Standards and Industrial Research, and National University Hospital of Singapore.

Xue Li was educated in Guangxi, China and was in the first group of five persons to be authorized to tutor the Teaching of English as a Foreign Language (TOEFL), and the Business English (Cambridge) Courses (BEC) – indeed she introduced BEC to China. She gained first-hand knowledge of the issues facing managers who jointly wish to set up ventures in China whilst working as a 'go between' in an Import/Export agency; and also through working as an interpreter for English-speaking firms looking for business in China.

Gary N. McLean graduated from the University of Western Ontario (BA) Teachers College, Columbia University in business education (MA, 1965; Ed.D, 1971), and United Theological Seminary in New Brighton, MN, in 1983 (M.Div.). He is now a professor and coordinator of human resource development and adult education, as well as a professor in business and industry education, in the Department of Work, Community, and Family Education, College of Education and Human Development, University of Minnesota, St Paul. He is a frequent speaker, and has written over 100 journal articles and 20 textbooks. He is immediate past editor for *Human Resource Development Quarterly*, general editor for *Human Resource Development International*, North American editor for the *Journal of Transnational Management Development*, and consulting editor (and previous executive editor) for the *Journal of Education for Business*. He has been an independent consultant, primarily in training, organization development, strategic planning, and quality transformation.

Roger Pyatt was educated in the UK and worked for two major UK industrial and computer organizations, and a USA international, before carrying out research in international industrial marketing and purchasing at the University of Manchester Institute of Science and Technology. Between 1988 and 1998 he taught in Hong Kong, including 1990 to 1998 at The University of Hong Kong School of Business, where he established and directed the Southeast Asian Strategic Network Studies (SASNS) of Mainland China, Thailand and Vietnam. He has been an independent marketing consultant for American, Australian, British, and Hong Kong firms, and currently manages a bio-technology business operating across Asia and in Australasia. Dr Pyatt earned his PhD at the University of Queensland.

Frank-Jürgen Richter is Director for Asia at the World Economic Forum, and has lived, worked and travelled extensively throughout Asia. He has previously held executive management positions with multinational companies, and is a frequent speaker on issues related to Asian economies, international management and global competition.

Jan Selmer is Professor of Management at School of Business, Hong Kong Baptist University, Hong Kong. He received his doctoral degree in business administration from Stockholm University, Sweden. Living and working in Asia for the last decade and a half, his research interest lies in cross-cultural management with a special focus on the Asian region. He has published nine books and numerous journal articles in refereed journals including *International Business Review*, *International Journal of Human Resource*

Management, International Journal of Intercultural Relations, Journal of Business Research, Journal of International Management, Journal of Organizational Behavior, Journal of World Business, and *Management International Review*. His latest book, *International Management in China: Cross-Cultural Issues* was published in 1998 by Routledge, UK. In August 1996, he organized the world-first international academic conference on 'Cross-Cultural Management in China'. Professor Selmer is also an active consultant in cross-cultural training for multinational corporations, such as ABB, Ericsson, Esselte, Motorola, and Singapore Airlines.

Rick Tamaschke is a Reader in the University of Queensland Graduate School of Management. He is a graduate of Monash and Queensland Universities. He is a member of the Australian and New Zealand Academy of Management, the Australian Institute of Management and the Graduate Management Association of Australia, as well as life member and state vice-president of the Economic Society of Australia. Rick specializes in international business, strategy and operations management, Rick has worked in Canada, New Zealand and the United Kingdom. He has also been a frequent visitor to Singapore in connection with the University's MBA programme. He has published extensively, mainly on strategy and policy related subjects, with particular emphasis on Australia's competitiveness on the home and world markets, including Asia, Europe and the CIS. He has frequently addressed professional conferences on these subjects and has acted as a consultant to business and government.

Malcolm Warner is Professor and Fellow at Wolfson College, Cambridge, and at the Judge Institute of Management Studies, University of Cambridge, UK. Formerly he was a Scholar, then later a Research Scholar of Trinity College, Cambridge: he also received his doctorate from that university. He is the author of a number of books on Chinese management and is the Editor-in-Chief of *The International Encyclopedia of Business and Management*.

Verner Worm received his PhD from Copenhagen Business School. He is an Assistant Professor at the Asia Research Center of Copenhagen Business School. His research focuses on Sino-foreign management issues and international human resource management. Dr Worm is the author of the book *Vikings and Mandarins: Sino-Scandinavian Cooperation in Cross-Cultural Settings* which was published by Copenhagen Business School Press in 1997.

1 Affirmation of the Central Role of Human Resource Management in Asia

John B. Kidd, Xue Li and Frank-Jürgen Richter

Not too many years ago, in the evolution of industry and commerce, it was sufficient for the operations managers to employ someone to 'hire and fire' personnel according to the market demands on the operations of the firm. In boom times more workers were hired, and in lean times they were fired. This 'boom and bust' mentality caused much unrest for the lower staff echelons, who worried about holding their jobs, their income and thus their individual life-style arrangements. It was problematic also for the senior management, once they considered the deeper issues; they found their new employees did not understand the working ways of their firm as well as the staff they had recently fired.

Equally problematic though, in Asia, was their managers' intent to have a constant, 'for life' work force. Their human resource managers, in reality these were usually the senior executives, often required loyalty and emotional commitment from their workers. Thus the staff agreed to live in a community in which they would not exploit each other, but rather they would attempt to co-evolve through the sharing of a common purpose, visions and values. The Western expectation is of a constant depletion of the work force each year just like a regular triangle having a broad base (the mass of young, untrained workers), decreasing linearly until there is only one chief executive. Whereas in Japan we would see basically a rectangular shape (the initial cadre being held in employment until there is rapid retirement of the less able after 55 yrs); followed by the typical triangular shape to yield a single, but quite old, senior executive. Their low labour mobility is in stark contrast to firms in the USA, where in recent years the New Economy even increased mobility. Japan has been the focus of much research into its labour ethic since it proclaimed the practice of lifetime employment. This provided a rationale for huge investment in people – such as on-the-job training – since senior managers were confident in their belief that employees could improve their capability and ability, and that an employee would not be lured away by a competitor.

1

Now the post-crisis environment is driving Asian firms to adapt to the globalization of the economy, proactively to adjust employment practices and to reconsider traditional inter-companies relations like the *keiretsu* in Japan, the *chaebol* in Korea, and the Overseas Chinese networks in Southeast Asia. It is now thought that lifetime employment (the Asian model) may have hindered flexible adjustments necessary to absorb changes in demand and to foster competition (Steffensen and Dirks, 1997). We thus see a potential convergence of the Eastern model (looking towards employee retention) and the Western model (once inclined to staff exchanges to create flexibility and cross-fertilisation of knowledge).

More recently, in the West especially, the Human Resources Management (HRM) function has been seen to take up the responsibility of ensuring the general staff carries through the knowledge management initiatives of the chief executives. The HRM staff may do this by ensuring that conversations occur between the middle managers and the workers so they become engaged in organizational learning. Their rationale for these 'conversations' can be demonstrated through training courses that may be in-house, or delivered

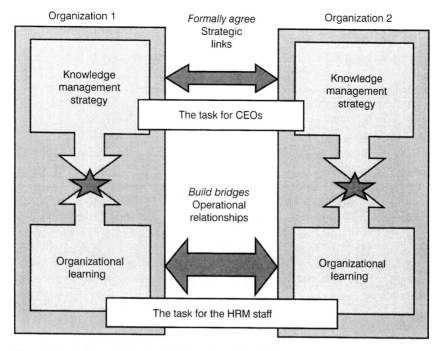

Figure 1.1   Joint work for the HRM staff and the CEOs

by an external consultancy. We illustrate this in Figure 1.1 which links the activities of the chief executives and their workers in 'knowledge management initiatives', firstly in their own firm and then between firms in their alliances. We will return to this figure shortly.

Generally speaking, we have seen considerable shifts in the attitudes of Western managers, production workers and consumers from the 1920s through to the present day as manufacturing systems became more complex. The initial pressure on firms was simply to become more efficient and achieve economies of scale (Chase, 1997): it is not surprising that industry aggregation and 'massification' took place in the early days of 'boom and bust' labour policies. Early in this period Dewey identified two forms of knowledge – *knowing how* (that insight gleaned through methodical work practices) and *knowing about* (suggesting one might reflect on one's situation and consequently learn) (Dewey, 1922). These concepts linked with the tenets of what was then the new Gestalt psychology, in which it was said that complex actions could be pursued through being divided into micro-routines which themselves may be followed without recourse to conscious thought. Thus we find the logical basis of Fordism which channelled human activity into the chores of the production lines (Baumard, 1999).

In post-Fordism, developing through the 1980s in firms in the developed nations, we find great pressure to operate production systems in a 'lean way', so as to achieve continuous improvement, and even operate in teams. In particular, the Japanese and the Swedes had already done this for decades – though they were not alone; there were many 'counter-examples' of American organizations also inclined to teamwork principles from the early nineteenth century onwards, but these tended to be ignored by the mainstream management literature (Grint, 1994). It took a book by Womack, Jones and Roos (1980), *The Machine that Changed the World*, to highlight these issues, to stimulate CEOs and literally to change the world.

Japan, it might be said, 'joined the modern world' through its industrial reconstruction after its devastation in the last World War. We noted previously their inclination towards 'life-time' employment. Yet, broadly speaking, most of the production systems and processes across Asia have lagged far behind the Western models – except where there is a joint venture company, or perhaps in the high technology sectors. Unsurprisingly, in the latter sector, we often find the local management cadre have Western education and have utilized Western production processes. In general, however, there has been a tendency thoughtlessly to import Western management models in the hope that they will work satisfactorily in their new local (Asian) environment – but in most cases this has proved not to be the case. We must understand the local conditions in order to make sense to all concerned – not rush into a programme of change management without concern for the staff involved and without the incorporation of their cultural expectations into the joint programme.

We recognize that with globalization as extensive as it is that firms, in whatever corner of the world, will be not be exempt from being co-joined within a world-wide supply chain. To enable production to take place contracts may be exchanged, but the nature of such an exchange of 'vows', as it were, will vary greatly depending on the location of each firm. In all these situations we may presume that the CEOs in the alliance may have taken time to understand their joint needs; their lower staff will not have that advantage. They are thrown into alliances, needing great support from their HRM staff. This is an issue which is addressed in many chapters of this book, as authors draw upon examples to illustrate how 'cultural literacy' is of fundamental importance in making alliances work in the way in which their CEOs intended. The authors also note that the alliances are not wholly between the advanced and developed nations firms, they also take place within Asia itself as firms venture outside their own borders.

This book is not focused upon Knowledge Management (KM) or Organizational Learning (OL) in a formal sense, but these concepts are the base upon which much of the development of HRM will rest. To return to the illustration of Figure 1.1, we recognize that the staff of all firms must engage in change processes to survive and to progress in the fast-moving modern world. At first such initiatives will begin 'at home' in the native firm. By developing staff who are conversant with change, with OL and with KM, it is more likely they will acquire the interpersonal skills of 'survivors', and they will be happy to co-venture with others abroad. These locally learned skills in KM and OL will be of paramount importance in the assimilation of the management methods and models that are promoted by other managers and their staff in partner firms in Asia. If all the staff concerned can not understand their process models, which undoubtedly will be different between each firm, the alliance will be fragile. It is thus important that the HRM function be well developed in each partner firm so as to be ready for the alliance and thus be able to manage better the issues developing during its merging.

THE DEVELOPMENT OF 'ORGANIZATIONAL' TRUST – BRIDGE BUILDING

Multinational enterprises (MNEs) must decide upon their ethical stances – especially if it is understood that members of another culture would see one or more courses of action as unethical. Using the best decision ('best' according to one of the partners) may backfire – but will operating at the lowest common factor yield sufficiently high returns for the firm? Does the MNE have to accept that the company's home culture should dominate the outpost culture? Or should the outposts be seen as operating within a differentiated network, as Nohria and Eccles (1992) noted? Under their scenario a degree of trust has to be developed between the outposts and the HQ, as each will uphold different norms as being (culturally) proper in its own host region. By adhering too strongly to local norms, managers in a joint venture will inevitably face culture clashes as each grates upon the other, and distrust will become a destructive force. We have suggested the basis for learning, and the heavy task of the HRM staff is to 'build bridges' – firstly within their local firm and then to cross boundaries into their alliance firms. It is not enough to have the CEOs agree on principles, nor is it enough to have initiatives develop from the grass roots, as there has to be a coherent up–down learning pro-gramme. It is here that the HRM role becomes central to the learning process of the alliance – and this is an issue of great concern throughout Asia where man-agers have to grapple with the merging of local customs with those imported from outside.

Ralston *et al.* (1999) have suggested the New Managers (in China, and in general in Asia) are exhibiting 'cross-verging' – insofar as they maintain their Confucian background yet work ever more readily as individualistic entrepreneurs as does the Western manager. They are not converging to or diverging from Western mannerisms in their projected management style. However, they may become known as the Chinese 'Me Generation', fully reflecting the one-time *yuppie* philosophy of the West, and so be referred to as *chuppies*. If this is so, it will herald an attitude which is detrimental to the development of trust in the globalized organization. We recall the popular dislike of the behaviour of the Western yuppies. Now in the West, the yuppie culture has departed to leave a feeling that me-ism does not engage with the organizational strength and the togetherness that is the base of OL and KM.

The West has discovered a need to find 'trust', in contrast to its earlier materialism and its somewhat uncritical acceptance of transactional cost theory, or agency theory, which might lead to academic 'perfection' but in practice holds many loopholes. But, if the East is to turn in its growth phase to me-ism, the average MNE will have great difficulty raising trust as a general concept throughout its organization if it now apparently supports individualistic greed (and thus personal untrustworthiness) at its periphery. Further, many staff in Asia will hold on to their Confucian roots, which in their inclination towards the whole almost abhor individualistic acts – so they in turn will be confused by the *chuppies*. Yet they yearn for the high salaries and the trappings of materialism that would lift them from their perceived life of toil and relative deprivation.

SHARING DATA, INFORMATION AND CONCEPTS

We know from the earliest of times that people around the world have become specialized in certain tasks within their group. For instance, whoever was best at organizing hunting would have known who in the tribe was good at running, or at carving up the proceeds of the hunt. Inevitably those who did the detailed work would, in their turn, have recognized their leader, the person who naturally assumed the mantle of authority. It is not really different today, except that in modern industrial, commercial or military operations the work roles are highly specialized and the authority structure is often detailed and it is certainly precise in the West (Gallagher, 1993; Calori and de Woot, 1994; Brodbeck *et al.*, 2000). It is only in rural areas that we continue to see 'jacks of all trades' – inevitably because they have to survive against the elements of nature in small isolated teams.

However, it is difficult to imagine a world in which information is freely shared – probably because man has kept information to himself for his own survival since time immemorial. The logic of the *prisoner's dilemma* demonstrates that data sharing can often be best overall, for the good of the community; and the pragmatic evidence within the Internet, Intranets, and Extranets now adds to this theoretical justification. Recently, with the advent of Knowledge-based Systems and the deeper study of cognition, we have seen that it continues to be difficult to elicit data, information or knowledge from people. They have a poor perception of the data available to them; 'if only we knew what we know' applies both at the level of the individual and the organization. In addition, they find it just as hard to perceive that which others need, in offering supportive actions, for instance. Following on, while we might agree upon certain mathematical models for data aggregation, we know that different groups of people perceive their complex world differently, and thus contrive their aggregations differently. They even work with systemic models that are quite different, and which reflect their national psychological background. So much so that sometimes these lead to disputes, as the actors in a project wallow in a Babel, not only of language but also of concepts (Kidd and Li, 2000). To an extent the study of history is useful in understanding how we have reached our present position, but 'if you don't know where you want to get to – any road will lead you there' (Chinese proverb).

We must therefore concentrate on developing the skills and knowledge in the HRM field in order to help our enterprises formulate and achieve a cross-cultural, cross-border, multinational focus. This may be partially supported by encouraging 'story telling'. This form of collectivism, of story telling, is in fact a form of organizational learning. For instance, skills from hunting – let us say, tracing and tracking – are passed on by those with these particular skills, and so youngsters in the tribe can learn by hearing these 'war stories' from the past. In a sense, we may describe the tribes' elders as the archetype of HRM managers, since they were responsible for 'organizational learning' as they discharged their duties by setting up campfire meetings. The 'story' is a powerful learning tool, even in modern business society, and should be given due recognition by human resources managers (Bruner, 1990; Thorndyke, 1977). Further, the CEOs have also to be appraised of the need for their staff to 'waste time talking' in order to gain strength collectively. It is here again the HRM functional staff have to build bridges, as illustrated in Figure 1.1, as they interpret the visions of the CEOs for the workers to engage in directed organizational learning, in meaningful discourse.

At one time during the development of Western firms there were many confrontations between the workers' unions and the representatives of management. The go-betweens were the negotiators (often the HRM staff), who had to secure a compromise. Naturally it is much better if the HRM staff can sense unrest before it flares: they say 'anyone can put out a fire, but few can detect the initial smouldering'. And so it is that the HRM function has had to change from a fire-fighting group – mediating between angry people – and become a group of educators. Just as in their early tribal days, they have to explain and to educate concerning the systemic interactions between opposing forces. And they have to be able to model, understand and explain complex systems in an attempt to forecast the effects that result from technological, structural or ecological change. The modern HRM group has to be able to do its job across national boundaries with its targets (remote staff) holding very different mores and personal expectations than those staff operating in their home country. The enterprise model has become complex and ambiguous, and those who work in it have to be better trained to cope with this ambiguity.

We must accept the increasing complexity and global reach of business, commerce and their systems, and we have to do more than simply show willingness to change business systems to meet the needs of the consumers. Processes have to be changed swiftly in the global enterprise structure as niche markets expand, top out and die. In parallel, while these changes are taking place 'on the shop floor', the education of all businesspersons has become more intense. At one time it was sufficient, it seemed, to take a man from the army and put him in command of a firm. As he had been trained in command and control, the business should run like clockwork with the machines and the blue-collar workers complying with schedules. But this is not sufficient to meet the new demands for flexibility. To create flexibility all the staff should understand the corporate mission and how best to achieve it as a dynamic operation. Generally we might see this as a reasonable market-led response to complexity, since the HRM function of firms has the difficult task of maintaining the skills and knowledge levels of all their staff.

In the complex and fast moving workplace we have to ensure all staff are well trained and can integrate with each other – we can illustrate some of these issues in Figure 1.2 and so develop the notions of Dewey (*op cit.*). To begin with we have to train staff in the use of their tools – such as the ubiqui-tous personal computer in the office environment (with its many uses, from computer-aided design to humble word processing), or the machines on the shop-floor (frequently also with their individual computer control systems). These tools should also be the best available, which is not such an easily managed task given their rapid obsolescence in our consumer-driven techno-logically intense environment. Once that training is done we can see our way forward to training the staff in the scheduling aspects of the business – describing why meetings and production schedules have to be met, with all the quality and resource implications of 'getting it right first time'. We would note at this stage how the workload of one firm interacts with the work of other firms in the supply chain – those firms who are producing other items, or who are acting as logistics providers as 'the chain' strives to meet the demands of customers. This figure proposes a clear way to understand the vision of the firm – but our modern firm may be co-located in many places around the globe. Consequently any local vision must encompass global visions, but set appropriately – 'think global, act local' – which is one of the *raisons d'être* for this book.

Finally, a major question in creating communities of practice is how to get staff to be volunteers, rather than conscripts, in offering to share their knowledge. This is the culmination of the learning cycle in Figure 1.2. We suggest that as time progresses the individual, beginning gradually, will 'broaden their shoulders' over time as they learn and, in concert with the others, will be able to contribute responsibly to an organization's capacity to learn. To promote this process the HRM staffs have to be capable, sensi-tive and persistent. They must also have the backing of their senior staff. Throughout this book we will return to this concept of training staff to be volunteers in their organization's learning programme, in being sensitive to the needs of the others, and to their behavioural models.

So far in this chapter we have taken the viewpoints from the process changes taking place in a Western firm – after all, the Industrial Revolution began in the West in the 1800s. But now, with intense globalization, indigenous

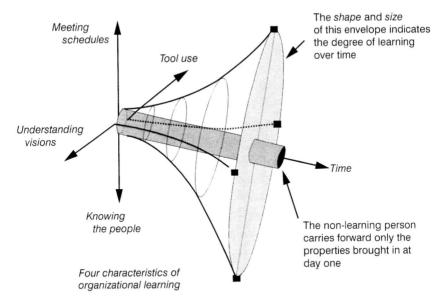

Figure 1.2   Modern HRM imperatives

firms of any nation are free to grow, make alliances and venture abroad. In all cases their HRM managers have to help align their out-reach staff with the firms' vision, especially when some research indicates that strategy has little connection with profitability (Griney and Norburn, 1975), or when it seems 'any old decision' will suffice (Langer, Blank and Chanowitz, 1978). The HRM staffs also have the difficult task of re-aligning the personal visions of their staff when mergers and acquisition take place. It is a difficult task to get 'us and them' to think in the same way, to be able to venture jointly, when once the two firms might have been competitors.

In Figure 1.3 we illustrate the intensity of globalization using two data sets compiled by UNCTAD (the United Nations Conference on Trade and Development). One set of data shows the rapid rise in global annual foreign direct investment (FDI). In detail, in data not presented here (UNCTAD, 1999), we find that much of the FDI is between developed nations, especially between the US and Europe – but that does not rule out firms in the developing world engaging in modest flows across their borders. The second set of data is linked to the first – it shows the rise in the annual value of Mergers and Acquisitions (M&A). Like the FDI figures, there has been a rapid rise in M&A in recent years as firms find they can expand more easily and faster by acquisition rather than by incremental growth. Often this M&A activity is

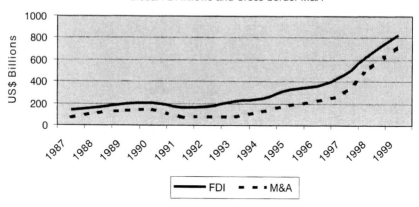

Figure 1.3   Drivers of globalization
Source: UNCTAD press release TDA/INF/2847, 15 April 2000.

across-border as the firms extend their reach into new markets, and as host firms look outside to acquire more know-how and better technology for their mutual benefit. We should note that UNCTAD advises that while the FDI and the M&A data seem to be strongly correlated, the relationship between the two data is not constant over the years. There is considerable structural difference dependent on the general well-being of the global economy.

From these data we might appreciate that firms will frequently be working with others from abroad, and often we will see firms from the US and from Europe engaged in business with firms in Asia. This does not exclude firms from different countries in Asia having alliances outside their own borders – and naturally they will find their new partners are quite different from firms inside their own country, with different psychological needs and drivers.

It is fitting to say we recognize that much of Asian culture has some of its present behaviour settled upon centuries of religious precepts. Perhaps the greatest pervasive influence is Confucianism, though we recognize that in Malaysia, Thailand, and points West this is not fully so. We wish to insert a quote from Dieter Albrecht's Chapter 13 in the present volume, as it is neatly put:

> The fundamental Confucian assumption is that men only exist in relation-ship to another. It is considered natural that these relationships, even those between friends, are hierarchical and based upon seniority. Women are only marginal figures. In fact, the Chinese conceptual framework of behaviour shows its unique delicacy in well-developed power games between friends, colleagues and enemies. The Western concept of the

omnipotence of the individual is alien to the Chinese, who define them-selves in an interactive context. With benevolence as the central concept and 'loving other men' as its starting point, it embraces the spectrum of daily human virtues, valuing childlike love, courteousness, decency, honesty, fidelity, fraternity, truthfulness and the sense of shame – the Eight Rules of civilization. Because Chinese tend to ignore or break rules and regula-tions, Confucius set up a meticulous system of regulations to be followed, the Five Cardinal Relations (*wu lun*) that characterize the male-dominated hierarchical relationship between people. There is no direction for how to treat foreigners. In a self-centered, isolated society, this is not a problem that emerges until China's confrontation with the West during colonial times. The slogan on the entrance to the Confucius' mansion in Qufu, Shandong Province, 'It is nice to receive friends from afar', implies the welcoming of friends and foreigners as well.

Well, it may be nice to see foreigners as friends, but it is not always the case in the modern world. Indeed in our sister book (Kidd, Li and Richter, 2001) we have some discussion upon the missing 6th Rule of Confucius, since he needed to have taught the Chinese how to deal with true outsiders, those who are the expatriates of today.

STRUCTURE OF THE BOOK

We believe one of the strengths of this book is that it does not incline totally to the viewpoints of the Western firm undertaking business in Asia, although the last four chapters specifically discuss the HRM activities of Western firms in China. The first eight chapters illustrate the diversity of HRM activity in Japan, the Republic of Korea, Malaysia, Hong Kong, Thailand and China. They form a good base for the managers of firms in these countries to study the issues their HRM function may have to face when venturing abroad, or when involved in an inward investing venture from another Asian country. It is our intention to offer précis of the chapters that follow to give just a hint of their richness in combination. These will be based strongly on the words the original authors used, with interjections from us, the editors.

Human Resource Management of Asian Firms

Chapters 2 and 3 are located in Japan and in their different ways stress the need to manage knowledge – one through accepting the need for entrepreneurs, and the other directly in reviewing how the Research and Development (R&D) function contributes to knowledge generation.

Philippe Debroux (Chapter 2) writes on 'the Rise of a Venture Business Culture and the Changes in Human Resource Management in Japan' and so comments on the need for the traditional firms and the State to incline to a new mind-set, one which allows for people who 'upset the boat' by following their radical ideas, and who thus need to work in environments that allow such ideas to flourish rather than be forever set in the consensual ways of tradition. He notes how the State and local governments have set up schemes to promote new venture firms and to support the Small and Medium enterprises (SMEs) that in turn support the large well-known firms. There are tier after tier of SMEs who really do not advance their technical and managerial skills, but who rely on the tradition of being a supplier to, say, Toyota, and are proud of this. It is these firms, and those called 'spin-offs' in the West which need the new financial supports to develop their overall skills. And here, we include their HRM function, which might be internal – but in the SME there may be too few staff to support the function – or it may be externally supplied to help a whole sector.

Alexander Fliaster (Chapter 3) focuses on the 'Deployment of Knowledge Workers in Japanese Corporate R&D at the Turning Point Towards the Knowledge-Based Economy'. Here we see that many Japanese firms spend much more still on R&D, notwithstanding the financial crisis in Japan and the earlier one which affected the globe, but East Asia in general. He highlights the dilemma in Japanese firms that for the corporate HR management this means on the one hand that its routines should secure the socialization, mutual loyalty, and emotional commitment to the company in order to foster the cooperation between knowledge workers. But on the other hand, corporate HR management has to foster workforce diversity and, in particular, promote intellectual elites and high performers in order to enable creative problem solutions; even to promote staff mobility between firms. It is not an easy task to attempt 'revolt' while maintaining a semblance of stability to act as a refuge in the stormy times of change.

There is a change of country in the next chapter as we re-focus on a highly industrialized nation, Korea, which has, like Japan, several difficult structural adjustments to make.

Gary N. McLean (Chapter 4) looks to the 'Human Resource Development and Human Resource Management in the Chaebols of South Korea in Response to a National Economic Crisis'. He notes, as do other authors, that this government has not yet established its own definition for HRM. In part it is made quite difficult as large numbers of Koreans have studied in the US, and there is considerable influence of the US directly in Korea, and so the definitions of HRM have been largely imported without any attempt to indigenize the definitions. These interact, for instance, within Korean labour laws, and there are many cultural differences that impact upon specific interventions. He says, as did Debroux earlier, that the education and training programmes of universities had to change. The recruitment modes of the Chaebol also changed to take more interns for direct placement in jobs, rather than put them into in-house indoctrination programmes while the firm considered which position to place them in.

In contrast to the busy Japanese and Korean scenes depicted above, the following three chapters focus on the needs of firms in Eastern and South-East Asia as they cope with more industrialization.

Roger Pyatt, Neal M. Ashkanasy, Rick Tamaschke and Trevor Grigg (Chapter 5) write on their research into the 'Transitions and Tradition in Chinese Family Businesses: Evidence from Hong Kong and Thailand'. Their research focuses upon the 'Chinese' who are working in two regions – but outside the traditional mainland China. One group resides within that crescent of countries bordering the South China Sea (*Nanyang*). Mostly these are the economies that form the ASEAN zone. The China Coast group includes those in the predominantly Chinese communities of Hong Kong, Macau and Taiwan (now, of course, we find only Taiwan as separate from the Beijing government rule). The resulting organizational forms are distinctly different from Western companies, or even other Asian organizations such as the Japanese *keiretsu* or the Korean *chaebol* which were discussed in Chapters 2 to 4. They describe the nature of *quan-xi* (Cantonese: connections; or *guanxi* in Mandarin) organizations and the nature of their 'opaqueness', looking at the ways in which the Chinese Family Business has developed in these two regions. They conclude, in part, that knowing the underlying values can minimize intercultural conflicts and knowing the underlying 'brainstyle' can minimize interpersonal conflicts. (Note the link with the last chapter in the book by Dieter Albrecht.) Both aspects are basic approaches to family, work and relationship and have to be recognized when making decisions, and so have a common denominator. They require the willingness of a person to get more aware of himself or herself. Moreover, successful intercultural management is not a one-time-event, it is a process of constant self-examination if true understanding and acceptance of the other cultural or corporate identity is the goal.

Niti Dubey-Villinger (Chapter 6) looks directly at firms in Thailand and their business world in 'Thai Business Culture: Hierarchy and Groups, Initiative and Motivation'. Immediately we find that Thai management and business culture is unique in certain respects. It retains elements of other Asian cultural practices. On one hand, there is the noted Thai propensity for *sanuk* (literally, 'fun') or the carefree attitude that characterizes *mai pen rai* ('never mind/don't worry'). On the other hand, certain elements of Thai culture are similar to those observed in other Asian traditions. There is group orientation, the emphasis on hierarchy and personal connections or networks that have also been attributed to East Asian societies (Japan, China, for example) and, in particular, the Confucian background. From these basic grounds we learn that Thai management or business culture presents specific characteristics which might be called uniquely Thai, and stem particularly from their culture. The most significant observations are connected with hierarchy and group orientation through harmonious relationships; and there is a very strong need to gently build up trust. In this we see the HRM function having to educate carefully the 'fast, abrupt, aggressive' developed world manager to be less so; and to educate the Thai manager to be less disturbed at these incoming traits in the foreign managers – to be more able to 'stand-up for themselves, and to speak out'. Appropriate behaviour has to be learned.

Vinda Chainuvati and Cherlyn S. Granrose (Chapter 7), following on, express how Thai managers may be better educated, which is revealed in their chapter on 'Career Planning and Development of Managers in Thailand'. They discuss a study that was carried out in Thailand in 1991 – accepting this was before the Asian economic crises in which Thailand was particularly hard hit. Nevertheless their study gives good insights into the education needs of a developing nation, and they offer concluding remarks on the present-day situation. At the time of their study, rapid economic growth created many employment opportunities that could not be filled by the number of available Thai managers. Many multinational companies wanted to assign expatriate managers from their home offices to Thailand in order to help alleviate the managerial shortage. However, the control on immigration through The Alien Work Permit Act limited the number of expatriate managers in Thailand which is a simple way for governments to protect jobs for Thai managers. In times of economic hardship, such as the last years of the 1990s, it is still a valid method for protecting jobs. They found generally in Thai firms the concept of career management and planning was not fully developed. But in concluding they say, 'In sum, in the face of the new economic and environmental situation, it can be anticipated that the careers of managers in Thailand will have to make some changes'. Senior (expatriate) managers can expect that their managerial employees 'will continue to value good interpersonal relationships, and being able to take care of their families'. They can expect that Thai managers are willing to work hard and would like further education to achieve goals if the firm can demonstrate a connection between this hard work and personal long-term career objectives. In other words, we see some echo with the previous paper in which the Thais are seen as a fun-loving people who can only perceive that a modicum of hard work is needed to maintain their personal family arrangements. The work-rate of 'hard driving' expatriates seems not to be welcome.

In her second chapter, Niti Dubey-Villinger (Chapter 8) looks to current training needs in 'Training in Thailand: Current Trends and Cases from the Service Industries'. The chapter begins with a discussion of the state of training in Thailand using government initiatives and training companies as examples, giving an overview of the types of training employed and methods utilized, with implications for the future. Given Thailand's strong tourism orientation, the chapter has as one main focus, training in the hospitality sector. Training and development is viewed as effective when based on more interactive training approaches, possibly involving on-the-job training. Thus continual training, especially in keeping with trends in the sectors concerned, was deemed necessary and valuable for the development of staff and the maintenance of international standards. Culturally rooted behaviours were identified by some managers, especially in cross-border organizations, as playing a role in developing the topics and strategies for training and its possible outcomes.

Malcolm Warner (Chapter 9), in his chapter 'The Future of China's Human Resource Management in its Asia Pacific Context: A Critical Perspective', provides a direct link to the ensuing China focus whilst looking broadly at the region's policies for HRM. He notes briefly that after the 'Liberation' in 1949 when the Chinese Communist Party took power, state-owned enterprises (SOEs) dominated Chinese industrial production and its HR over a period ranging from the early 1950s to the late 1980s. Such work-units (*danwei*), as they were called, embodied the so-called 'iron rice-bowl' (*tie fan wan*) which ensured 'jobs for life' and 'cradle to grave' welfare for many urban industrial SOE workers. Now the situation has changed greatly throughout China, where many firms and collectives have an HRM system in a sense more comparable with Western or other Asian ones now being embedded in a more market-driven framework. He suggests also, for the SOEs, that there may be an evolution of people-management from personnel administration (*renshi guanli*) as typical of most SOEs, to human resource management (*renshi ziyuan guanli*) as seen in the leading-edge joint ventures – though he suggests caution in being too optimistic. In his wider review he concludes that if indeed there is a common direction in which industrial relations or HRM systems in Asia Pacific, including the Chinese, are moving, *it is most likely to be towards adaptation to business restructuring, deregulation, and liberalization vis-à-vis the challenges of globalization.* Down-sizing of the workforce is now a common experience in all Asia Pacific economies so their policies have a similarity; but all countries are not moving at the same pace – there is much variation.

Human Resource Management of Western Firms in China

Having had an opportunity to review the HRM policies adopted in a broad
range of enterprises, sectors and countries in South East Asia we now move
on to consider China directly. Having seen in Chapter 9 a comparison of the
changes in China with respect to the Asian-Pacific nations in general, we wish
to see how Western managers cope with these changes.

In Part II, Brij N. Kumar, Birgit Ensslinger and Susanne Esslinger (Chapter 10) write upon 'Cross-Cultural Human Resource Strategies in China and
India' so drawing us into a comparison of China and India through the eyes
of the German manager. They state that staffing key positions around the
globe in foreign subsidiaries with the right people at the right time is perhaps
a challenge greater than any other managerial job, and the strategic role of
cross-cultural human intelligence deployment must be recognized. In
common with Chainuvati and Granrose in Chapter 7, they report on their
research, which indicates that as in most Asian countries, the managers'
nationalities become a dominating factor within the legal and cultural frame of
the host-country, which usually supports assignment of local nationals. On
the other hand, to the extent that Asian subsidiaries also become a part of
global networks, *a priori* favouring of local managers becomes counter-
productive. Their findings show that even though the market-based prospects in China are stronger than in India, deployment of German expatriates
in the former is more intensive. They find local Chinese staff are less used to
the overseas marketing methods, whereas India has a long tradition in multinational companies (MNCs) operations. On the other hand the German
operations in India have a stronger resource-based orientation so have a
higher local executive deployment than in China. German MNCs apparently
find it (still) difficult to leave management in the hands of Chinese managers
which often must be recruited from the staff of the acquired state-owned
enterprises, so they conclude that the higher use of German expatriates in
China than in India is basically due to the lesser experience and qualification
of Chinese local personnel in staffing key positions in the respective host-
country subsidiaries. Yet in India, the problem is not so much of the qualifications of local staff, but rather the difficulty of building up reliable and trustful
relationships with the Indian partners and subsidiaries in order to run local
operations without numerous expatriate assignments. We see herein the
need for subtle and sensitive (global) HRM policies – how they handle three
sets of nationalities, the Germans, the Indians and the Chinese when they
look to similar problem identification and solution.

Verner Worm, Jan Selmer and Corinna T. de Leon (Chapter 11) discuss
the 'Human Resource Development for Localization: European Multi-

national Corporations in China'. Under the planned economic system of pre-1978 China, the labour market was abandoned because it was considered a capitalist phenomenon. It was the belief then that in the state-operated enterprises (SOE), there was no need for a 'manager' in the Western sense of someone who has the ability to take initiative in overseeing operations. In a planned economy, the managerial role was confined to executing orders given by the government bureau above the firm, reducing it to a mere production unit. Consequently, by the time European Multinational Corporations (EMNCs) began to enter China, the non-existence of a labour market and lack of need for managerial qualifications meant that managerial skills were absent among Chinese staff. We believe there is still a great need for the development and deployment of the concepts of HRM in China, despite the investments leading to the high growth rate over the last 20 years, which is partly explained by China's great success in attracting foreign direct investments (FDIs). By the end of 1998, the PRC government had approved more than 300,000 foreign invested enterprises (FIEs), of which half operate with actually utilized FDI in excess of US$ 260 billion. However, management training did not exist until 1980, and the majority of cadres and professors at that time remained sceptical to applicability of Western management knowledge to China. Consequently, any EMNCs human resource development (HRD) of Chinese managers had to start from the basic foundations, to enable the *gradual* replacement of positions currently held by the expensive expatriates. The authors consider a number of case studies to illustrate these and other issues, concluding in part that in most EMNCs, interdepartmental communication is weak and difficult to implement, since the Chinese are comfortable with hierarchical communication. On the one hand, expatriates should be trained in understanding indirect modes of communication. On the other hand, the Chinese should be trained in communicating more explicitly (which is indeed similar to findings in other nations and stated elsewhere in this book). Thus, they continue, in order to enhance management localization and thereby reduce the number of expensive expatriates, HRD should be a critical business issue that is completely integrated with other objectives. HRD plans should coincide with the business development plans in China, in order to facilitate the successful transfer of knowledge from expatriates to locals. And, finally, relevant and comprehensive information on the functioning of the Chinese market and its development is crucial for any localization programme. Since the market economy in China is undeveloped, most EMNCs are not able to make even rough estimates of their China business for the next five years. Nonetheless, in the new millennium, more mid-term or, when possible, long-term strategic business planning has to be applied in China operations, so as to secure long-term success in the midst of tremendous changes.

Brigitte Charles-Pauvers (Chapter 12) looks in detail at the 'Management of Human Resources in JVs in China', using a research framework to measure organizational commitment in French/Chinese joint ventures (JVs) and SOEs and to make comment on the use of these instruments in cross-cultural situations. Generally speaking, very little research has been carried out on the concept of commitment in an international perspective. The validation of measurement scales, in a different context from the original one (essentially from North America), is further complicated by the fact that the cross-cultural aspects to be taken into account concern two well-apart cultures: Asian and Western. Moreover, most management concepts and work-related attitudes and behaviours have been tested mainly in Western countries, especially in North America. Yet, the cultural differences between North American, European, and, to a larger extent, Asian contexts have to be taken into account, to avoid the parochial dinosaur. (See also a chapter by Bird and Osland in Kidd, Li and Richter, 2001, taking into account just this point from a US perspective.) Starting from the studies of Allen and Meyer (who questioned the nature of organizational commitment), Charles-Pauvers notes that such commitment often encompasses an exchange relationship in which individuals attach themselves to the organization in return for certain rewards or payments from the organization. Her results concern the Chinese context and highlight their strong inclination to organizational commitment, which is related to the perceived fairness of the leader. But some limits need to be underlined – the samples are not fully representative of the country studied (given China is huge) – and, as the data were collected in a definite region, the results need to be confirmed by further studies to ensure generalisability. Nevertheless, this research is a first attempt to use Allen and Meyer's model, and it finds there was good agreement; and her results confirm other Sino-HRM studies. There are clear indicators for the HRM function in both the joint ventures and the SOEs who wish to work together, one of which is that we cannot expect the Western model to be imposed on the Chinese situation, since the Western model, in general, tolerates job-hopping by individuals, whereas in China this is still unwelcome. Yet we are reminded of our early chapters where both Debroux and Fliaster note the changes needed in Japan which would support personnel mobility.

Dieter Albrecht (Chapter 13) concludes this book with a notion of how the Western firm and the Asian firm can jointly learn to work better together. In 'Culture and *BrainStyles*®™: New Alternatives for Human Resource Strategies to Develop Chinese–Western Cooperation' the author begins with strong statements. He notes that many Western managers think that their newly arrived, highly qualified co-workers will 'muddle through' to find their way in the new country. Thus half of the assignments of American companies in China fail because these so-called foreign experts and the business people are unprepared for their job abroad. The situation on the Chinese side is similar. It is said there is an 'inadequacy' of Chinese managers – this is changing and their entrepreneurial spirit is being fostered. Nonetheless, future conflicts with them seem inevitable, as there is an expectation for cooperation with foreigners who do not understand and accept the cultural differences. In this chapter the author compares two approaches for understanding behaviour. First, he elaborates on the cultural environment in China, *the mental software*, as Hofstede (1984) expressed it. Then, the author introduces a system for describing their *mental hardware*, or their *brainstyles*. He says that knowing how the genetic hardware creates four different *brainstyles* is helpful for the formulation of a successful human resource strategy that can take advantage of cultural or corporate conditions. Thus a process of self-examination can minimize intercultural conflicts by knowing the underlying values; knowing the underlying *brainstyle* can minimize interpersonal conflicts. Both types of knowing are basic approaches to family, work and relationships that have to be recognized when making decisions. This author advocates awareness training and the development of communication skills that can bring clarity and reduce (unrealistic) mutual expectations. These aspects will allow each to deal with another in an intercultural and corporate environment more productively and harmoniously.

We hope through reading these authors' scholarship and practical advice, you, the reader, will have been made more aware of how we have to change our approach to the management of our human resources when looking to send managers into a new country. Often these expatriates will be Western managers going to Asia, yet more and more frequently we will see inter-Asian joint ventures (indeed there are very many Japanese/Chinese joint ventures already). Soon we will see more Chinese managers coming to the West, bringing with them specific skills and knowledge, and setting up their own joint ventures.

This book will help all managers involved in the process of exchanging 'sticky' knowledge, be this about the psychology of how to develop relationships, or maybe precise knowledge of a technical nature. What is important to recognize is that we have to be volunteers in the process of organizational learning. If we feel we are conscripts we will not be willing to share our personal knowledge with others – as they may gain some advantage over us. Clearly throughout the book our authors have been at pains to explain how we have to take care to understand the others around us. If we do that, we are sure that our ventures will be more rich and harmonious.

References

Baumard, P. (1999) *Tacit Knowledge in Organizations* (London: Sage).
Brodbeck, F. C. and 44 co-authors (2000) 'Cultural variation of leadership prototypes across 22 European countries', *Journal of Occupational and Organizational Psychology*, 73, pp. 1–29.
Bruner, J. (1990) *Acts of Meaning* (Cambridge, MA: Harvard University Press).
Calori, R. and de Woot, P. (1994) *A European Management Model: beyond diversity* (New York: Prentice Hall).
Chase, R. L. (1997) 'Effectively using Intranets for Knowledge Management', *International Journal of Business Transformations*, 1(1), pp. 30–40.
Dewey, J. (1922) *Human Conduct and Nature: An introduction to Social Psychology* (London: George Allen and Unwin).
Gallagher, W. (1993) *The Power of Place* (New York: Poseidon Press).
Griney, P. H. and Norburn, D. (1975) 'Planning for Existing Markets: perceptions of executives and financial performance', *Journal of the Royal Statistical Society, Series A*, 138, pp. 336–72.
Grint, K. (1994) 'Reengineering history: social resonances and business process reengineering', *Organization*, 1(1), pp. 179–201.
Hamabata, M. M. (1990) *Crested Kimono: Power and love in the Japanese business firm* (Ithica, NU: Cornell Press).
Hofstede, G. (1984) *Culture's Consequences: International Differences in Work Related Values* (Beverly Hills, CA: Sage).
Kidd, J. B. and Li, X. (2000) Worse than the Tower of Babel – the Opacity of the Others' Concepts: a note upon Oriental and Occidental Paradigms, presentation to the INROP IV conference *Paradoxes of Project Collaboration in the Global Economy: Interdependence, Complexity and Ambiguity*, Sydney, January 10–12th, published in CD-ROM proceedings by University of Technology, Sydney.
Kidd, J. B., Li, X. and Richter F.-J. (2001) *Maximising Human Intelligence Deployment in Asian Business: The Sixth Generation Project* (London and New York: Palgrave).
Langer, E., Blank, A. and Chanowitz, B. (1978) 'The mindlessness of ostensibly thoughtful action: the role of "placebic" information in interpersonal interaction', *Journal of Personality and Social Psychology*, 36, pp. 635–42.
Nohria, N. and Eccles, R. G. (1992) Face-to-face: Making networked organizations work, In Nohria, N. and Eccles, R. G. (eds) *Networks and Organizations: Structure, form and action* (Boston, MA: Harvard Business School Press) pp. 288–308.
Ralston, D. A., Eggri, C. P., Stewart, S., Terpstra, R. H. and Kiacheng, Y. (1999) 'Doing Business in the 21st Century with the New Generation of Chinese Managers: a study of generational shifts in work values in Asia', *Journal of International Business Studies*, 30(2), pp. 415–28.
Steffensen, S. K. and Dirks, D. (1997) 'Between Efficiency and Effectiveness: technological change, restructuring, and human resource management in Japanese firms', presentation to the 14th Euro-Asia Management Studies Association Conference, October, Metz, France.
Stock, G. N., Greis, N. P. and Kasunda, J. D. (1999) 'Logistics, Strategy and Structure: A conceptual framework', *International Journal of Physical Distribution and Logistics*, 29, pp. 224–39.
Thorndyke, P. (1977). 'Cognitive structures in comprehension and memory of narrative discourse', *Cognitive Psychology*, 9, pp. 77–110.

UNCTAD (1999) *Global Investment Report*, Geneva, UNCTAD.

Womack, J. P., Jones, D. and Roos, D. (1980) *The Machine That Changed the World*, Based on the Massachusetts Institute of Technology [5-Million-Dollar, 5-Year Study] 'On the Future of the Automobile' (Boston, MA: MIT Press).

Part I
Human Resource Management of Asian Firms

2 The Rise of a Venture Business Culture and the Changes in Human Resource Management in Japan

Philippe Debroux

INTRODUCTION

Japan is now reconsidering the basis of its economic and management system. The necessity of developing competitive advantages in new industries has been identified but a crucial question is how it will affect the way that industry has organized itself to maximize quality, efficiency and flexibility. Despite a number of entrepreneurial success stories, the Japanese economy has been largely controlled and driven by large established companies during the postwar period. It is said that an entrepreneurial culture was not so necessary because a group-based industrial organization could generate about the same dynamism and outcome. New blood was deemed necessary but merely to complement the activities of established interests. This is shown by the extremely low mobility of firms in many industries, compared to the USA, during the last forty years (Ostrom, 1999). The success of Japanese industry until the end of the 1980s may have vindicated that opinion. Nevertheless, the structural low growth period of the 1990s indicates a need for change in that respect. Both the dynamism coming from existing small businesses and the development of a venture-type business culture may be key factors in the renewal of Japanese economy to put it back on a sustainable growth path.

Public authorities are encouraging existing small businesses to shift towards higher value added products and services through a number of support programmes. Many of them are already adapting to the globalization of the economy, the changes in the labour market and a reconsideration of traditional inter-companies relations. The development is observed of internal and external venture businesses and organized entrepreneurship. Vertical and horizontal inter-firm relations transform the supply base structures through strategic outsourcing. Relations often transcend conventional modes of inter-firm coordination structures and lead to the creation of networks of competency. They regroup those willing to cooperate extensively to develop technologies, share information technology resources and commercialize common original products, specialized sophisticated know-how and patents. These developments are bound to bring a new dynamism to the Japanese economy but public authorities believe that new businesses must also be created in much larger numbers than before. Despite remaining difficulties, the idea of forming start-ups is more readily accepted by the population. While many salaried people are struggling to find their marks in a new management system, a growing number of young graduates and mid-career executives, men and women, are considering more seriously than before the creation of their own company. Their initiatives are supported directly through public financing and consulting programmes, encouragement given to the collaboration between companies, the central and local authorities and the academic world, and indirectly through financial liberalization and other regulatory changes. The evolution of the labour market induced by changes in management practices and demographic trends also push the authorities to accelerate the reform of the educational system. At national and regional levels, examples flourish of collaboration between universities, business and administration. Public national universities have been given more autonomy to optimize their technical and human resources. A change of their status is in the offing that should allow a commercialization of their research expertise and prepare the ground for the formation of spin-off companies. Measures are taken to adopt new curricula at all levels of the educational system in order to foster creativity. The students' selection process by universities is reconsidered to make it less exclusively driven by entrance examination based on rote learning. New programmes are launched to upgrade the qualifications of salaried people and make them more self-reliant in a labour market where the long-term job guarantee in one company is disappearing. Courses specifically devised to respond to the growing demand for specific expertise by would-be entrepreneurs open in a growing number of universities.

SOCIO-ECONOMIC CONSTRAINTS AND THE NEED FOR REFORM

Evolution of the Public Policy *vis-à-vis* Small Companies

Japan suffers from acute production over-capacity in a number of industries and services while many niche markets remain under-exploited or neglected. This indicates that the weak domestic demand may be partly caused by a lack of adequate response to the needs of consumers. It makes the ascent of entrepreneurial firms all the more necessary to challenge established large companies, force them out of their protected markets and provide a new dynamism to the economy. Public authorities show a growing concern over the declining number of small and middle size enterprises (SME). As defined by the Small and Medium-Size Enterprise Basic Law of 1963, a small and medium-sized enterprise in the manufacturing sector is a firm with 300 or fewer employees or with a capitalization of 100 million yen or less. It is true that quite a number of traditionally dependent subcontractors are transforming themselves into more independent entrepreneur-type firms, diversifying their partners while maintaining the stable relationship with their main customer (*Chusho Kigyo Hakusho*, 1999). But a myriad other small firms are unable to remain competitive on open markets. They have little managerial expertise and financial resources, limited information about overseas markets, and a lack of firm-specific assets. Either they will disappear or they will barely survive in competing on price on low value added products' markets. Japanese policy-makers are concerned because a rapid decline of small businesses means less overall economic dynamism. Indirectly, the consequence will be that, in a period of rising unemployment, they may not be able to offset the job losses in large firms. They will not play the role of second labour market for the retrenched mid-career employees and of absorbing the new entrants on the labour market (Somucho, 1998). Establishments with less than 100 people employ two-thirds of all workers. Since mid-1993, smaller firms (especially those with 5 to 29 employees) have reported steady declines in employment as separations have dominated the picture (Japan Economic Institute, 20 November 1998). That is why the revival of SME is considered as indispensable to putting the economy back on track.

Reflecting the awareness of a need for an upgrading of their technological and managerial capabilities, policies were devised in the 1990s. They have incorporated a wide range of components such as special financing for investment in equipment that will assist in shifting to new product lines, tax write-offs for such equipment, advisory services and other services for companies wishing to invest overseas (*Chusho Kigyo Hakusho*, 1994). In many respects, although useful, the programmes have continued to be driven by the obsession of Japanese authorities to avoid any hard landing causing a surge in unemployment and regional growth unbalance. Of course, a large number of bankruptcies of SME per year had always been expected and employment is naturally more mobile than in large concerns. Nevertheless, much akin to the financial-type convoy system, even very weak players had to be supported somehow to stay on the market if possible. Such concern largely reflected the highly political sensitivity *vis-à-vis* changes in a number of industries close to the ruling party. The Liberal Democratic Party's (LDP) leading money contributors continue to be construction companies. So, it is not surprising that they were and still are the principal beneficiaries of LDP-led governments' pump-priming of public works projects. Times are changing, though. Expensive subsidy programmes and government-guaranteed lending have both an economic and a political cost. Such expenses are unsustainable and growth of the public debt obliges any government to be cautious in this respect. It is not possible to help all struggling small businesses, and programmes are more focused on those that can contribute to the revitalization of the Japanese economy.

The new programmes, although still somewhat tilted as usual towards well voting industries and regions, show a departure from the traditional system. Measures are introduced to control the use of public financing and to increase the accountability of the firms. For the first time in 36 years, the government worked to revise the Minor Enterprise Basic Law and other existing measures that have formed the basis of the nation's policy on SME. The latest law aimed at revitalizing SME took off in 1999. The main feature of the new support scheme is its numerical target showing the willingness of the authorities to control the use of the funds. A company receiving support under the scheme must draw up a plan to increase its value added by at least 3 per cent a year for three to five years through the development of innovative products and services and the introduction of new production methods and management styles. Recipient firms are required to achieve their respective targets (*Chusho Kigyo Hakusho*, 2000). The numerical target generated fierce debate at hearings on the scheme held by the Ministry of Foreign Trade and Industry's (MITI) Small and Medium Enterprise Agency. Conflicts of interest were often hidden under the blanket-type support programmes, but now that more differentiated ones are put into place, they come to the fore. For instance, food and timber industry representatives were demanding that the figure be lowered, while ambitious managers in other industries were calling for a higher target (*The Daily Yomiuri*, 14 July 1999).

Quite a number of existing small companies are indeed successful and they may partly compensate for the growing number of those unable to keep track with the market changes. They will take advantage of the new public support programmes while managing the restructuring process on their own. However, it will be insufficient in terms of employment and revitalization of the economy to rely only on them. The number of small-businesses bankruptcies is rising again following the phasing-out of the loan-guarantee programme. It was boosted in the autumn of 1998 because failures were reaching disturbing levels and, immediately, the rate of bankruptcy decreased. However, the programme ran out of money one year later and, since then, about 3,000 firms that had received government-backed bank loans have gone under (Japan Economic Institute, 9 June 2000). The recent rise in bankruptcies is as spectacular as the earlier decline, showing clearly that the underlying problems of Japan's small businesses have not yet been resolved. Too many companies are still operating with excessive costs, very high debt burdens and small or no profit. The expansion for one year of the loan-guarantee programme merely postponed the day of reckoning. The government paid for it but it is obviously not a sustainable situation. It explains the recent shift in emphasis from the role of rescuing and encouraging existing companies to the nurturing of start-ups.

BUILDING BETTER LINKS BETWEEN ACADEMIA AND BUSINESS

Reform in the Educational System

Programmes to support existing businesses and start-ups, the birth of a venture capital industry and new capital markets focusing on venture businesses, and the introduction of management tools such as stock options will remain useless if there are no would-be entrepreneurs around. The average age of new Japanese entrepreneurs has risen over time. In the mid-1960s, about seven years' experience as an employee was the standard norm and more than 60 per cent of entrepreneurs created their companies in their twenties or thirties. This compares with an average of 35 to 40 years old nowadays. The rise can be partly explained by higher financial entry barriers as capital requirements grew due to the increase in land prices and the cost of high technology equipment (Altbach, 1997). However, another reason of the shortage of would-be entrepreneurs is to be found in the inadequacies of the educational system. Changing economic conditions force large firms to restructure, eroding rapidly the guarantee of lifetime employment. There is a growing mismatch between the labour market and the needs of established companies and start-ups. This leads to a slow fading away of institutional credentialism, the hallmark of the Japanese educational system. Of course, firms' reliance on new graduates is likely to continue, albeit with a growing weight of mid-career recruitment. The external labour market is expanding but it is still far away from covering all the companies' needs. Large companies will continue to recruit in elite schools those who will be groomed to become senior managers. In the case of natural science graduates, especially, recruitment through professors in a limited number of specific universities is likely to remain the norm at the postgraduate level. The informal contract with certain universities minimizes the risk and subsequent monitoring cost. Firms can reasonably believe that they will not be recommended candidates who do not have the characteristics they are expecting. So, both sides have no reason to damage a long-term new graduates demand/supply relationship if there is no urgent need for change (Debroux, 1997). However, the elite was always very small and large companies are taking advantage of the crisis to make it even smaller and more exclusive. The number of employees who, without belonging to the elite, were recruited as new graduates in specific universities and enjoyed the benefit of long-term job guarantees with a career of generalists is shrinking rapidly. For the vast majority of those who will be recruited from now on, companies are likely to give less importance to the educational credential.

The change in career attitudes of students and young employees is induced by such reform of management practices and the indecisive course of the Japanese economy. Getting into the 'right' university becomes a less important factor in terms of career choices, and making a career in a large firm will not necessarily be considered as the best option by new graduates. For young graduates it becomes critical to develop specialized, marketable skills at school and in the earlier stages of the career. At the same time, it may be that it is no longer so popular to join a big corporation or official organization straight out of school because more challenging alternatives are now not completely out of reach. For the second time since the Second World War, entrepreneurship, especially (but not exclusively) if it is Internet-related, is getting very popular. To create one's own company is becoming a professionally and socially acceptable career choice. This time it is not as in the immediate war aftermath when there was such a scarcity of good salaried jobs that it forced many people in their twenties to start on their own. Although it is true that current would-be entrepreneurs are also driven by economic factors, i.e., the difficulty in finding a job or in keeping it, their initiatives also indicate changes in the state of mind of many Japanese people who are not in so dire straits. Having understood the limits of the current Japanese management system not only to provide adequate jobs but also to offer the right environment for self-achievement and use of creativity, they are looking for other ways of making money, building a career and finding satisfaction at work and in private life. As in the USA and now in many European countries, this leads to the rapid growth of networks of entrepreneurial start-ups, symbolized for example in the Shibuya 'Bit Valley' regrouping internet-based new businesses. Most of the Bit Valley entrepreneurs had the right background to become elite salarymen. Some of them actually entered into large firms and left; others never tried, and started their own business just after or even before graduation (Arai, 2000).

Nevertheless, only a very small minority of would-be entrepreneurs can be expected to achieve their goal in any circumstance. The difficulties are compounded by the inadequacies of the Japanese education system to prepare them to make such a jump. According to a recent survey, there is an increase in new businesses created by people under the age of 29 and those between 45 and 59 (*New Business Hakusho*, 1999). This confirms the change in attitude of younger people and the growing autonomy (spontaneous or forced by necessity) of those of managerial age. For instance, young women have difficulties in being hired as regular employees on a permanent basis. Moreover, there are very few qualified jobs available for female university graduates in their thirties and forties when they want to come back on the labour market (Debroux, 1999). Some are attracted by the SOHO (Single Office Home Office) concept, the micro-companies they could manage from home or with little space and capital investment (*Nikkei Sangyo Shimbun*, 1999). The number of women-owned or women-run firms reached 60,593 in 1999. However, about 70 per cent of women's companies remain one-woman affairs, or very small firms with only a couple of employees (Teikoku Data Bank, 1999). Despite a number of success stories (Tamura, 1995), women may end up disappointed and trapped into new forms of low-paid low value-added subcontracting work if they do not have enough expertise to develop new products and services on their own. That is why a number of them are looking for graduate schools programmes. However, there are still very few universities offering relevant training, explaining how to make a business plan, develop a marketing strategy, or use the opportunities offered by the capital market to raise funds. The large gap between the scope of the support programmes and the slow increase of new business is therefore understandable. The pressure is now on the educational system to produce graduates with the differentiated skills required by the restructuring in established companies and the entrepreneurial drive.

This is not the first time that public and private concerns push for a restructuring of the education system. In 1984, Prime Minister Nakasone established the National Council on Educational Reform to study and recommend changes. The Council issued three recommendations in 1987, which collectively became called the Third Reform of the Education System. The advisory group, also known as the Ad Hoc Council on Education Reform, proposed that all participants in the education system change their policies to encourage creativity and individual talents, opportunities for lifelong education, and the ability to meet the demands of internationalization and the information age. The recommendations were strongly opposed by a number of people inside the Ministry of Education, schools officials and teachers' unions. As a consequence, the Third Reform led to only very peripheral changes. In the late 1980s, educational reform was forgotten in the then 'bubble' fever and it is only the prolonged downturn of the 1990s that is pushing the issue back to the fore. In the past few years significant movement on educational reforms issues has been observed. Moreover, additional changes are being contemplated or already are scheduled (Choi, 1999). Over the last few years, several advisory bodies of the Ministry of Education have submitted recommendations, calling for significant changes. The Curriculum Council's July 1998 Report proposes that greater creativity be introduced into elementary and high school programmes by reducing the annual classhours and increasing the number of elective or general courses. The Council stresses that rote memorization will play a lesser role in delivering the new curriculum, to be replaced with learning accomplished by demonstration and experimentation (Ministry of Education, 1999). The University Council suggests that universities produce creative, innovative and highly skilled graduates by focusing on developing programmes based on four principles:

- qualitative enhancement of education and research aimed at fostering students' ability to achieve individual goals
- more flexibility in educational and research systems to ensure the autonomy of universities
- improvement of the administrative structure to facilitate responsible decision-making and implementation that foster institutional autonomy
- differentiation of universities and continuous improvement of education and research by establishing a plural evaluation system.

The University Council pushes also for the expansion of the number of graduates programmes, especially those modelled on the MBA (Master of Business Administration), but also less ambitious ones. In view of the increased career mobility and the growing entrepreneurial aspirations, there is a reckoning that more diversified and higher-level curricula should be developed to satisfy the needs of those eager to come back to school. The Ministry of Education's Vocational Training Division is shifting its emphasis away from the development of blue-collar-worker types of skills to upgrade the practical expertise of white-collar workers to international standards. A new Business Career Scheme was devised geared to professional-level qualifications, such as finance, tax accountancy, legal affairs, public health, small business management consultancy, etc. Already in 1993, evening schools and daytime evening schools were allowed to offer doctoral courses. More day and night master courses are now made available. In fiscal 1998, the number of new postgraduate master students reached 5,177. In April 2000, specialized graduate schools were opened offering two-year master programmes. This is a departure from the graduate schools traditional objective of producing academics, especially in social sciences. The objective is to provide practical training for advanced vocational specialists. Universities are expected to hire professors having a practical experience in their specialized field. Practical educational methods, such as case studies, debate, fieldwork, etc., have to be adopted. The shift reflects the current willingness to develop a 'model' for employees that is more self-reliant than before under a stable long-term employment in one firm (*Japan Labour Bulletin*, May 2000).

The Central Council for Education suggests important changes in the entrance examination system. The students should be allowed to choose their university according to individual interest and career plan. Universities should publicize their educational objectives and explain in detail the characteristics and quality they require in students, so that the latter can determine which place best matches their needs. Entrance examination is bound to remain a key element of selection but the Council urges the institutions to include into the process a range of subjective factors. The spirit of the process should be one of 'mutual choosing', replacing unilateral selection by the university (Ministry of Education, website, 1999). In the current socio-political and economic climate, such reforms are more likely to be accepted than in the 1980s. Not only the labour market but also the demographic trends are pushing for changes in the educational system. The number of 18-year-olds peaked in 1993 at 2.3 million and is expected to decline by 1 million by 2010. This decline will change the balance between applicants and openings at universities. The Ministry of Education predicts that by the year 2009, every student who wants to go to university will be able to attend the institution of his or her choice. This development is unlikely to eliminate completely the need for entrance examinations because it can be expected that the demand to enter the best universities will continue to exceed supply, but it will surely greatly reduce their importance for the large majority of the students and universities alike. It means that the educators should be able to refocus their efforts towards teaching students to think more creatively and encouraging individual talents (Ministry of Education, 1999).

For many universities, public and private, there will be no other choice anyway but to reform and propose attractive curricula if they are to avoid being wiped out of the market or forced to merge with other institutions. Already Kawai Juku, one of the largest *juku* (cram schools preparing for the entrance examinations) that make very precise statistical schools and universities ranking, is putting a number of universities in a so-called 'F' category. The *juku* are unable to make any quantitative measurement of the relative difficulty of entering those universities. They cannot calculate the *hensachi* (deviation value), the sacrosanct comparative figure, cornerstone of the pyramidal education system and key factor of the school choice (and subsequently career) for the immense majority of students and parents. The 'F' category means that in some universities any applicant, whatever his or her level, is now likely to be accepted. This is the clearest sign possible that universities are entering into a very difficult period because they may not be able to attract enough students without lowering their standards. For the time being, the problem is the most serious in small countryside universities, but many bigger one in the cities have seen a dramatic drop in the number of applicants and will have to react rapidly (Nihon Watakushiritsu Gakko Shinko. Kyozai Jigyodan, 2000). To differentiate themselves and respond to the demand, some of them propose courses on the development of start-ups at the undergraduate and graduate levels, and/or geared towards salaried people (Matsuda, 1997). In 1995, only five universities were offering courses on entrepreneurship. In 1999, 70 universities were offering such programmes. Most of them are still in the early stage of providing basic education on company formation, growth and risk finance, completed by lecture series made by entrepreneurs and summer internship programmes to familiarize the students with the business world.

Japanese universities are just reaching the stage of idea contests, and studies on the elaboration and implementation of a business plan. With rare exceptions such as Waseda, Tama and Keio Universities, they have not yet reached the stage of incubator, i.e., they do not have yet the support system for actual business creation and development inside the institution (*New Business Hakusho*, 2000). To reach higher stages would require students with a higher level of specialized knowledge. That is why the University Council is favouring the increase of students into postgraduate programmes of the MBA and Management of Technology types. The push for high-level postgraduate programmes reflects first the doubt that new industries can be developed only in large companies and second that the internal training they have provided so far is good enough to compete with the entrepreneurial US ventures and large companies. Large Japanese companies need MBA-type managers, and entrepreneurs with such a background are also crucial in the increase of the number of technology-oriented new businesses (*New Business Hakusho*, 2000). The objective is to emulate the USA where is it said that about 50 per cent of the graduate students in prestigious universities intend to create their own business. In 1998, only 3.6 per cent of Japanese entrepreneurs had a postgraduate degree, compared with 26.6 per cent in the United states in 1996, a situation considered to be due to the shortage of management oriented programmes at postgraduate level (*Japan Labour Bulletin*, May 2000).

New Links between Business and Universities

The wall between business and the academic world is crumbling. Concerned about the 'hollowing out' of local industrial bases, local governments and business associations encourage the contacts by promoting exchange of marketing and technological information (*Asahi Shimbun*, 20 April 1998). Japanese corporations are studying the business model that emerged from Silicon Valley during the late 1980s and the public authorities are boosting the trend. Some 40 companies, including NTT, the Japan Development Bank and Toshiba, are members of Smart Valley Japan, a group of 400 companies created to foster the entrepreneurial spirit (*Japan Times*, 15 April 1999). Many start-ups have been created in Japan during the last 20 years but the most successful cases such as Tsutaya, Recruit, Pia or Persona have been in the retail and other service industries. They have created many jobs but most of them of relatively low level. Moreover, those companies are only active on the Japanese market. They do not have the ambition of conquering the world markets. The gap between Japan and the USA in terms of R&D-oriented new companies, creating high value-added employment and aiming towards the world market, is growing, and causing official worries. It is true that there are many examples of innovative and successful small and medium sized businesses (especially among the medium sized firms) developing new products and markets in traditional industries (Odagiri, 1998). Nevertheless, public authorities are pushing strongly for the creation of 'elite' ventures in new industries such as information technology or biotechnology. These themselves are expected to create high-level jobs but are also expected to have spillover effects. Public authorities are looking anxiously for outlets for the middle-age-manager victims of the restructuring. Admittedly, some may have difficulty in keeping pace but many others are considered as having the right managerial expertise to help start-ups and also to help inexperienced universities launching spin-offs to develop a sound management structure (Ministry of Education, 1999).

The Japan External Trade Organization (JETRO) is trying to bring together US and Japanese venture businesses to strike deals. In Northern California, Stanford University's US–Japan Technology Management Center and the International Business Incubator in San José perform similar functions (*Japan Times*, 15 April 1999). The willingness to promote a collaboration between the academic world, business and the administration appears strongly since 1995. Many examples of local public authorities–universities–SME collaboration in R&D activities have been noticed lately all over the country. For example, the Shizuoka prefectural government and the Shizuoka Science and Technology Promotion Foundation have begun to promote technology transfers from the prefecture's universities and institutes to local small businesses. The partners hope to coordinate the seeds of technology developed by the academic institutions to fit with the needs of small firms. Relying on the newly approved technology transfer law (see later), the Osaka Industrial Council decided to open a liaison office in October 1998 that will recruit university researchers to serve as consultants to local businesses and support the pursuit of joint research projects (Choi, 1999).

The gap is very wide between the resources used or accounted for by the university system and its measurable contributions to practical technology. On the one hand, more than one-third of Japan's researchers are employed at universities. They spend about one-fifth of all research funds, but the entire Japanese university system filed only 128 patents applications in 1997 (Choi, 1999). Facing tight budgetary constraints, universities need external resources to finance their research. On the other hand, large and small companies are seeking more interactions with researchers to pull themselves out of recession. In a number of high-technology industries, even large Japanese firms do not have the researchers they need to develop innovative technologies, but they could find them in universities (*The Japan Times*, 6 December 1998).

The problem was in government regulations limiting interactions between professors at national universities and companies. Traditionally, professors employed by a national university were barred from employment by companies as well as from participation on corporate boards and executive committees. The restriction extended even to retired professors. It was also illegal for a professor at a national university to start a company or a joint or private venture that might commercialize his or her research. Small companies have been consistently disadvantaged by the lack of a functioning labour market. The mobility restrictions still reinforced the impediment to their potential function as restructuring catalysts. Large Japanese firms are still cornering the market on the best young graduates. This lure of the big companies has to decrease to give SME access to first-class human resource as well. It could be done by offering the possibility of moving from one company to another, or back and forth from the university to the business world. The removal of the regulations on private partnerships, including the participation of personnel of public universities, would make the creation of one's own company a credible possibility. A recently approved law directly addressed the barriers that prevent professors from entering fully into the private sector. The Law Promoting the Transfer of Research Results from Universities to Private Entities was passed in May 1998 at the Diet and was put into force in August 1998. Through this law, the tight restrictions are replaced by a more liberal framework. The law also attempts to tackle questions relating to patent rights and the government rights to limit business affiliations. At this stage, it is not clear though whether the Ministry of Education intends to impose a standard interpretation on all its universities or whether it will allow each institution to tailor the new legislation to its needs.

In recent years, some informal and *ad hoc* responses have cropped up in universities. A number of professors have pushed the limits of the restrictions by serving as consultants to firms or to associations of companies. Some government research institutions have encouraged their employees to enter into commercial spin-offs. For example, the Science and Technology Agency-funded Institute of Physical and Chemical Research (RIKEN) approved new guidelines in January 1998 that allowed its researchers to start their own venture companies and to act as directors of firms as long as they are not paid for this work. In addition, the RIKEN rules allowed staff-linked companies to have offices on the Institute's premises (Choi, 1999). At the public university level, the restriction means that while a number of private universities have actively pursued commercialization of their research for a number of years, national universities are just beginning to explore this area. What can be observed so far is a flexible and pragmatic approach. Tohoku University, the Tokyo Institute of Technology, Tsukuba University and Hokkaido University have set up venture capital funds to invest in the commercialization of their researchers' ideas. They are also developing more systematic approaches to protect and capitalize on the intellectual property developed by their staff. Encouraged by regulatory changes, Japanese universities are creating technology licensing organizations (TLO) with the authorization of the Ministry of Education and the Ministry of Foreign Trade and Industry (MITI). However, the difference between private and public universities remains a problem. Nihon University's TLO was allowed to be located inside the organization because it is a private university. In the cases of national public institutions, it was not possible to do so. National universities do not have a legal standing and they cannot make an application for a patent. The TLO are thus created outside of the university as limited companies by researchers investing a small amount of money as individuals. Afterwards, they can entrust the commercialization of their research to the TLO, from the patent application to the licensing. The situation would change only significantly if a new status of 'independent entity' were given to national universities, allowing them to manage their own resources. The project is currently discussed at the governmental level but many obstacles still have to be overcome. Ambiguity remains as far as the sources of funds available to the new entities. Quite a number of people, inside and outside the academic world, are reluctant to accept that national universities operate according to the rules of the markets because they may have difficulty in fulfilling their broader role in society at large. Moreover, the idea that public money utilized to finance research may just become private profit is unpalatable to many. Rules on intellectual property rights and on the use of funds must be precisely devised in order to create a fair ground for all stakeholders.

The objective of the TLO is precisely to induce a cycle of innovation rewarding the parties while providing money for further research. Currently, about 90 per cent of the patents coming from research in national universities are the individual property of the researchers. However, it is almost impossible to sell them to companies. In most cases, they are given away to the private research partner for a small amount of money. The TLO is supposed to create a more transparent system and to reward the parties more fairly. In the case of CASTI (Tokyo University), for research bringing a revenue lower than 10 million yen, the researcher receives 30 per cent; the laboratory 30 per cent; the department of affiliation 15 per cent; the university, another 15 per cent and CASTI, 10 per cent. The TLO have started a membership system for companies receiving technology transfers as a priority. The system is different from one case to another, reflecting policy differences. In the case of Techno Arch at Tohoku University, membership costs ¥50,000 (about US$ 500) and at Kansai Area it is ¥100,000 (US$ 1000). They have, respectively, 200 and 60 members. The objective is to attract a large number of companies, mainly SME. In the case of CASTI, membership costs ¥5 million, well above the means of most SME. The merit is that companies can have access to the technological information in a patent application within two weeks of the application. So far, seven large companies have signed up (*Shukan Diamondo*, 10 April 1999).

It is too early to predict the success of the TLO. For the time being, it is reported that they have problems recruiting members (notably at Kansai Area). It takes years to get the approval for a patent and the costs are very high. The recognized TLO can receive up to ¥20 million (about US$ 20,000) of public money a year for a maximum of five years as a bridge to cover the lead time between the patent applications and the revenue they may generate. However, the subsidies do not cover the total cost and the TLO could be in severe trouble if they are unable to attract more members, a difficult task in a period of economic crisis. So, they are under pressure to show results as soon as possible (*Asahi Shimbun*, 17 April 1999). From 2000 on, professors will be admitted as members of the board of a TLO, removing the constraint preventing a key stakeholder in the scheme from participating in its management. One big problem currently is the shortage of people able to manage the technology transfers. Ownership rights are not always clear in the case of national universities. Furthermore, at national and private universities alike, there is often no central office in charge of pursuing patent rights or otherwise licensing the results of research. Keio University which also created a TLO in spring 1999 decided to hire as professor and adviser a former specialist of the Patent Office. But the manpower shortage is not limited to legal issues. There is also a lack of marketing expertise. That is why CASTI has decided to outsource its representation abroad to a private company. Recruit has been trying for three years to commercialize Tokyo University research results. Overall, it means that universities have to cultivate both technological and internal managerial expertise to succeed (*New Business Hakusho*, 2000).

CONCLUSION

The anti-competitive business practices which limited the entrance of both foreign and new Japanese companies in some industries are crumbling. Supply sources are more diversified than before and the unwritten rules that a customer buys only from established sources are breaking down. The extreme stability of corporate Japan after the war reflected the deep conservatism of consumers. 'Bigger is better' is what Japanese consumers always used to believe when it came to the purchase of a good or a service. As a consequence, the attractiveness of offerings by newcomers was limited. Now, customers yearn for something new. Although still limited overall, the recent success of foreign and newly established Japanese manufacturers, service providers and retailers offering original products and services and using original sales methods shows that times are changing. True, a number of failures and some opposition can be expected. Restructuring in companies may cause serious socio-political problems, such as bankruptcy, an unemployment surge or regional imbalances. Political leadership is so weak that it is difficult to create a strong momentum for reforms. As a result, they may slow down or even stall for a while. The entrepreneurship boom may just fade away because of difficulties in creating the right business environment. Huge obstacles remain and it is too early to make any assessment of the results. Probably 5 to 10 years will be necessary to observe significant changes. Nevertheless, the transformation of Japanese society and business environment is at work and should eventually bring to the fore a completely different environment from the one observed during the last 50 years.

40   *Rise of a Venture Business Culture in Japan*

References

Alexander, A. (1998) 'Structural Change and Economic Mobility in Japan', *Japan Economic Institute*, no. 44A, 20 November 1998.
Altbach, E. (1997) 'Small and Medium-sized Businesses in the Changing Japanese Economy', *Japan Economic Institute*, no. 31A, 15 August 1997.
Arai, K. (2000) *Bit Valley no Kodo* [The Pulse of the Bit Valley] (Tokyo: Nikkei BP).
Asahi Shimbun (1998) 'Chusho Kigyo to Kenkyusha Musubimasu' [Collaboration between SME and researchers] 20 April, p. 10.
Asahi Shimbun (1999) 'Ugoki Dashita Daigakugijutsu no Minkan Iten' [Moves towards transfer of university technology to the private sector] 17 April 1999, p. 16.
Choi, J. (1999) 'Research and Development in Japan: Squeezing More for Every Yen', *Japan Economic Institute*, no. 29A, 31 July 1998.
Chusho Kigyo Hakusho [Small and Medium Enterprises White Paper] (1994, 1996, 1997, 1998, 1999 and 2000) (Tokyo: Ministry of International Trade and Industry, Small and Medium Enterprise Agency).
Debroux, P. (1997) 'Human Resource Policy in Japanese Companies', *Journal of General Management*, vol. 23, no.1 (Autumn).
Debroux, P. (1999) 'Women at Work in Japan: Opportunities and Threats Offered by the Recent Management Changes', *Journal of the Asian Academy of Management*, vol. 4.
Diamondo Shukan (1999) 'Susunda Daigaku wa koko made Henshin Venture Soritsu no Zenshikake' [Projects to foster venture businesses undertaken by changing universities] 10 April, pp. 72–3.
Dirks, D. (1997) *Employment Trends in Japanese Firms: The Japanese Employment System in Transition*, Working Paper 97/3 (Tokyo: German Institute for Japanese Studies Economic Section) pp. 35–53.
Japan Times (1999) 'High Tech Entrepreneurs take New Venture Dreams to the US', 15 April, p. 5.
Japan Economic Institute (2000), *Report No. 22B*, p. 9.
Japan Labour Bulletin (2000) vol. 39, no. 5, pp. 2–3.
Matsuda, S. (1997) *Kigyoron* [Theory of Enterprise] (Tokyo: Nihon Keizai Shimposha).
Ministry of Education (1999) *Jinzai (Human Resources) Support Programmes 1998: A Collaboration between Schools and Business NOW*.
New Business Hakusho (1996) (Tokyo: Chusho Kigyo Research Centre, Ministry of Finance Publishing Bureau).
New Business Hakusho (1999) (Tokyo: Chusho Kigyo Research Centre, Ministry of Finance Publishing Bureau).
New Business Hakusho (2000) (Tokyo: Chusho Kigyo Research Centre, Ministry of Finance Publishing Bureau).
Nihon Watakushiritsu Gakko Shinko. Kyosai Jigyodan [Japanese Private Universities Promotion and Support Association] (2000), Survey on the Future of Private Universities, Tokyo.
Odagiri, H. (1998) 'Midsize companies now playing larger role in Japanese economy', *Nikkei Weekly*, 8 June, p. 15.
Ostrom, D. (1999) 'The Search for New Corporate Superstars: Japanese Firm Mobility in the 1990s', *Japan Economic Institute*, no. 12A, 26 March.

Ozaki, E. (1996) *Jinji. Chingin Seido no Kadai to sono Kaiketsusaku* [Issue and Solution to Changes in the Human Resource and Compensation System] (Tokyo: Seikei Kenkyujo).

Somucho (Management and Coordination Agency) (1998) *Shinki Jigyo no Soshutsu* [Creation of New Enterprises] April (Tokyo: Government Printing Office).

Tamura, M. (1995) *Josei Kigyokatachi* [Female Entrepreneurs] (Tokyo: Nihon Keizai Shimbunsha).

Teikoku Data Bank (1999) Survey on Women's Entrepreneurship, Tokyo.

The Daily Yomiuri, 14 July 1999, p. 10.

3 Deployment of Knowledge Workers in Japanese Corporate R&D at the Turning Point Towards the Knowledge-Based Economy

Alexander Fliaster

STRUCTURAL CHANGE AND VALUE CHANGE AS DRIVING FORCES OF HUMAN RESOURCES (HR) MANAGEMENT TRANSFORMATION

In recent years, Japanese companies have been engaged in a painful process of restructuring and modernization in order to regain competitiveness in the global economy. Certainly, one important reason for this modernization lies in the current economic crisis, which is the worst in Japan's postwar history. For instance, the nation's unemployment rate in February 2000 rose to a postwar high of 4.9 per cent, especially due to the increase in the number of bankruptcies among medium and small-sized companies and to having intensified corporate restructuring, and Japanese officials are concerned that the unemployment situation will further deteriorate (*Asahi Shimbun*, 31 March 2000). Many Japanese companies are now calling into question even fundamental basics of Japanese-style management such as a long-term psychological contract with corporate-specific human resources (HR).

However, to understand the change process in the management and deployment of HR in Japanese companies by putting it down only to the cyclical recession seems insufficient. The fundamental problem is not the periodical adjustment of an economic cycle alone but rather that Japan's society has reached the turning point from a mature industrial mass-production economy to a knowledge-based economy. The emerging knowledge-based economy makes the old competitive strategies obsolete by developing new rules for competitive success. The key source of structural advantage is no longer physical resources such as production equipment or office buildings, but software and service assets such as goodwill, know-how, and patents (MITI and Andersen Consulting, 1999).

Additionally, there is also a process of value change which is interdependent and at least of the same key importance as the structural change. In fact, the new economy is not only about information and telecommunication technologies and deregulated markets, but also about more labour mobility and increased emphasis on entrepreneurship and performance rather than on cohesion, hierarchy and seniority. Traditionally, Japanese society has been work-oriented and group-oriented, made up of 'company people' (*kaisha ningen*) who are fiercely loyal to the company. These people possess strong perseverance, sense of cooperation and common knowledge and skills suited to mass production of standardized goods (EPA, July 1999). The concepts of mass consumerism and stability, which have been symbols of the Japanese postwar economic growth, have deeply infiltrated not only corporations but also the family, the educational system and the community, pushing the life-styles of each member of society towards uniformity (e.g., Morishita, 1999). But in the 1990s, this economic and social system, characterized by uniformity and the 'catch-up and pass' mentality, reached a complete dead-end (e.g., Keidanren, 1996). For the necessary structural change, a value change is first required: the old egalitarian approach should give way to an emphasis on individuals. Distinctive personalities, non-traditional experience, and talented individuals should be more appreciated in Japan, and the awareness of the necessity of this value change seems to be spreading in the Japanese business community.

In other words, in the knowledge-based economy, as opposed to mass production, *another kind of person steps into the limelight as creator of competitive advantage.* In terms of corporate HR deployment this need for differentiation and the fostering of individuality means in particular the diversification of employment contract. According to the MITI's Discussion Agenda, the new economic system, among other things, should take a neutral position with regard to job switching and should promote greater job mobility, especially among white-collar workers (MITI/PPO, 1999).

In what follows, the change in how the knowledge workers in Japanese companies are deployed will be analyzed, embedded in the context of the transformation of Japanese-style HR management as a whole. For better understanding of what the differences in the competitive rules in the old and the new economy are and what system of HR management becomes inevitable for creation of competitive advantages in the latter, the theoretical framework will first be discussed.

PEOPLE-BASED INNOVATION IDENTITY OF JAPANESE COMPANIES AND DEPLOYMENT OF KNOWLEDGE WORKERS IN THE TENSION FIELD BETWEEN UNITY AND DIVERSITY

In the knowledge-based economy, innovations result from the organizational capability to generate, select, and integrate various knowledge components and the people who possess them. In other words, creating new products needs 'a community of interacting individuals with different backgrounds and mental models' (Nonaka and Takeuchi, 1995, p. 73).

Therefore, the management of *intraorganizational community of differences* or, to put it in a more philosophical manner according to Luhmann and Heidegger (as quoted in Fliaster, 2000, p. 311), this is the *unity of diversity* which becomes increasingly important for sustainable competitiveness.

For better understanding, this management dilemma can be embedded in the framework of the theory of social systems. The problem the Japanese HR management must solve now is in essence a Japanese version of the basic problem of every social system: to establish a new balance between the necessary integration and the differentiation of the members of the system (Marr, 1989; Fliaster, 2000). In terms of corporate HR management this means especially that, on the one hand, its routines should secure the socialization, mutual loyalty, and emotional commitment to the company in order to foster the cooperation between knowledge workers. But on the other hand, corporate HR management has to foster the workforce diversity and, in particular, promote intellectual elites and high performers in order to enable creative problem solutions (Figure 3.1).

Basically, this tension field does not represent the 'either–or' logic of dichotomy but rather the integrative 'both–and' approach: an extreme uniformity causes stagnation, a too wide differentiation may cause loss of inner cohesion.

Figure 3.1   HR management routines in the tension field between community and diversity
Source: Following Fliaster, 2000, p. 312.

Consequently, the management of this tension has to be dynamic and include steady monitoring and periodical corrections of the balance according to the corporate-specific development and trends in business environment. Against this theoretical background, the situation in Japanese companies can be considered in more detail. For a better understanding of what is changing in the Japanese-style management of knowledge workers at the turning point towards the knowledge-based economy, the attention should be at first directed to the 'starting position', that is, to the strengths and weaknesses of Japanese management of knowledge and knowledge workers in the 'old economy'.

A huge number of empirical studies conducted in the 1980s and early 1990s allows one to summarize the innovation style typical of Japanese firms as an 'operations-oriented' strategy which focuses more on the incremental refinement of organizational processes, while placing considerable emphasis on accumulating experience that contributes to the existing intraorganizational capability and know-how; change, therefore, tended to be incremental and more continuous (e.g., Kagono *et al.*, 1985). These incremental continuous 'day-to-day' innovations have been carried out by cooperative efforts of 'company people', many of them employed for the long-term and who have developed primarily corporate-specific, often tacit knowledge. To put it differently, Japanese employees have carried out mostly firm-specific and factory-specific innovations (e.g., Clark and Fujimoto, 1991; Bowonder and Miyake, 1992, p. 320). Thus, the system of long-term employment contract and the organization-specificity of knowledge fostered each other. Under this pattern of Japanese 'companyism', which restrains interorganizational mobility, while fostering it intraorganizationally, many people could not become professionals but rather have become 'all-purpose employees' and 'intra-company-specialists'. Even the interaction of Japanese corporate researchers with their colleagues within the company was closer than their interaction with someone outside of the company (e.g., Asakawa, 1995; Niimura, 1996).

The emphasis the Japanese top managers have put on the intraorganizational mechanisms of variety amplification such as job rotation deals very much with the low interorganizational mobility, that is, with the impossibility of injecting new ideas into the organizational knowledge context through employee turnover – as American firms do (e.g., Sullivan and Nonaka, 1986). Additionally, ethnic and cultural diversities as 'natural' sources of 'requisite variety' and therefore important enabling conditions for organizational knowledge creation (Nonaka and Takeuchi, 1995, p. 220) are relatively low in Japan, especially compared to the US, where the immigrant legacy is one important source of the vitality and pioneering spirit (Hayashi, 1988, p. 51).

From the above, it might be concluded that in the tension field between unity and diversity Japanese companies have created an imbalance in the past: the pendulum has swung massively in favour of uniformity. This mismatch turned out to be very dangerous in the emerging knowledge-based economy. In fact, it is the product innovation in high-technology industries, and creative research as its essential precondition, that are increasingly becoming the key competitive weapons. The development of new products and markets requires, however, the revitalization of diversified people with different ideas, not the organizational coherence of a homogeneous group (Kameyama, 1992).

To foster innovation, therefore, Japanese firms should start to consciously accept 'people with diverse idiosyncrasies and backgrounds, people who for whatever reason do not blend in smoothly with their environment' (Sugahara, 1994). Accordingly, if one analyzes the recent transformation of the Japanese-style HR management, one can consider that the pendulum is swinging in favour of more diversity. As indicated above, this change process is affecting not only separate HR management routines but also many other aspects of what can be called *'innovation identity of the company'*, that is, the idiosyncratic collective capability of employees to create knowledge in a specific way, as well as their commitment to this way of knowledge creation (Fliaster, 2000). Some of these aspects of change are summarized in Table 3.1.

With this in mind, the manner in which Japanese companies modernize the key routines of HR deployment in order to amplify diversity and promote knowledge creation, will be discussed in detail. But at first, the question of how Japanese companies adapt the *number* of knowledge workers, especially in R&D, in the years of economic recession, will be briefly taken into consideration.

CHANGES IN THE DEPLOYMENT OF KNOWLEDGE WORKERS

Increasing the Number of Researchers as a Means of Building Up the Innovation Potential

According to the survey on private enterprises' research activities by the Science and Technology Agency (STA), in 1997/98, 35.1 per cent of Japanese enterprises responded that in the previous two to three years, the relative importance of R&D for their management strategy 'increased'; 37.5 per cent stated that it 'increased somewhat'; a further 21.2 per cent responded that it had not changed. Only 5.7 per cent stated that it 'declined somewhat' or 'declined'. In knowledge-intensive industries, this data is even more impressive: for instance, in the pharmaceutical industry about 62.3 per cent of

Table 3.1   Modernization of knowledge-worker-based 'innovation identity' of Japanese companies

Level of modernization	From ... only =>	=> Towards more ...
'Self'-definition of the people.	Relatedness, interdependence, ability to maintain harmony with social context.	Individuality, independence, self-responsibility.
Innovation style as a foundation of competitive advantage.	Cumulative refinement of processes and products through cooperative efforts.	Development of new products and markets through originality, creativity, and fusion of knowledge components from former separate fields.
Corporate membership.	'Company people', e.g. Generalists =>	Professionals, e.g. knowledge workers with distinctive, market-related skills and values.
HR management routines fostering.	Homogeneity, conformity.	Diversity, variety.

Source: Following Fliaster, 2000, p. 309.

companies stated that the importance of the R&D increased (STA, 1998). This rhetorical appreciation of the importance of R&D as a means of overcoming the recession and restoring competitiveness is reflected in the following 'hard facts' of HR deployment policies.

According to the *World Competitiveness Yearbook 1999* published by the Institute of Management Development in Switzerland, Japan is ranked 2 among 47 countries in terms of total R&D expenditure as a percentage of GDP, and 3 in terms of total R&D personnel nationwide per capita (IMD, 2000). As indicated in Table 3.2, despite the economic slump, the number of researchers in Japanese companies has even been increased in recent years. Thus, the Japanese managers did not sacrifice the capacity for knowledge creation and long-term growth for the sake of a short-term costs reduction.

Of course, hoarding people cannot alone guarantee innovation. But it is also evident that in many high-technology industries the so-called 'critical mass' is very high because, for the promotion of R&D projects, companies need many specialists in various fields of knowledge. Moreover, not only do Japanese companies deploy more researchers but they also try to optimize the organization of R&D, that is, to improve the HR deployment. Between

Table 3.2   Increasing number and share of researchers in the Japanese corporate R&D

Financial year	R&D personnel in Japanese companies (total)	Number of researchers in Japanese companies	Share of the researchers on the total R&D personnel in Japanese companies (per cent)
1992	564,600	342,400	60.6
1993	585,700	358,100	61.1
1994	585,200	369,000	63.1
1995	579,200	378,100	65.3
1996	575,400	385,800	67.0
1997[a]	570,600	387,200	67.9
1997[b]	592,100	403,000	68.1
1998	589,200	407,300	69.1
1999	615,800	431,800	70.1

[a] The data from 1992 up to 1997a exclude software industry;
[b] The data from 1997b include software industry.
Sources: Fliaster, 1999; Management and Coordination Agency of Japan, 1999.

1994 and 1997, 37.9 per cent of private Japanese companies had already carried out a major restructuring of the R&D organization, and a further 10.8 per cent are planning to carry out such a major restructuring in the future. The goal which most of them (53.4 per cent) pursue by this restructuring is increasing the efficiency of their R&D organization (STA, 1998, figs 3–12, 3–13).

An additional positive effect of the increasing number of corporate researchers can be mentioned when taking into account that the main instrument of HR development in major Japanese companies is job rotation. Job rotation has made it possible to increase the share of employees with technological competence not only in the R&D department but in marketing, production, etc. as well. It ensures that the efficiency of interdepartmental coordination and cooperation which is necessary for innovation, specifically for interdisciplinary product development teams, has also increased.

On the other hand, as may be inferred from Table 3.2, the decreasing share, that is, the true shortage of research assistants responsible for assisting with experiments, performing secretarial and clerical duties, etc., can pose a threat to the performance of R&D activities. Indeed, about 84 per cent of all Japanese researchers described themselves as not having enough research assistants (STA, 1996). This shortage is responsible for the fact that in Japanese companies highly-qualified knowledge workers must allocate their time among various administrative and other routine tasks which can impede the achieving of the desired research results, that is, creation of new products and technologies. In private Japanese companies, about 18 per cent of researchers spend up to 1 hour, about 36 per cent spend from 1 to 2 hours, and a further 39 per cent spend more than 2 hours each day on tasks other than creative research (STA, 1996). Therefore, Japanese companies have to improve their system of research assistance in order to optimize the deployment of the expert-based innovation potential they build up.

As indicated above, selecting and deploying knowledge workers appropriately is even more important than increasing their number. In what follows, diversification of the R&D personnel and its recruitment will be analyzed in detail.

Promoting Diversity through Diversification of HR Management Routines

In the past, the stability of R&D personnel in both the basic and applied research centres of large Japanese companies was very high (Sato, 1989, p. 31). Now, the diversification of every single aspect of HR deployment, that is, time of recruitment, selection criteria, etc., works as a 'floodgate' to regulate the level of diversity in the intraorganizational context of ideas and values (Fliaster, 2000).

Diversification of the Recruiting Time

Traditionally, large Japanese corporations accepted only newly graduated applicants, hiring them only after graduation in the spring. In particular, a survey by Keidanren 500 member companies found in the mid-1990s that only 13.4 per cent of the companies hired workers throughout the year (*Nihon Keizai Shimbun*, 13 June 1996).

Against this background, Keidanren asked large Japanese companies to hire workers all year round. According to a survey conducted in 1995 by the Keidanren member companies, nearly half have begun or may soon begin to hire in seasons other than spring (*Japan Update*, 1996). To name examples, leading distributors like Jusco Co., Ltd, Daiei Inc. and Ito-Yokado Co., Ltd, have already introduced full-season periodical employment; Toyota and other manufacturers are also hiring engineering graduates in the autumn (*Japan Labour Bulletin*, 1996).

Diversification of the Schools and Universities from which New Recruits Graduate

What Japanese recruitment personnel traditionally wanted to know was not what abilities the student developed and displayed while in school but primarily the school's name; a survey by Keidanren 500 member companies found that only 7.5 per cent did not ask applicants the name of their university (*Japan Update Bimonthly*, 1996). Japanese companies traditionally have a number of schools they give preference to in a pyramidal array. For instance, in the beginning of the 1990s among the members of the board of directors of Mitsukoshi, about 80 per cent were former students of Keio University (Wiersema and Bird, 1993).

Many leading Japanese corporations have traditionally hired students who were recommended by the schools they designated (see, e.g., *Japan Labour Bulletin*, 1996). Employees in the corporate R&D are also involved in this network system under which visits by R&D personnel to their own *alma mater* and other informal practices are frequent. Moreover, many large corporations encourage young employees to meet with prospective job applicants from the schools they graduated from and arrange introductions to staff members in the HR department (*Japan Update Bimonthly*, 1996). These 'old boy' systems were already being criticized in Japan at the end of the 1980s because of the fear that R&D centres could become filled with people from a very limited number of universities (e.g., Sato, 1989, p. 30). Because many large companies feel that this system results in an homogeneous personnel and discriminates against people with unconventional curricula vitae, changes are under way. Major Japanese companies – Toyota Motor Corp. and Nippon, Steel Corp., among others – have been asked by Keidanren to abandon this method of recruiting by not asking the name of the school that the candidate attended, demonstrating through their action that they are not prejudiced (*Nihon Keizai Shimbun*, 13 June 1996; Keidanren, 1996).

In consequence, to diversify the values and knowledge of the workforce some leading companies have introduced a system under which new applicants were solicited from the public regardless of which university they graduated from or whether they were recommended by colleges (*Japan Labour Bulletin*, 1995, 1996; *Japan Update Bimonthly*, 1996).

In 1996, Keidanren also asked its members to 'make every effort to employ a diverse workforce by increasing employment opportunities for candidates who have studied abroad and for people with prior work experience' (Keidanren, 1996). To take an example, Tohoku Electric Power Co. declared that it plans to cut back on recruiting college graduates and instead hire more mid-career employees: about half the company's recruits will be mid-career employees or those who studied abroad (*Nihon Keizai Shimbun*, 19 June 1996). As shown below, especially in the R&D area, where the variety of knowledge and diversity of knowledge workers is of the utmost significance, in many leading companies this diversification process is under way.

Diversification of Contract Forms for Knowledge Workers

Unlike in American or European companies, in most large Japanese corporations, no exact job descriptions existed. In Japan, putting newly hired young people into specific positions was not a precondition for hiring: young people were employed by specific companies, not for specific jobs (see, e.g., Nakamura, 1992). When large Japanese companies hired young people, they did not buy skills for the purpose of filling certain specific job openings but literally engaged 'individuals as a whole – and their lifetime potentials and commitment – in order to train and mould them to fit the needs and goals of individual companies' (Ozawa, 1982, p. 8). This approach is also being reconsidered: according to a 1995 Keidanren survey of its corporate members, more than half of the respondents reported that they already or may soon allow at least some employees to select job fields for the development of more specialized careers. Among others, Sony offers general recruits a choice of career paths: 'Seeking to attract and effectively utilize those young people who aspire to develop skills in specific areas, it has divided its office positions into 10 categories and lets new employees select the one they think best suits them. By fostering more specialists, Sony believes, it can cope better with the complexities of modern society' (*Japan Update Bimonthly*, 1996, p. 12).

Other large firms experiment with new contract forms also for development engineers, who traditionally play a key role in the Japanese-style knowledge creation process. For instance, Nissan Motor Co. announced the introduction of a one-year contract system for some volunteers, initially from among some 400 designers and engineers. Contracts will be renewed every year, but the company has the right to terminate them in the case of poor performance. Nissan will also be able to vary salaries according to responsibilities. For these employees, the attraction are salaries some 20–30 per cent higher than those of regular lifetime employees (*Nihon Keizai Shimbun*, as quoted in Fliaster, 2000, pp. 340–1).

Similarly, Fujitsu Ltd has begun to hire mid-career employees on a contract basis in a full-fledged manner and allows new recruits with special abilities to select a 'contract-based employee' course. The course is tailored to those who do not want to be employed on a lifetime basis but who want a high salary. The company is seeking professionals with creative ability and business experience and will negotiate with them flexibly to set a contract period, forms of employment and salary (*Japan Labour Bulletin*, 1995). Needless to say, such contracts mean not only new legal arrangements, but also a new form of *psychological* contract which is based on the principle of mutual independence, with the emphasis put first on monetary or monetizable exchange factors (Fliaster and Marr, 1998). In other words, in addition to the well-known, long-term psychological contract of loyal 'corporate servants,' there is in large Japanese companies also an emerging somewhat short-term contract of 'mercenaries', even among the knowledge workers.

The longer and more extensively the new differentiation routines are practised, the more it becomes obvious that they strongly affect the whole system of corporate management and its underlying basic assumption concerning what a 'good employee' should be. The point of view that Japanese people 'must wean themselves from their dependence on the company, putting their ties with it on the proper level of give and take, and re-establish their individuality as the central element of their lives' (Takeuchi, 1997) describes very well how the 'new type of Japanese employee' is being defined by many Japanese companies and management scholars.

This type of contract can be useful especially if companies launch into a new field of technology or new product market where the risks are high and it is advantageous to be free of the rigidity of lifetime employment (Kameyama, 1992). However, hiring researchers under fixed-term employment contracts is not yet common in Japan (Figure 3.2).

Diversification of Knowledge Workers' Professional Experience

The job market for mid-career recruits has been rather underdeveloped in Japan, because 'the practice of evaluating the vocational abilities of job hoppers and unemployed persons in order to actively employ them, has not yet taken root at large and middle-sized companies, thus putting mid-career employees at a disadvantage in the labour market' (Nakamura, 1992). At present, many Japanese companies start to hire more knowledge workers who already have the specialized skills to fill specific posts. In particular, about 44 per cent of private Japanese corporations now hire researchers who were previously employed in other organizations (STA, 1997). Innovative companies such as Sony frequently recruit mid-career employees as a kind of corporate custom: 'Counter-culture inside the firm created the organizational chaos that stimulates creative activities for generating a variety of information throughout the entire company' (Nonaka, 1988, p. 58). Fujitsu and Tokyo Electric Power Co. are other well-known Japanese companies which practise the mid-career hiring of highly-qualified engineers (*Nihon Keizai Shimbun*, 15 April 1997).

Recent hiring plans of Japanese companies are shown in Figure 3.2.

In order not to go beyond the limits of this chapter, only a short comment on Figure 3.2 will be given here. Although persons with a postgraduate degree or higher are becoming increasingly important for promoting R&D activities, roughly 60 per cent of Japanese private corporations do not hire

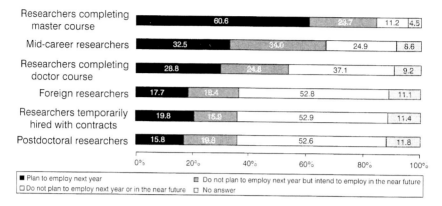

Figure 3.2   Forecasts for researchers to be employed in private Japanese companies in the near future
Note: The above shows responses to the question, 'Compared to this year, do you except to employ next year more or fewer researchers completing master course, mid-career researchers, researchers completing doctor courses, etc?'
Source: Science and Technology Agency of Japan (STA), 1999, fig. 3–5.

researchers who have completed a doctoral course, while upwards of 80 per cent have no established system of special compensation for doctorate researchers. Therefore, to make full use of the capabilities of this group of talented researchers, Japanese industry must strive to hire greater numbers of, and improve the compensation for, doctorate researchers (STA, 1997). However, as shown in Figure 3.2, many private enterprises have as yet no plans to employ doctoral or postdoctoral researchers. In this regard, the changes in Japanese HR deployment seem not to be rapid enough compared with the speed of the global technology-based competition.

New Recruitment Criteria for Knowledge Workers

As indicated above, among recruitment criteria it is not the specific set of professional abilities but rather the 'long-range potentiality' and 'contextual ability' (Maruyama, 1989, p. 427) that have traditionally played the crucial role in large Japanese companies. Prospective employees have not been viewed 'as multifunctional cyborgs from whom a company purchases a single skill such as riveting or selling ability. The corporation and the new employee both… [understood] that the firm hires the whole individual' (Hayashi, 1988, pp. 73–4). Therefore, the screening criteria used by firms for selecting recruits have been 'not professional knowledge nor technological skills useful for specific jobs, but general knowledge and culture, eagerness for work, the desire to work, understanding and judgement, cooperativeness, health and physical strength. In other words, what . . . [has been] emphasized . . . [was] whether the recruits can efficiently improve their abilities through systematic education and training systems, to what extent they possess trainability, and furthermore, whether they can work in cooperation' (Nakamura, 1992).

These recruitment criteria seem to be deeply rooted not only in the long-term employment system but also in the specific features of the 'interdependent contextual definition of self', that is, the specific kind of self-definition which is typical of Japanese culture and puts emphasis on the ability to adjust, maintain harmony with the social context, and fit in, rather than on the ability to express, realize and validate unique internal attributes (see, e.g., Fliaster, 2000). This cultural embeddedness explains the crucial role which is being played by the process of value change for modernizing corporate HR deployment routines.

In recent years, Japanese employers' organizations asked companies to indicate the kind of employees they were seeking, not only by recruiting for specific job classifications, but also by giving greater attention to the evaluation of individual skills categories such as 'subjects studied in school', 'individual's perception of problems', 'personality', etc. – all of them the features of 'professionals' rather than those of 'company people'. In particular, if one looks at the relevant recruitment criteria for the knowledge workers in the R&D in detail, this trend can be observed very clearly (Figure 3.3).

Given the above discussion, it is little wonder that Japanese companies stress the role of originality. What is more surprising, however, is the low ranking of cooperativeness. According to the Japanese HR management tradition in the era of mass-production, the 'person who rises more rapidly' in Japanese corporations was 'the one who can cooperate with others' (Vogel, 1979, p. 150). In the emerging knowledge-based economy, cooperativeness is even of greater importance for organizational knowledge and R&D than formerly, simply due to the increasingly integrated and interactive nature of today's innovation process in many fields of technology. Against this background, it can be suggested that the figure above does not demonstrate that Japanese companies began to ignore the key role of cooperativeness. It rather seems to show that Japanese companies think that the cooperativeness is mostly given, and put an emphasis exactly on the skills they find many R&D workers are lacking in.

As mentioned above, the structural change towards the knowledge-based economy is strongly affected by new information and telecommunication technologies. To develop and extensively use these technologies, a type of people as well as a type of organization are needed which are very different from those required by mass-production. In particular, the production of software

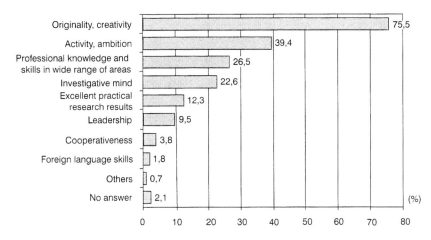

Originality, creativity	75,5
Activity, ambition	39,4
Professional knowledge and skills in wide range of areas	26,5
Investigative mind	22,6
Excellent practical research results	12,3
Leadership	9,5
Cooperativeness	3,8
Foreign language skills	1,8
Others	0,7
No answer	2,1

0 10 20 30 40 50 60 70 80

(%)

Figure 3.3 What do the Japanese private companies request from the researchers they employ?
Note: Up to 2 answers possible. Data except from temporarily hired researchers.
Source: STA, 1998, fig. 4–7–1

requires meritocracy rather than a group consensus approach, and task-oriented organization rather than hierarchical organization (Imai, 1988, p. 227). In this field, American companies seem to have a 'natural' competitive advantage over the Japanese: in the development of software, 'stars' matter, and in the heterogeneous American culture, the ability to be distinct is highly valued.

So, Japanese organizations have to do very much to increase the valuation of individual talents. In addition to what has been discussed above, they also have to modify their compensation policies for incentivizing the most innovative knowledge workers and fostering job performance. Traditionally, in many Japanese companies, 'even the most brilliant engineer proceeded up the salary ladder at the same pace as his peers. The principal rewards for outstanding performance were intrinsic (the respect of supervisors and peers) and long-term (the opportunity to go abroad for advanced study, for example, and the prospect of staying in the central lab rather than transferring to the division)' (Westney and Sakakibara, 1986, p. 225). At the end of the 1980s, a survey conducted by the project team from Kobe University revealed that around 30 per cent of Japanese engineers felt that they were not suitably evaluated in the forms of promotion and salary compared with clerical staff who were also university graduates and had been employed for the same length of time as the engineers (Okubayashi, 1989, p 40.) Thus, there are many things yet to be changed in Japanese HR management.

**Promoting Professionalization through the Modernization
of HR Development**

As products and technologies become more system-like, innovation is being
often carried out by fusioning knowledge among the various fields of discip-
lines. In many 'hybrid' fields of technology like optoelectronics and mecha-
tronics, the competitiveness of Japanese companies is traditionally very high.
As indicated above, one of the factors which have strongly contributed to this
competitive advantage lies in the specific system of job rotation. Typically,
'internal technology transfer in the Japanese firms seems to follow the maxim
that to move information, you move people' (Westney and Sakakibara, 1986,
p. 223), and Japanese engineers, 'who have been extensively job-rotated...
know how to combine knowledge... and talents from many departments'
(Maruyama, 1989, 427). Interestingly, according to empirical surveys, to
develop skills and foster section managers also in the areas of HR management, marketing and accounting, Japanese managers stress not only the
experience in the current area but experience in other areas, while their
American colleagues emphasize the range of work experience in the current
area of responsibility (Sato, 1999). At the same time, one of the most essential
preconditions for the extensive use of job rotation is the readiness of 'company people' to accept the deployment in different departments and fields of
specialization.

To put it another way, extensive job rotation has impeded the *specialization*
of knowledge workers in Japanese companies. Therefore, it is not surprising
that in last few years innovations such as adoption of a special career path
providing greater opportunity to individuals with sophisticated expertise
(Keidanren, 1996) have been fostered in Japanese firms. Simultaneously, to
bring the qualifications of professionals in line with the challenges of the
knowledge-based economy, professional skills of the knowledge workers
have to be steadily updated. According to a survey conducted in 1995, to
which 570 companies with an average of about 3,300 regular employees
responded, 61.6 per cent of Japanese firms with engineers on their staff said
training engineers was vital to expediting development of new products and
new business areas. But at the same time, training those in charge of new
product development was deemed inadequate in 40.3 per cent of the
responding firms. Also, the fact that inadequately trained people are posted
to the research and engineering jobs is acknowledged by 36.2 per cent.
Furthermore, 45.2 per cent admitted to a lack of staff members responsible
for training engineers (Kawakita, 1996). Doubtlessly, the awareness of a
problem is the first step towards its solution, and it can be supposed that the
leading Japanese firms will do their best to go this way.

CONCLUSION: MUTUAL FOSTERING OF HR MANAGEMENT CHANGE AND VALUE CHANGE

From what has been discussed above it can be concluded that the fundamental problem of Japanese HR management as well as knowledge management lies now in the fact that core employees who were selected, trained as generalists and deployed for sharing and generating corporate-specific knowledge in the traditional businesses of the industrial society, have to be reorganized, retrained, promoted and motivated with the aim of creating innovations in new industries and services of the knowledge-based economy through creativity and entrepreneurship. Against this background it is all but surprising that in the last few years, 'Japanese companies have started introducing Western "individualism" to encourage creative self-transformation' (Nonaka, 1988, p. 45).

This 'introduction of individualism' is being accomplished through the diversification of the HR deployment system discussed above and being fostered not only for economic reasons but also by the value change in Japanese society. Now the logic underlying the 'company servant' mentality is being eroded, and the young generation in particular puts increased emphasis on the interorganizational, market-oriented employability, that is, on the special skills and abilities. Many Japanese seem to desire a new system which allows a greater diversity of lifestyles, and where 'starting again' and 'changing direction' are possible (see, e.g., EPA, 1995). Whether Japan is *really* 'in transition from collective to individual values', as suggested, for example, by the IMD (2000), is at the moment an open question, but doubtless the result of this transition will strongly affect the economic system of the country. In particular, this value change may affect the innovation capacity – and its core components, creative capability and cooperativeness – of the Japanese and, thus, of the companies who deploy them. Analyzing this process will become one of the most important tasks in the future study of Japanese human resource deployment and innovation management.

References

Asakawa, K. (1995) *Managing the Knowledge Conversion Process Across Borders*, INSEAD Working Papers Series, 95/91/OB, INSEAD, Fontainebleau, France.

Bowonder, B. and Miyake, T. (1992) 'A Model of Corporate Innovation Management: Some Recent High-Tech Innovations in Japan', *R&D Management*, vol. 22, no. 4, pp. 319–35.

Clark, K. and Fujimoto, T. (1991) *Product Development Performance: Strategy, Organization and Management in the World Auto Industry* (Boston: Harvard Business Press).

Economic Planning Agency (EPA) (various years) *Kokumin seikatsu hakusho* [White Paper on the National Lifestyle]. http://www.epa.go.jp/
Economic Planning Agency (EPA) (July 1999) *Ideal Socioeconomy and Policies for Economic Rebirth*. http://www.epa.go.jp/99/e/19990705e-keishin-e.html
Fliaster, A. (1999) 'The Japanese-Style Management in the Midst of Recession: What can the European Firms Really Learn Now?', Paper presented at the 14th LVMH Conference, 'Crisis and Transformation in Asia: Implications for Western Corporations?', held at the INSEAD Euro-Asia Centre, Fontainebleau, 6 February.
Fliaster, A. (2000) *Humanbasierte Innovationsidentität als Managementherausforderung: Ein interdisziplinäres Erklärungsmodell des japanischen Wissensmanagements* (Frankfurt am Main: Peter Lang Publishing Group).
Fliaster, A. and Marr, R. (1998) 'Towards New Human-Based Competitive Advantages: Reconceptualizing the Psychological Contract as an Innovation Challenge for Japanese and European Human Resource Management', *Proceedings of the 15th EAMSA Conference*, November 1998, Taiwan, R.O.C.
Hayashi, S. (1988) *Culture and Management in Japan* (Tokyo: University of Tokyo Press).
Imai, K. (1988) 'Industrial Policy and Technological Innovation', in R. Komiya *et al.* (eds), *Industrial Policy in Japan* (Tokyo), pp. 205–32.
Institute of Management Development, Lausanne (IMD) (2000) *The World Competitiveness Yearbook 1999*.
Japan Labour Bulletin (1995) 'Trends in Diversifying Recruitment', vol. 34, no. 10 (October). http://www.jil.go.jp/bulletin/index.htm
Japan Labour Bulletin (1996) 'Diversifying Recruitment in Companies', vol. 35, no. 12 (December). http://www.jil.go.jp/bulletin/index.htm
Japan Update Bimonthly (1996) 'Companies Cast Their Recruitment Nets Wider', published by the Keizai Kôhô Centre, July 1996, p. 12. http://www. keidanren.or.jp/
Kagono, T., Nonaka, I., Sakakibara, K. and Okumura, A. (1985) *Strategic vs. Evolutionary Management: A U.S.–Japan Comparison of Strategy and Organization* (Amsterdam: North Holland).
Kameyama, N. (1992) 'Management Restructuring and Multi-Faceted Manpower Procurement – Development of Annual Pay System and Contract-Based Employee System', *Japan Labour Bulletin*, vol. 31, no. 7 (July). http://www.jil.go.jp/bulletin/index.htm
Kawakita, T. (1996) 'Japanese In-House Job Training and Development', *Japan Labour Bulletin*, vol. 35, no. 4 (April). http://www.jil.go.jp/bulletin/index.htm
Keidanren (1996) 'Keidanren Proposes on Developing Japan's Creative Human Resources – An Action Agenda for Reform in Education and Corporate Conduct', 26 March. http://www.keidanren.or.jp
Management and Coordination Agency of Japan/Statistics Bureau & Statistics Center (1998) *Heisei 10-nen kagaku gijutsu kenkyû chôsa kekka sokuhô (yôten)* [Results of 1998 Survey of R&D (Summary)], 28 November. http://www. stat.go.jp/
Management and Coordination Agency of Japan/Statistics Bureau & Statistics Center (1999) *Heisei 11-nen kagaku gijutsu kenkyû chôsa kekka sokuhô (yôten)* (Results of 1999 Survey of R&D (Summary)], 25 November. http://www. stat.go.jp/
Marr, R. (1989) 'Überlegungen zu einem Konzept einer "Differentiellen Personalwirtschaftslehre"', in *Individualisierung der Personalwirtschaft: Grundlagen, Lösungsansätze und Grenzen*, ed. by H. J. Drumm (Bern: Haupt), pp. 37–48.
Maruyama, M. (1989) 'Practical Steps for Interactive Innovation', *Technology Analysis and Strategic Management*, vol. 1, no. 4, pp. 423–30.

Ministry of International Trade and Industry (MITI) & Andersen Consulting (1999) *Change in the Employment Structure Brought About by the IT Revolution*, September 1999.

MITI, Policy Planning Office, Minister's Secretariat (1999) 'Toward a Competitive and Participatory Society', *Journal of Japanese Trade & Industry*, vol. 18, no. 6 (108th issue) (November/December).

Morishita, Y. (1999) 'A New Vision of Japan Must Emerge to Face the New Century', *Messages from Monthly Keidanren*, December 1999. http://www. keidanren.or.jp/

Nakamura, M. (1992) 'Hiring Practices in Japan', *Japan Labour Bulletin*, vol. 31, no. 2 (February). http://www.jil.go.jp/bulletin/index.htm

Nihon Keizai Shimbun (1996a) 'Keidanren to ask firms not to hire based on university', vol. 1, no. 109 (13 June), WWW-edition.

Nihon Keizai Shimbun (1996b) 'Tohoku Electric Power to hire more employees in mid-career', vol. 1, no. 113 (19 June) WWW edition.

Nihon Keizai Shimbun (1997) 'Fujitsu plans major recruitment of mid-career engineers in FY 1997', vol. 2, no. 339 (15 April), WWW-edition.

Niimura, Y. (1996) 'The Changing Reality of the Japanese-Style Employment System', *NIRA Review*, Autumn.

Nonaka, I. (1988) 'Self-Renewal of the Japanese Firm and the Human Resource Strategy', *Human Resource Management*, Spring, vol. 27, no. 1, pp. 45–62.

Nonaka, I. and Takeuchi, H. (1995) *The Knowledge-Creating Company: How Japanese Companies Create the Dynamics of Innovation* (New York; Oxford University Press).

Okubayashi, K. (1989) 'Social Status of Professional Engineers in Japan', *Annals of the School of Business Administration*, Kobe University, no. 33, pp. 24–41.

Ozawa, T. (1982) *People and Productivity in Japan* (New York: Pergamon Press).

Sato, H. (1999) 'Comparison of Career and Skill Development Among White-Collar Employees in Three Countries', *Japan Labour Bulletin*, vol. 38, no. 2 (February).

Sato, H., Koichiro, I., Shigemi, Y. and Davis, S. T. (1989) 'Organization and Administration of R&D Personnel in Japan', *International Journal of Manpower*, 10, pp. 3–43.

Science and Technology Agency (STA) (various years) *Kagaku gijutsu hakusho* [White Paper on Science and Technology], financial years 1996/1997/1998. http://www.sta.go.jp/

Science and Technology Agency (STA) (1998) *Minkan kigyô no kenkyû katsudô ni kansuru chôsa chôkoku (Heisei 9-nendo)* [Survey on Research Activities in Private Companies (Fiscal Year 1997)], August 1998. http://www.sta.go.jp/

Science and Technology Agency (STA) (1999) *Minkan kigyô no kenkyû katsudô ni kansuru chôsa chôkoku (Heisei 10-nendo)* [Survey on Research Activities in Private Companies (Fiscal Year 1998)], August 1999. http://www.sta.go.jp/

Sugahara, M. (1994) 'Five Fatal Symptoms of the Japanese Disease', *Japan Echo*, vol. 21, no. 2 (Summer). http://www.japanecho.com/

Sullivan, J. and Nonaka, I. (1986) 'The Application of Organizational Learning Theory to Japanese and American Management', *Journal of International Business Studies*, pp. 127–47.

Takeuchi, Ya. (1997) 'End of the Line for Japan's Corporate Feudalism', *Japan Echo*, vol. 24, no. 4. http://www.japanecho.com/

Vogel, E. F. (1979) *Japan as Number One: Lessons for America* (Cambridge, Mass: Harvard University Press).

Westney, D. E. and Sakakibara, K. (1986) 'The Role of Japan-Based R&D in Global Technology Strategy', in *Technology In The Modern Corporation: A Strategic Perspective*, ed. by M. Horwitch (New York: Pergamon Press), pp. 217–32.
Wiersema, M. F. and Bird, A. (1993) 'Organizational Demography in Japanese Firms: Group Heterogeneity, Individual Dissimilarity, and Top Management Team Turnover', *Academy of Management Journal*, vol. 36, no. 5, pp. 996–1025.

4 On Human Resource Development and Human Resource Management in the Chaebols of South Korea in Response to a National Economic Crisis

Gary N. McLean

INTRODUCTION

From 1997 until, some would argue, today, the Republic of Korea (ROK), more widely known in the world community as South Korea, has been going through a significant economic crisis. Much of the blame for the crisis has been laid at the feet of the chaebols, the large, family-owned conglomerates that dominate the ROK economy. The historic meeting of the heads of the ROK and the DPRK (Democratic Peoples' Republic of Korea, or North Korea) on 13 June 2000, and the hoped-for unification of the peninsula by many from the South, lends urgency to the need to stabilize the economy. The purpose of this chapter is to address the role of both human resource development (HRD), as it is emerging in the ROK, and human resource management (HRM), as it has existed and is evolving, in a time of national economic crisis, specifically within the chaebols.

In spite of many visits to the ROK, where I conducted research projects and workshops, consulted within ROK chaebols, and worked with numerous Korean doctoral students, I am clearly a beginner in understanding the ROK. I bring with me certain biases based on my own ethnocentricity. In the culture of the US, the role of the professor is not, fortunately, to have the answers, but to facilitate reflection and exploration on the part of learners, of which the professor is one. I hope you will be able to view my role in this light in this chapter. I am very grateful for the assistance and input from many of my Korean friends, colleagues, and scholars, but I take full responsibility for the errors and misinterpretations that may exist within this chapter.

WHAT ARE HRD AND HRM WITHIN THE
KOREAN CONTEXT?

Unfortunately, or fortunately, depending on your perspective, no universally accepted definition of human resource development or of human resource management exists. As Weinberger (1998) concluded:

> The field of HRD is disciplinary in nature, on that point there is no disagreement. What is not agreed upon is a unifying definition of the theories that underpin this field. It is not suggested that psychology with a learning emphasis, systems, economics and performance are the only fields that impact HRD, simply that they are primary. (pp. 82–3)

The ROK has not yet established its own definition for HRD, nor, for that matter, HRM. As with so many other educational concepts, given the large numbers of Koreans who have studied in the US, and the influence of the US directly in Korea, the definitions, at this point in time, have been largely imported with few attempts to indigenize the definitions. Of course, within the broad definitions, specifics will be different, given differences, for example, in Korean labour laws and cultural differences that impact specific interventions. Park Moon-soo (1998, personal communication), Director of Knowledge Management for Samsung Life Insurance Co. Ltd., indicated that HRD in Korea is almost always equated solely with Training and Development. Kwon Dae-bong (1998, personal communication), Professor, Corporate Education and Adult Education, Korea University, concluded that there were many synonym terms used in Korea for HRD:

> ... education and training, training and development, human capital development, humanware development. Humanware is a comprehensive human skill that enables one to produce goods and services by utilizing existing hardware and software or creating new ones with other people.

However, during the short tenure of Moon Yong-lin, Professor at Seoul National University, as Minister of Education, Human Resource Development was elevated to a national priority. It is probable that this emphasis will continue, even though the personnel in this office have changed rapidly during 2000.

A sampling of definitions developed in the United States follows. The first apparent use of the term 'human resource development' is ascribed to Nadler (1970): 'HRD is a series of organized activities conducted within a specified time and designed to produce behavioral change' (p. 3). At that time, it is clear that HRD was seen, basically, as a synonym for Training and Development. However, over time this concept has expanded. Writing under the auspices of the American Society for Training and Development, McLagan (1989) defined HRD as 'the integrated use of training and development, career development and organization development to improve individual and organizational effectiveness' (p. 7). Out of this definition emerged the Human Resources Wheel, whereby the field of Human Resources is graphically displayed as 11 segments of a 'pie', in which three segments are allocated to Human Resource Development, four to Human Resource Management, and four overlap the two areas, as follows (slightly modified):

- *Human Resource Management and Development*
  Recruitment, Selection, and Staffing
  Performance Management Systems
  Human Resource Strategic Planning
  Organization/Job Design
- *Human Resource Development*
  Training and Development
  Change Management/Organization Development
  Career Development
- *Human Resource Management*
  Human Resource Research and Information Systems
  Employee Relations
  Employee Assistance and Safety
  Compensation and Benefits

This view of HRM is clearly offered from an HRD perspective. Scarpello, Ledvinka and Bergmann (1995), however, suggested that HRM be defined as the management of an organization's employees. The *purpose* of HRM is to foster organizational policies that enhance the contribution employees make to the effectiveness of the organization (p. 2). When focusing on the functions of HRM, the authors included training, career management, and organization development, all areas that McLagan (1989) excluded from HRM and included in HRD.

Chalofsky (1992) defined HRD as 'the study and practice of increasing the learning capacity of individuals, groups, collectives and organizations through the development and application of learning-based interventions for the purpose of optimizing human and organizational growth and effectiveness' (p. 179). The faculty in HRD at the University of Minnesota has a working definition of HRD as: 'HRD is a process of developing and/or unleashing human expertise through organization development and personnel training and development for the purpose of improving performance' (Swanson, 1995, p. 208). All of these definitions, from within the context of the USA, focus on performance within the organization. Based on my research, and in an attempt to provide a definition that is more globally accepted, McLean and McLean (2000) have suggested the following definition for HRD:

Human Resource Development is any process or activity that, either initially or over the long-term, has the potential to development adults' work-based knowledge, expertise, productivity and satisfaction, whether for personal or group/team gain, or for the benefit of an organization, community, nation, or, ultimately, the whole of humanity.

It has been my experience that HRD is defined much more broadly in other parts of the world. For example, when I was working in the Liaoning Province Human Resource Centre in the People's Republic of China, HRD for the staff there included the whole Human Resource Wheel. My experiences in Thailand suggest that HRD has a broader emphasis that extends beyond the organization to the community. Though not clear from the Korean literature, it appears that HRD has traditionally been seen as part of HRM, but in recent years, with the establishment of HRD programmes within Korean universities, HRD is beginning to establish itself as a separate field of study and application, most commonly found in Schools of Education, rather than in Business Schools where most, if not all, HRM programmes are found. It will take some time before it becomes clear whether this separation of the two areas of human resources will survive in Korea, as they have now survived for decades in the US, or whether there will be pressure exerted to bring them back together in the business schools of Korea.

WHAT IS THE ROLE OF THE CHAEBOLS IN THE ECONOMY OF THE ROK?

The word 'chaebol' is used negatively, but almost universally, in Korea to refer to the highly diversified conglomerates that tend to dominate the Korean economic scene. Used originally to refer to the millionaires who owned the companies, they now refer to the companies themselves (Gong, 1999). Gong, president of the Korea Centre for Free Enterprise, recounts numerous accusations that have been directed toward the chaebols: 'The prime cause of the Korean financial crisis; inefficient organizations which can survive only through special privileges, users of bribery and cosmetic accounting; monopolists and oligopolists; reckless investors that ignore profitability, and so on' (p. 34). Gong then goes on to conclude, however, that 'many of these accusations are based on groundless myths' and that there may, in fact, be good evidence to show that the chaebols 'may be efficient' (p. 34).

Chaebols are family-owned and run. 'Twenty-nine out of the top thirty chaebols have been managed by the founder-shareholders or their sons' (Gong, 1999, p. 38). One source ('Yes But What Exactly is a Chaebol?' (on-line) 2000) suggested that 'the top four superchaebol have sales which account for somewhere between 40 and 45 per cent of South Korea's Gross National Product' (p. 2). And Ehrlich (2000) claimed that, as of August, 1999, 'chaebol heads or their allies still held almost 35 per cent of equity in the top 10 chaebols' (p. 31).

Because of the regulatory power of government, Gong (1999) pointed to the potential of the government to 'plunder' the chaebols. In response, the chaebols used bribery to compromise government officials, thus leading to the corruption that has characterized many of Korea's past governments. Gong's (1999) conclusion was:

> Ultimately, we do not know whether the chaebol are desirable or not. What we can do is to persuade the government and the general public to give up rescue programmes financed by tax money, the prohibition and the regulation of tender offers, and the control of bank loans.... If chaebols still survive in spite of such institutional changes, then they must be the product of other factors. (p. 38)

SHORT-TERM/LONG-TERM VIEW

Humans in the 'West' tend to be impatient. They want what they want *now*! Unfortunately, that's not the way the world works. Our socialization process teaches us that we control the world, that we have dominion over the earth. We are shocked, surprised, and angered when we discover that that's not the way the world works. So, when a crisis hits, we want it solved immediately! The ROK, with its Confucian tradition (as explained fully in an earlier chapter), is prepared to take a long-range view of the world and of change. Its national flag incorporates what we might see as ambiguity in the *taegeuk* (what we have come to understand as the concept of yin-yang). In this symbol, Koreans see complementarities coming together to form a whole – a concept that is difficult for those of us socialized to look for a single answer and to attempt to 'resolve' any ambiguity that might exist.

Figure 4.1   The national flag of the Republic of Korea

Beck (1997) described the national flag this way:

> The circle in the center divided equally with each part resembling a comma represents the *yin* and *yang*. The upper red section represents the *yang* or positive cosmic forces and the lower blue section the *yin* or negative forces. The main idea represented by the pattern is that while there is constant movement within the sphere of infinity, there is also balance and harmony. The four trigrams in each of the corners represent the four elements that make up the universe: heaven, earth, fire, and water. (p. 2)

Unfortunately, when a country finds itself in economic crisis, such as is found throughout much of Asia today, with impact felt literally around the world, our inclination is to 'fix it'. And so the International Monetary Fund (IMF), with concepts and principles that do not emerge from an Asian way of thinking, stepped in with its remedies. Just as the crisis did not occur over-night (Engardio, Moore and Hill, 1996, outlined its progress before it hit), there are no quick, lasting fixes – not economically, not politically, not from the IMF, not from Western nations, not from the World Bank, and not from HRD and HRM. Unless, and until, there is an understanding of the root causes of the problems, and these are addressed directly, the crisis may abate temporarily, only to return at a later time. The crisis may become worse. HRD and HRM have important roles, but they will occur over the long-term, not the short-term. As Louis Emmerji, then President of the OECD Development Centre, concluded in his preface to Salome and Charmes (1988),

> In-service training [read also HRD] does not offer a miraculous solution to the problems of development. But it is one of the most effective ways of achieving a better match between training and employment and for making life-long education more widely accepted. (p. 8)

All of this argues that, even though Korea has made what appears to be a very quick recovery, with a growth rate exceeding 10 per cent in 1999, my fear is that this is a superficial and artificial recovery. Until Korea and its chaebols are willing to make lasting, deep, long-term changes in the problems outlined in the following section, Korea will likely be on the road to another crisis.

WHAT ARE THE ROOT CAUSES OF THE CRISIS IN THE ROK AT THE MACRO-LEVEL?

Given that the world's brightest economists cannot agree on the causes of the crisis, and that the proposed solutions from the IMF and the World Bank are greeted with less than unanimous applause (see, for example, 'Asian Unionists Denounce IMF's Policy Remedies', *The Nation*, 1998), it would be foolhardy for me to try to suggest all of the root causes. Rather, let me attempt to identify those root causes that are amenable to HRD and HRM interventions, with a very brief presentation of other possible root causes.

Historically, Korea has had a high rate of economic growth. Kirk (1994, pp. 32–53) and Ungson, Steers and Park (1997, pp. 168–76), as cited in Lee (1998–9, p. 26), provided a number of reasons for this growth rate, emphasizing the role of HRM: 'Employee loyalty, "can-do" spirit, "work hard" ethics, and familial, paternalistic management.' Lee (1998–9) explained that there have been major changes in the 'Korean employee's work values, attitude, and behavior' (p. 26), leading to reduced commitment to a hard-working ethic, labour unions that have challenged management authority, and globalization that has opened up the domestic market to foreign competitors' (p. 26). As a result, the ROK slipped in competitiveness from 26th in 1995 to 38th in 1999, according to the International Management Development (Kwang, 1999, p. 67).

Ehrlich (2000) reflected the thoughts of many by claiming that 'it was mismanagement that sparked [Korea's] economic crisis' (p. 31), and he concluded that, in the area of corporate governance, 'progress... remains stalled'

(p. 31). He went on to explain: 'more needs to be done to rein in the excesses of corporate leaders – on whom the crisis may be blamed, for their penchant to borrow easy money for dubious expansion' (p. 31) – in almost direct contrast to the arguments against these claims put forward by Lee (1998–9). Kim Nam-hee (2000, personal communication) argued that part of the explanation for the crisis is that the earlier growth rates were driven by 'quantity, not quality'. As the gap between quality and quantity grew, the crisis became inevitable.

Certainly, Korean politics has been marked over decades with corruption. This could well be another source of the crisis, as a 'corrupt and unstable political system makes it difficult to solve problems in infrastructure and education' (Engardio *et al.*, 1996, p. 62).

On a micro-level, there remains a shortage of higher education programmes in human resource development. So students leave the ROK to study in the United Kingdom, Australia, and the United States, taking valuable foreign exchange currencies with them and, in some cases, taking their own talents with them as they decide not to return home. Those few programmes that do exist are rather inflexible in meeting the needs of potential students, by offering only full-time, day-school programmes, when many of those desiring such an education need to be part-time students attending evening classes because of commitments to employment during the day. This situation is beginning to change, but slowly, as demand for such programmes increases and as competition from the development of new programmes grows. Part of this problem, though, stems from the continuing emphasis Koreans put on traditional higher education, emanating from the most prestigious universities. Part-time, adult, evening degree programmes or correspondence and distance education courses have many cultural barriers to overcome.

From a long-term perspective, there is a shortage of an indigenous research base. As my Korean graduate students focus on HR in the ROK, as a way of bolstering the research base that exists there, they consistently find that there are few research studies published on HR in the ROK, and many of those that are published suffer from research deficiencies. I have asked where the journals are that provide Korean professionals with research on HR. I have asked where the professional organizations are to support the development of a community of HR researchers in the ROK. Both questions have been greeted with silence. And the problem may simply be that there is not a good data base available for identifying those research studies that do exist within the Korean context (though this is improving with the web), thus making them inaccessible to both scholars and practitioners. A further issue might well be that much of the research that has been done on Korean

HR has been done in other countries and may never find its way back to Korea or ever get translated into Korean for ready access to practitioners there.

Surely there are more causes of the current economic crisis that are amenable to human capital development intervention. Other causes that are perhaps outside of the scope of HR include such concerns as debt/equity ratios, bank practices that have allowed such ratios to occur, government subsidies to prop up financially troubled organizations, accounting practices below international standards, barriers to foreign direct investment, and so on. Korea's Finance-Economy Minister, Kang Bong-kyun, claimed that the 'primary reason that Korea was forced to borrow from the IMF was the lack of foreign exchange liquidity' that 'stemmed from a structural weakness... characterized by high cost and low efficiency, accumulated in the course of the nation's energetic economic growth' ('Nation Builds Firmer Economic Foundations', *Business Korea*, 1999, p. 21). Kwang (1999) rejected the liquidity argument, suggesting that 'the root of the problem involved the inability of the Korean government as well as the domestic financial and business sectors to adapt to the new world order marked by unprecedented global competition' (p. 66). The view of the IMF, itself, was that the 'crisis was marked by massive capital outflows, a sharp depreciation of the won, and severe distress in the corporate and financial sectors' (IMF, 1999, p. 1). They have also concluded, however, that 'policies adopted under the programme have successfully restored external stability, rebuilt reserves, and initiatied reform of the financial and corporate sectors' (IMF, 1999, p. 1).

HOW HAS HR RESPONDED AND WITH WHAT SUCCESS?

There is no question that Korea has responded in a vibrant way to the crisis – in 1999, Korea's growth rate had returned to 10.7 per cent ('Business as Usual', *Far Eastern Economic Review*, 2000). The same editorial, however, concluded, 'Little has changed' (p. 74). In contrast, many arguments have been put forward that major changes in HR (both HRM and HRD) have been, at least in part, responsible for the significant turnaround.

Almost immediately after the IMF recommendations in 1997, major shifts occurred in organizations. Downsizing, re-engineering, new employment policies and practices, renewed emphasis on training and development, and new reward systems all came into play, 'moving away from traditional lifetime employment and seniority practices' (Lee, 1998–9, p. 27).

One area that has seen dramatic change since the financial crisis has been in recruitment. Traditionally, Korean chaebol have recruited large numbers of graduates from the country's most prestigious universities twice a year. Graduates were selected based primarily on their university performance, performance on assessment tests administered by the company, and the prestige of the university, though other, relationship-based factors (family home, connections) may have been present, but to a lesser degree in recent years. These new employees were then put in long-term training and orientation sessions lasting from six months to a year before decisions were made about job assignment. With the onset of the financial crisis, the chaebols no longer had the luxury of hiring large numbers of graduates for unspecified jobs, yet there was still a need to hire highly-skilled graduates, particularly in the areas of science, technology, engineering, economics, and management. Thus, in order to hire a smaller number of the top graduates in a very competitive recruitment environment, the chaebol have been forced to develop more systematic recruitment plans, using many approaches, including the use of summer internships, television commercials, campus visits, company tours, and company–university partnerships (research, scholarships, grants, at least in part to improve the image of the company). They have also re-emphasized their relationships with university professors, especially using top executives with alumni relationships with the prestigious universities, to exert pressure on professors to recommend the most talented graduates and to assist them in recruitment. In 1999, several chaebols resumed the practice of visiting the United States (and other countries) to recruit Korean students to return to Korea, extending their concepts of 'prestigious universities'. I have seen many of these practices first-hand as chaebols attempt to recruit Korean graduate students from our programme, even including females which is a rarity for the Korean chaebols. Lee (1998–9, p. 35) claimed that fewer than 8 per cent of the chaebol hires in 1995 were female. Perhaps the necessity for hiring the best graduates, combined with changing cultural norms, may influence this number positively in the future.

Lee (1998–9) also concluded that the financial crisis and recent increases in global competition have forced the chaebol to shift from 'education-based to performance-based selection criteria' (p. 36), leading either to the elmination of examinations and mass interviews to at least a reduced emphasis, with increasing emphasis on the assessment of personality traits ('creativity, positive attitude, and outward-looking characteristics') and capability, including 'simulated exercises or discussion sessions'. Given the inability of other countries to create valid personality-trait prediction criteria, however, this may not be the most effective approach for the Korean chaebols.

Lee's (1998–9) final area of transformation in HR, while not elaborated upon, included 'employee evaluation, promotion, and compensation practices' that 'are also undergoing change, with a shift in emphasis from seniority to ability and performance' (p. 39). He recognized the difficulty of the many changes facing the Korean chaebols and the fact that they may take many years to achieve. However, 'unless Korean businesses achieve such a successful transformation, they are not expected to regain the competitiveness they once enjoyed in the world market, and they may find it hard to survive in the new global-competition world' (p. 39).

Labour relations, which most expected to deteriorate rapidly with the crisis, did not materialize to the extent expected. In fact, Beck (2000) concluded that the reason for this is that 'Kim Dae-jung came into office with labour's support and trust', in part by expanding 'the social safety net without exploding the government's budget deficit' (p. 1).

Within HRD, in the one year between 1997 and 1998, Cho, Park and Wagner (1999) cited a survey from Korea's *Human Resource Development* magazine indicating a cut in training investments of 12.5 per cent (p. 98). In a follow-up interview with HRD managers from six of the chaebols, they found that 'one of their most urgent needs was to align HRD with business issues' (p. 98). To accomplish that, the interviewees said that 'HRD practitioners must design and deliver programmes in restructured organizational development, reallocation of workers, change management for leaders, and marketing and finance-related courses' (p. 98). HRD costs were reduced by 10–68 per cent in these chaebol through 'cost-effective or profit-making training activities, including consolidating training departments, outsourcing, marketing, shortening training periods, developing customized programmes, and using out-placement programmes funded by the government', resulting in training staff cuts of from 4 to 110 people (p. 98).

Park Moon-soo (2000, personal communication), Director of Knowledge Management for Samsung Life Insurance Co., Ltd, shared these observations on Samsung. Samsung, one of the leading chaebols, followed the lead of other chaebols by restructuring itself in 1998; the unit most hit by the restructuring was HRD. This caused a lack of loyalty and other legal problems between the company and the staff who were forced to leave. Problems in managing the remaining employees in HRD also resulted.

As recovery began in 1999, the company has had to focus on HRD, with a heavy emphasis on training, with a feeling that 'we have tried to start from scratch again'. Staff have been sent abroad for learning and experience opportunities. They have been encouraged to acquire MBAs and to undertake local specialized projects.

However, there is a major difference in what Samsung is doing now and what it did before 1998. Previously, there was a heavy emphasis on selecting and training the 'right' staff. Now, the focus is on 'loyalty-fulfilled members', that is, they select people with potential and train them to fit into their organization.

Park concluded: 'Investing in HRD has had good effects in re-establishing our company's relationships with its staff, and it has improved the credibility of HRD.'

Kim Han-sung (2000, personal communication), a member of the HRD Department with SK, another chaebol, indicated that some HRD departments in some of the chaebols have tried to be independent through outsourcing, by trying to sell their training products in the public market. But their marketing efforts appear not to have been successful. They still depend on their company and their colleagues for their training fees.

SK has experienced a shift in the focus of its training efforts. There is now increased emphasis on training those who have been identified as 'high potential'. Thus, training is no longer provided for everyone. Rather, 'each individual must take responsibility for his or her own development'. Another shift has been to focus on individual task expertise rather than general management skills as before. Another shift has been to expand distance learning. Since it is 'not easy to gather people together at the training center, we are replacing many of our off-line programmes with on-line learning'. Finally, while most HRD staff are focused on training at present, as the boundary between HRM and HRD becomes blurred, 'not only training but also OD approaches are being viewed as more desirable'.

Moon Yong-lin (2000, personal communication), formerly professor at Seoul National University, and recently the Minister of Education for South Korea, shared examples of HR transformation in two companies following the financial crisis of 1997. The first is a company within the Samsung group – Samsung Electronics – that supports the observations of Park Moon-soo, and the second is Pacific Co., Ltd.

Samsung Electronics Co., Ltd since 1998 has laid a foundation for becoming a technology- and marketing-oriented company through extensive renovation, including the restructuring of HR. A new, more efficient Human Resource operation and management system was formed by the successful combination of HRD and HRM. The company now aims at offering training that directly influences business outcomes. Each training institute attached to the company has improved its training system to meet the most urgent needs of the company. It has also made efforts to nurture experts and highly skilled marketing managers with customer-oriented thinking. At the same time, the company has continued with many technical innovations. As a result of these efforts, Samsung Electronics Co., Ltd received the Employer Professional Development Award presented by IEEE in 1999.

Pacific Co., Ltd redesigned and expanded its training programme to meet existing challenges, to survive through the economic crisis. Programmes that were previously offered only to its employees were expanded to include all agents. These programmes allowed the company to instil the company's ethics and marketing skills so trainees would become more professional. With well-equipped workers, the company experienced a dramatic increase in sales and profits, emerging from its financial difficulties.

Korea Telecom (Korea Telecom HRD Group, 1998), while projecting a decrease in its overall training impact, nevertheless proposed a number of changes in its organization and focus. Specifically, four focused aims were created for the HRD Group as follows (verbatim, including Korean English):

- Bring up *Multi-Pro Personnel* who are equipped with core technologies which can be used in various fields.
- Foster *Creative Personnel* who flexible, creative and innovative mind toward solving problems.
- Nourish *Global Personnel* who contribute to global management activity and mantles corporate vision.
- Cultivate of *Ethics Personnel* who carry out the social responsibility of corporate. (p. 3)

The Korea Telecom HRD Group also created a vision of its 'Training Direction' as follows:

- Concentration on Management Innovation
  - Train people to practice value, profit, and money oriented management
  - Customer satisfaction & management enforcement training
  - Ensure the successful growth of team system
  - Maintain the corporation's values and management innovation.
- Accumulating Core-Competency for Employees
  - Overall management training for leaders
  - Business & technology management training for managers
  - Technology & job skill training for workforce
  - Basic communication technology training
  - Marginal member's productivity & flexibility, repositioning training
- Raising Economical and Competitive Training Capability
  - Reconfirm value & cost concept of training investment
  - Launch distance learning (through TV or www)
  - Continue to evaluate Quality of Education (QOE)
  - Benchmarking world leading company's training know-hows (p. 10)

Chang Young-chul (2000, personal communication), Professor of Management at Kyunghee University, was less positive about the changes that have occurred in the HR arena since the onset of the financial crisis. He saw few changes occurring in the way in which HR activities are conducted. He concluded that

> few companies have systematic metrics to evaluate the success or failure of their HRD and HRM practices. Furthermore, most HRD activities are not strategic in the sense that they are designed to meet certain strategic needs. Instead, most HRD activities are designed and implemented according to the temporary popularity of specific topics.

Kim Nam-hee (personal correspondence, 3 July, 2000) suggested that one response provided by HRD has been an increasing emphasis on globalization, reflected by increasing emphasis on foreign language instruction and providing international experiences for employees, to avoid some of the embarrassing situations that can occur in international trade when employees are not prepared for the interactions.

WHAT MORE SHOULD THE ROK EXPECT FROM ITS HR ACADEMICS AND PROFESSIONALS?

I approach this question as an outsider. Just as the US has much that it needs to be doing but isn't, so, too, does the Republic of Korea. I hope that readers of this chapter will feel free to open a dialogue with me about these suggestions and others that you have to add.

Let me cautiously suggest some ways in which HR can be useful in moving the ROK beyond its current economic crisis on a sound footing.

1. With the increasing demand for the very best employees and with limited numbers of hires allowed, and given the large number of Korean women now receiving higher education, we might well expect HRD and HRM in Korea to help the chaebols move away from their demographic homogeneity to affirm diversity, at least of gender. The younger generation has a different perspective regarding gender in Korea that will allow a slow, evolutionary increase in the number of women in employment in the chaebol. Changes in the culture will also allow such employees to remain on the job, even after marriage and childbirth, a major change from the current cultural expectations.

2. Korean chaebols need to put much more effort into research that would help in the identification of the most appropriate, systematic approaches to both recruitment and selection of employees that would be both valid and reliable in projecting the performance-based impact of such criteria.

3. Many have argued that the modifications made in the 1998 amendments to the Regulations on Securities Listing have not gone far enough (see, for example, Ehrlich, 2000). Several issues here could well be supported by strategic HR efforts that were aligned with the chaebols, themselves, perhaps moving the transformations out of the legal and governmental arenas to the organization development arena. Many of these issues have to do with the voice of the stockholder, avenues of stockholder redress, the role and identity of the chaebols' boards, and so on.

4. High-quality research focused on economic and HR problems within the ROK is needed to address questions of effectiveness and efficiency of expenditures on human capital – expanding the existing indigenous research base.

5. Training and development in business ethics, though the outcome of such is uncertain, may still be useful if directed at all levels of politicians and at all levels of supervision and management within Korean organizations. This needs to be followed with holding such individuals accountable for ethical behaviour in their professional and public lives. This will need to draw on the long religious values and traditions within the country, as well as the development of moral character within the Korean people.

6. Many countries have developed national awards that recognize a commitment to human capital development – such as components of the Deming Award in Japan and the Baldrige Award in the USA. The ROK may well wish to consider such an award focused solely on human capital development.

7. With the clear possibility that the ROK may be facing additional crises, HR may be a catalyst for consultation in the development of policies and reasonable responses to the need for quick downsizing. As an outsider looking in, it appears that there were no failsafe systems in place to step in when the need came for many companies to close their doors or reduce the number of personnel. While the government has made many changes in this area, it is not clear that enough has been done for future events of this nature, especially those focusing on the provision of training and retraining for those affected and for those continuing in poverty. While the Korean Research Institute for Vocational Education and Training (KRIVET) has taken the lead in providing information and support related to efforts in this area, more may yet need to be done for the future.

8. Education of politicians (and senior management personnel) in systems and strategic thinking is important. Is anyone doing this? Does organizational learning exist within the government? What has the government learned from the current crisis? Does it understand the interconnectedness of events, policies, actions, etc.?

9.	Leadership is needed in the development of a scholarly journal on HRD in the ROK, as well as contributions to the broader literature, such as *Human Resource Development International, Human Resource Development Quarterly,* and the *Journal of Transnational Management Development.* It is critical that Korea re-establish a scholarly journal to replace the now-defunct, Samsung-supported *Strategic Human Resource Development Review.* While practitioner journals have their place, and they do exist in Korea, scholarly journals are critical to the development and dissemination of indigenous research, theories, and models.

10.	Leadership is also needed in creating a community of HRD researchers and scholars. While practitioner professional organizations currently exist in Korea (e.g., the Korean Management Association), there is a marked lack of focused scholarship. Perhaps this would emerge as an Asian regional chapter of the Academy of Human Resource Development, or an Asian HR chapter of the Academy of Management, though it seems to me that HR is so important to the future of the ROK that there needs to be a professional HR research/scholarly organization that is country specific.

11.	Undergraduate and graduate programmes in HRD need to be established throughout the country that move away from the traditional higher-education model of full-time, day-time programmes to accommodate workers who need to be developing HRD competence. Such programmes also need to have a much broader perspective on HRD than is possible in those institutions which have simply made slight modifications in Industrial Education programmes. Distance-education approaches would meet the needs of potential students in locations away from existing institutions. Only when professionally prepared practitioners are widely available can the ROK expect to see an effective impact on the economy through in-service training, organization development, strategic planning, and other critical HRD activities.

Chang and McLean (in process) have produced another set of recommendations for training and development as Korea moves forward to regain its competitiveness:

1.	Need for paradigm shift in the mindset of training and development professionals:
	(a) Understanding business challenges
	(b) Developing capability to identify critical success factors of business
	(c) Collaborating with line managers to identify training needs
	(d) Developing cost-effective training systems

2. Need for future-oriented skill framework for both white-collar and blue-collar workers, by identifying future competencies and potential for contributing to the enhancement of competitiveness of the company.
3. Enhancing learning capability of an organization through facilitating the transformation of individual knowledge, skill, ability and behaviour into organizational competencies.
4. Integration of subject-matter experts into the education/development planning and course design/delivery processes. Too much reliance on education technology would end up with polishing and packaging education and training programmes with little impact on, or with few achievements in, the real business outcomes, particularly in management development. Clusters of competencies of HRD professionals include (1) business knowledge, (2) knowing leading-edge training and development theories and practices, (3) understanding a change models and applying them to a specific situation, (4) being credible through the accuracy of their work and the intimacy of their relationships.
5. Establishing the continuous learning systems in the workplace to improve individual knowledge/skill base as well as employability of employees.
6. Reawakening management to the value of a skilled, motivated and committed workforce so that intellectual capital will become an ongoing investment where employees are constantly learning, changing, challenging, and reinventing themselves and their organizations.
7. At the highest level, training and development roles should involve helping to build and manage the knowledge base of the firm so that the organization can become a learning system capable of generating new strategic assets and of ensuring people's full contribution to organizational transformation and growth.
8. National level support to boost the market-based forces enhancing security, learning, and involvement in the organization through good people management practices.

CONCLUSION

Long ago, I heard a story that was ascribed to a wise old man in a village in India. Two young men were annoyed that the elder was given so much respect by the villagers, and they set out to trap him. They came to him one day with a bird in their hands. They asked the elder, 'Is this bird dead or alive?' If the elder answered 'Dead', they would open their hands and let the bird fly away. If the answer was 'Alive', they would crush the bird. The elder pondered for a few minutes, and then said, 'The answer is in your hands.'

No wise person carries his or her responsibilities lightly. Presumably, readers of this chapter (and book) have an interest in human resources. The futures of HRD and HRM in the Republic of Korea, and, perhaps, the future of the country itself, are in our hands. How we respond to this challenge may well impact the future of the world.

References

'Asian Unionists Denounce IMF's Policy Remedies' (1998) *The Nation*, 12 January, p. B6.

Beck, P. (1997) 'Arranging the Elements: The Origins and Development of Taegeuk-ki', Paper presented at PACIFIC 97, San Francisco, CA. (Further information available from Korea Stamp Society, P. O. Box 8142, St. Paul, MN 55108.)

Beck, P. (2000) 'Reviewing President Kim's Two Years: Building a New Economy,' *Korea Times*, 25 February, p. 1.

'Business as Usual: Minority Shareholder Rights in South Korea' (2000) *Far Eastern Economic Review*, 6 April, p. 74.

Chalofsky, N. (1992) 'A Unifying Definition for the Human Resource Development Profession', *Human Resource Development Quarterly*, 3(2), pp. 175–82.

Chang, Y. C. and McLean, G. N. (in process) 'Corporate Training for Developing Sustainable Competitiveness in Korea' (manuscript is in draft format).

Cho, Y. J., Park, H. Y. and Wagner, S. (1999) 'Training in a Changing Korea', *Training and Development*, May, pp. 98–9.

Ehrlich, C. (2000) 'Arming Korea's Shareholders', *Far Eastern Economic Review*, 10 February, p. 31.

Engardio, P., Moore, J. and Hill, C. (1996) 'Time for a Reality Check in Asia', *Business Week*, 2 December, pp. 58–66.

Gong, B. H. (1999) 'The Chaebols – Myth and Reality', *Business Korea*, October, pp. 34–8.

International Monetary Fund (IMF) (1999) *IMF Concludes Article IV Consultation with Korea*, Public Information Notice No. 99/115 (Washington, DC: IMF).

Kirk, D. (1994) *Korean Dynasty: Hyundai and Chung Ju Yung* (Armonk, NY: M. E. Sharpe).

Korea Telecom HRD Group (1998) *Human Resources Development System* (Seoul).

Kwang, C. (1999) 'Public Sector Reform in Korea', *Korea Focus on Current Topics*, 7(5), pp. 66–77.

Lee, H. C. (1998–9) 'Transformation of Employment Practices in Korean Businesses', *International Studies of Management and Organisation*, 28(4), (Winter) pp. 26–39.

McLagan, P. (1989) *Models for HRD Practice* (Alexandria, VA: American Society for Training and Development Press).

McLean, G. N. and McLean, L. D. (2000) 'If we can't define HRD in one country, how can we define it in an international context?', in J. Woodall (ed.), *Defining HRD: The Debate So Far*, Economic and Social Research Seminar Series (Kingston, UK: Kingston Business School, Kingston University).

Nadler, L. (1970) *Developing Human Resources* (Houston, TX: Gulf).

'Nation Builds Firmer Economic Foundations' (1999) *Business Korea*, October, pp. 20–1.

Salome, B. and Charmes, J. (1988) *In-Service Training: Five Asian Experiences* (Paris, France: Development Centre of the Organisation for Economic Co-operation and Development).

Scarpello, V. G., Ledvinka, J. and Bergmann, T. J. (1995) *Human Resource Management: Environments and Functions* (Cincinnati, OH: South-Western College Publishing).

Swanson, R. A. (1995) 'Performance is the Key', *Human Resource Development Quarterly*, 6(2), pp. 207–13.

Ungson, C. R., Steers, R. M. and Park, S. H. (1997) *Korean Enterprise: The Quest for Globalization* (Boston: Harvard Business School Press).

Weinberger, L. A. (1998) 'Commonly Held Theories of Human Resource Development', *Human Resource Development International*, 1(1), pp. 72–86.

'Yes But What Exactly is a Chaebol?' (2000) (on-line). wysiwyg://25/http:/www.megastories.com/seasia/chaebol/chaewhat.html (3 pages).

5 Transitions and Traditions in Chinese Family Businesses: Evidence from Hong Kong and Thailand

Roger Pyatt, Neal M. Ashkanasy,
Rick Tamaschke and Trevor Grigg

INTRODUCTION

Redding (1995) argues that the twentieth-century rise of the Asian economies has been largely engineered by ethnic Chinese capitalists (see also Clegg, Redding and Cartner, 1990; Liu and Faure, 1996; and Whitley, 1992). Much of this rise has been accomplished by the *hua ch'iao* (referred to in this chapter as 'Sojourners'), the ethnic Chinese living in two Southeast Asian sub-sets. One group resides within that crescent of countries bordering the South China Sea (*Nanyang*). Mostly these are the economies that form the ASEAN zone. The China Coast group includes those in the predominantly Chinese communities of Hong Kong, Macau and Taiwan (Wang, 1994). The resulting organizational forms are distinctly different from Western companies, or even other Asian organizations such as the Japanese *keiretsu* or the Korean *chaebol* (Hamilton, Chen and Wong, 1991).

The first, that is the traditional, Chinese family business (CFB), can be described as a *quan-xi* (relationships) form (in Cantonese; also known as *guanxi* in Mandarin). In its purest form, the *quan-xi* organization is based upon immediate (extended) family or derivatives based upon socialization. In practice, a linkage of business relationships (distinct from Japanese-style consensus) is through *quan-xi*. Sociologically, *quan-xi* can be defined as 'personalistic, particularistic, non-idealogical ties between persons – based upon a commonality of shared identification' (Jacobs, 1985, p. 80). The second type comprises the *quan-xi-qiye* organizational form. The phrase is a combination of two Chinese words, *quan-xi* which means 'relationship' and *qiye* which means '(Western-type) enterprise' (Numazaki, 1991). [The standard translations of *quan-xi* and *quan-xi-qihe* are *guanxi* and *gunaxiqihe* respectively. We recognise there are differences between Mandarin and Cantonese but, for the sake of consistency in this book, we will use the standard form: eds.] This type is especially noticeable within the Coastal Chinese diaspora in Taiwan. Further, Chinese entrepreneurship does not necessarily exclude the development of larger bureaucratic organizations, however. In this respect, we posit that the corporations that they form are hybrid structures similar to the type identified by Semkow (1992). The coda we have adopted in this chapter for these publicly listed corporations under majority family control is the 'Quasi-corporation'.

In this chapter therefore, we will describe the way that the Chinese organization has evolved in the *Nanyang* and China Coast into more modern and international organizational forms, more suited to the competitive global environment of the twenty-first century, and discuss the economic and human resource implication of this transformation.

The chapter comprises three parts. In the first part, we briefly describe the history of the Chinese Sojourners in the *Nanyang* and China Coast groups, define key terms, and outline how Chinese organizations have adapted to the modern world of business. In the second section, we discuss epistemological and methodological issues relating to the study of 'opaque' business networks in Asia, and present qualitative and quantitative data to illustrate how forms of organization have evolved in the *Nanyang* and China Coast groups, especially new forms based on more Western business norms and formal rules of operation, and their economic and human resource consequences. Finally, we discuss the implications for business in East Asia and the global economy of the emergence of these organizational forms.

THE EVOLUTION OF THE CHINESE FAMILY BUSINESS

The Chinese organizations that Redding (1995) identified as pivotal in the rise of Asian economy are not at all homogeneous. Although all are known to favour collaborative organizational forms in distinguishing ways, they differ in structure, societal culture, history and domain, both from each other and from the Western norm (Hamilton *et al.*, 1991). Further, interest in this region remains high despite the diminution of the high growth rates of the 1970s and 1980s (Patten, 1997). This is because of the strong linkages between the capitalist economies of this region and the West established during the Cold War years. These include Western exports to Asia of technology products, Eastern exports to the West of low-priced manufactured goods, and reciprocal East–West capital investments (see Henderson, 1998; Rohwer, 1998).

The Chinese Sojourners

The Chinese in Southeast Asia, in essence, are an example of a 'Global Tribe'. The term was coined by Kotkin (1992) to describe a modern version of the Jewish Diaspora. Unlike their historical counterparts, however, contemporary tribes are connected by global communications with each other and the homeland, in 'the age of acoustic space' (McLuhan and McLuhan, 1989, p. 84). What characterizes the Chinese in particular is their highly entrepreneurial behaviour. In this respect, Wickberg (1965) has noted that there is general agreement in the literature that Chinese entrepreneurial behaviour is a mix of acute management of cash and finance, with informal vertically integrated networks to control a total market process. When coupled with *pang*,[1] this entrepreneurship has, over time, become associated with cohesion based upon social norms, especially within clans, lineage-groups, and dialect-groups. These cohesions serve to reduce uncertainty and transaction costs further. They also serve to generate economic growth, to integrate imperfect markets, to act as a means of internal credit control, and to obtain political cooperation (Leff, in Mackie, 1992a; Kao, 1993; Redding, 1990).

Culturally, however, Southeast Asian countries differ in their host religion and ethnic makeup. The Chinese in each country differ in their mix of dialect-groups (*pang*), although most groups originate from South China. Their political histories differ, and these histories offer important additional insights into the business behaviour of the Sojourners not considered in this chapter. Yet, at the same time, the Sojourners' overall 'Chineseness' is essentially the same, and institutions and business methods apply equally to both the China Coast set of Sojourners and the ASEAN block sub-set. The Thailand and Hong Kong ethnic Chinese discussed in this chapter operate in different cultural environments, and these countries also differ in their geographical proximity to mainland China, their current stage of economic development, levels and composition of imports and exports (trade), currency volatility, and rates of social, economic and technological development.

Hard economic and business expediency, in addition to ethnic loyalties, are reasons for much of the collaborative behaviour characteristic of the Sojourners (Redding, 1990). Social coordination allows the limitations of the traditional Chinese form of organizational behaviour to be transcended. In particular, Chinese family firms are noteworthy for their weak hierarchical organization structures, and distinguishing management practices which characterize and discern them from the Japanese *keiretsu*, the Korean *chae-bol*, or the Western norm (Redding, 1991; Whitley, 1992; Chen, 1995). These limitations include the danger of factions and cliques, stifling of initiative, limits to the boundaries of legitimate authority, the tendency for cooperative relationships to be small in domain, mistrust, the urge to control leading to capital starvation, and technical inadequacy (Redding, 1991). In addition to those normative benefits drawn from their networks, Chinese family firms enjoy vertical cooperation which incorporates many Chinese social norms about social order into the business world: willing compliance and perseverance, the stability of key relationships, and the manoeuvrability of linkages (Redding, 1991).

We argue in this chapter that much of the effectiveness of these organizations is based on trust. This is because, in an environment where markets are based on the price system, and administrative regulations determine hierarchies, trust in the context of opaque networks of relational contracts can be a source of sustained competitive advantage. Kay (1993) refers to such relational contracts as 'architectures'. In this respect, understanding the boundaries of trust and the architectures built by social contracts is an underlying feature of this study, which is one in a series named the Southeast Asian Strategic Network Studies (SASNS; see Pyatt, 1995a,b; 1996, 1999; Pyatt and Trimarchi, 1998).

CHINESE BUSINESS FORMS AND THE ROLE OF TRUST

The central concept of our chapter is the idea of *architectures*, comprised of networks of relational contracts within and around the firm that involve coordination, cooperation and commitment (Kay, 1993). The benefits of relational contracts typically include the development of organizational knowledge, and flexibility in response and information exchange within or between organizations. As applied to competing corporations, architecture can be a distinctive capability which, when applied to an industry and market, can be a source of competitive advantage for the firm (Kay, 1993). These relationships are based on trust, defined by Thorelli (1986) as 'confidence in the continuation of a mutually satisfying relationship and in the awareness of other parties of what this requires of their performance as network members' (p. 451). As such, trust is a vital supplement to these contractual arrangements, especially in oriental cultures (Kay, 1993).

Finally, we note that an important motivation for our research is that, although studies of Southeast Asian Overseas Chinese have provided new insights into East Asian capitalism (see Whitely, 1992), the intra-regional and international connections of Chinese businesses have received scant attention. In particular, we could find no measures of Southeast Asian Overseas Chinese relational contract architectures, nor any studies of intra-regional and international trust by ethnic Chinese. Thus, although Wong (1997) has identified the ability of ethnic Chinese networks to spread globally, and noted transnational commercial networks sustained by trusting behaviour and autonomy, no measures of the boundaries of trust and the nature of relational contracts in this region can be found in the literature to date. Our study was intended to begin to plug this gap in our knowledge of these organizational forms.

Trust in Competitive versus Cooperative Strategies

Contemporary views on management practice embrace a volume of accounts recording the extent of organizations working together (Lorange and Roos, 1992; Alter and Hage, 1993). The general term for those mutually reinforcing and advantageous, value-adding, and trust-based coordinations is 'win–win'. The social economic literature suggests that in generally low-trust societies (such as the Chinese), cohesion may be evident in certain places. This trust is not on a societal level, but is found selectively in forms such as business trading preferences, perhaps within small groups such as family firms or amongst a transnational elite. Kay (1993) has noted that trust mechanisms have been recognized over many centuries and in communities all over the world as a low-cost means of dealing with social and business relationships, supplanted only this century by aggressive individualism. The underlying management problem of the research described in this chapter, therefore, is that not enough is known and understood about the coordinations of the Sojourners, compared to our knowledge of the South Korean *chaebol* and Japanese *keiretsu*, or management in the rest of the world (Redding, 1990).

The paradigms of this new topology require research methodologies suitable for the task, whether or not they fit established research traditions. The term 'paradigm' refers to a network of concepts (see Kuhn, 1962). Kuhn coined the term 'paradigm shift' to mean a revolutionary change in scientific questioning, and this clearly applies in management studies, especially at the buyer–seller interface. The questions raised in macro-organization studies, and driven by the new paradigm, ask: What more can be understood about business markets by investigating interactions and relationships (Ford, 1990; Larson, 1992)? And what can be understood about organizations beyond markets or firms (Powell, 1990)? Answers to these questions are emerging, however. An actual understanding of coordinations includes not only their justification as an object of study but an analysis of how they work (see Thompson *et al.*, 1991). Also, managing the new organization requires a blueprint for alliances (Limerick and Cunnington, 1993). Steps for the successful management of global alliances are based upon collaboration

(Cauley de la Sierra, 1995) and the rise of regional economies is associated with collaborations beyond the nation state (Ohmae, 1995).

Researchers of the new paradigm (e.g., Easton and Araujo, 1993) consider that a significant, and major, method of contemporary business investigation is the use of comparative segmentation. Thorelli (1986) argues that network studies need to be holistic, and cannot be hindered by the tools associated with the more traditional, reductionist research traditions (see also Redding, 1990). Thus, inter-organizational relationships are better understood by a network approach rather than a transaction cost approach (Johanson and Mattsson, 1987). Further, since the basis for collaborating must also be investigated (Bleeke and Ernst, 1993), macro-organizational theories, rather than economic or political theories, are more likely to explain networks in specific environmental contexts (Hamilton, Zeile and Kim, 1990).

Other observers, such as Wilson and Mummalaneni (1986), have also emphasized the need for inter-organizational relationships to be studied in non-European settings and from a cultural perspective (Boisot, 1987). Ouchi (1980) has gone so far as to state that the organic solidarity of Asian entrepreneurial clans is a necessary subject for scholarly attention. This is in contrast with the conventional analysis at the macro-policy level, in that it is deemed necessary to consider how Southeast Asian and East Asian managers actually organize their own business activities (Hamilton *et al.*, 1990) and how they respond to social values (Donleavy, 1995). In this instance, more analysis of business systems in different Asian economic and cultural contexts is clearly an imperative (Whitley, 1992).

Finally, we note that values play an important coordination role within global tribes that sustain trust. In their intra-regional, economic study, Lim and Gosling (1983) identified cultural traditions, clannish and networked links, human resource policies, and language as factors underlying success across the 'Chinese zone'. Wong (1997) identified in addition the ability of ethnic Chinese networks to spread globally, and noted transnational commercial networks sustained by family-oriented trusting behaviour and autonomy. Thus, we conclude that, although cooperation is an important issue in Chinese business (Redding, 1995), research to date has yet to examine the boundaries of trust and the nature of relational contract architectures in the Sojourners' context.

Trust and Social Contracts

We have already noted that the central concept of the study we describe in this chapter is the notion of networks of relational contracts, or architecture (Kay, 1993). We expand on this notion in this section with a deeper look at the role of trust. Thorelli (1986, p. 37) has pointed out that, especially in oriental cultures, trust is such a vital supplement to contractual arrangements that it 'may even take their place'. In this sense, the firm is seen as a collection of contracts (see Alchian and Demsetz, 1972). The idea was extended by Klein (1983), and applied to inter-organizational relationships by Johanson and Mattsson (1987). From a legal perspective, relational contracts are associated with the work of Macneil (1980). In sociology, Macaulay (1963) is the seminal writer, and in economics these are referred to as implicit or incomplete contracts. Kay (1993) made an attempt to fit the relational contracts perspective within transaction-cost economics.

The specific concept of trust relationships in the management literature is associated with Fox (1974). The interaction between trust and management structures is discussed in the writings of Granovetter (1985) and Zucker (1986). Further, in social contracting, trust has been examined as a form of governance (Calton and Lad, 1995), and as a moral authority (Conry, 1995). Mutual interests generate trust and behaviour based upon standards which no one individual can determine alone. Trust reduces complex realities far more quickly and economically than prediction, authority, or bargaining (Powell, 1990).

Wong (1997) classified four forms of trust in ethnic Chinese society that relate to the economic performance of Chinese family firms: personal trust, network trust, systems trust, and moral trust. Where these qualities are practised, they shape human resource policies, add substantially to social capital, and thus underpin economic performance (Redding, 1990). In these contexts, we argue that it is *relational contracts*, and not classical contracts, which are common. From this, it follows that mutual trust is a form of relational contract. This behaviour acts as an external barrier of entry to competing networks (Dannhaeuser, 1981), and is therefore a powerful sanction against contract defaulters (Mackie, 1992b).

Finally, and for the purposes of the present study, we have refined our definition of trust into the concepts of *forbearance* and *reciprocity*. This is derived from the remarks of Buckley and Casson (1988, p. 32) where they state: 'that the essence of voluntary inter-firm cooperation lies in "coordination effected through mutual forbearance". Forbearance becomes possible only when there is reciprocal behaviour and mutual trust, which in turn only come about given an absence of opportunism.' This strongly suggests that trust is one dependent variable of forbearance, and the other is reciprocity. We note further that the opposite of forbearance is opportunism. As such, trust is developed over time as a series of mutually successful reciprocal exchanges, where each party can rely on the other not to take advantage of opportunities for unilateral advancement at the expense of the other.

SOJOURNERS IN HONG KONG AND THAILAND

In our research, we examine Sojourners in two locations: Hong Kong and Thailand. As we noted earlier, these Sojourners share different cultural backgrounds, but also have an essential 'Chineseness'. Hong Kong and Thailand offer examples of clear differences, and thus constitute a natural laboratory for studying CFBs and the role of trust, forbearance, and reciprocity.

Hong Kong has traditionally been closely aligned with Mainland China, and has therefore retained its extensive Chinese culture. Hong Kong is chosen for our study, however, as an example of an advanced economy of the China Coast diaspora. It is an immigrant community, built from Mainland Chinese who moved to the British colony from the 1830s to the close of the Second World War, or escaped the People's Revolution of 1949. There are also substantial numbers of non-Chinese expatriate workers from the West and the Philippines (6.6 per cent). The major Chinese dialect-groups are Cantonese (90 per cent of total), Hakka (1.6 per cent), Chiu-chow (1.4 per cent), Fukienese, and Shanghainese (*Asia Inc.*, 1996). Enright *et al.* (1997), for example, emphasizes that Hong Kong lies at the centre of the overseas Chinese business network.

Thailand is our second source of data. Thailand hosts the second largest intensive concentration of Chinese (after Malaysia) of the *Nanyang* diaspora, and is also a leading member of ASEAN. Thailand differs from Hong Kong because it is a developing economy with no dominant entrepreneurial clan. The Chinese in Thailand (8.3 million, or around 10 per cent of the population) are immigrants or their descendants. The major Chinese dialect-groups in Thailand are Chiu-chow (56 per cent of total), Hakka (16 per cent), and Hainanese (12 per cent). The remaining groups are mostly Hokkien/Fukien and Cantonese (*Asia Inc.*, 1996). We chose Thailand as an example of a developing economy of the *Nanyang* diaspora.

In summary, the Thailand and Hong Kong Sojourners that we studied operate in different geographic and cultural environments, and these countries also differ in their current stage of economic development, and make-up in imports and exports (trade), currency volatility, and rates of social economic and technological development. The particular research issue related to the relational contracts was to describe how distinguishable architectures have been developed in the Sojourner communities in each country, and to identify the stages involved in development of these architectures. Further, we expected to find that CFBs would differ in Thailand and Hong Kong. Since Hong Kong is a more advanced economy, and more subject to Western business influences, we expected to find that Hong Kong CFBs would be more aligned to Western business norms.

METHODOLOGICAL AND EPISTEMOLOGICAL ISSUES

Data for our study were collected from ethnic Chinese businesses in Hong Kong and Thailand. We employed a triangulated design (Jick, 1979) based on in-depth interviews with twenty Chinese garment-industry business leaders in each country, and an anonymous survey that involved 112 respondents in Hong Kong and 133 in Thailand, from whom 78 and 123 valid responses were received respectively. Our qualitative analysis of the interview data focuses on exposing and defining the relational networks, and expressions of reciprocity, trust, and forbearance in doing business with the four groups. The follow-up surveys attempted to expand the scope of the study by focusing on the 'telltale signs' of the networks discovered during the case interviews. The dependent measure from the survey reported in this chapter is the respondents' preference for doing business with four groups: local Chinese, local non-Chinese Asians, other Chinese, and Westerners. Full details of the study, the samples, and the methodology can be found in Pyatt (1999).

We noted earlier that research in this domain cannot rely on traditional approaches. In this section therefore, we focus on the epistemological and methodological issues underlying our study of the Sojourners, dealing in particular with the phenomenon of *opaqueness*, rather than presenting a detailed description of the methods *per se*, and justifying our triangulated approach. The notion of opaqueness is derived from Forsgren and Johanson (1992, p. 10), who noted: 'A feature of business networks is that they are opaque. This is a consequence of the invisibility of relationships.' In particular, we explicate the factors of opaqueness and relational contracts that underlie the development of our research methodology and the empirical process. The process of development aimed to study the telltale signs of networks, employing a series of case interviews.

Reviews of ethnic business studies by Aldrich and Waldinger (1990) and Braadbaart (1995), provide further guidelines for research in contemporary ethnicity and entrepreneurship. In the view of these authors, the foundation of such studies can be strengthened by careful use of ethnic labels and sensitivity to the interactions between ethnicity and entrepreneurship, and the adoption of an explicit research perspective that compares the samples taken of the phenomenon with the world at large. Aldrich and Waldinger also suggest that such studies should consider performance over time. Finally, Braadbaart has noted that cultural explanations for Chinese ethnic business are not free from methodological pitfalls and display some of the weaknesses noted in the review by Aldrich and Waldinger.

One flaw in culturally based research in East Asia that we have identified is that it largely rests on the questionable assumption that the Chinese Sojourners are culturally homogeneous. Indeed, based upon the ship's log of Chinese Admiral Cheng Ho (*c*. 1350), Chinese traders were already dispersed in a diverse diaspora of well-established settlements across the *Nanyang* by that period. Bond (1991), however, has questioned the assumption of Chinese cultural homogeneity, noting that Hong Kong Chinese are already culturally differentiated from Mainland Chinese. In this case, authors may easily attribute the business performance of overseas Chinese firms to unchanging Chinese values and aspirations, and thus fail to deal satisfactorily with the methodological issues raised by this rigidity.

We also question the assertion that the Sojourners enjoy a unique advantage by operating in family teams. We posit that the mobilization of kinship networks in the pursuit of economic goals is a commercial strategy that may be a widespread business practice around the world. In this regard, Powell (1990) has suggested that the Western historical norm is similar in form to the network phenomenon.

In our research, therefore, we set out to design a methodology that was both sensitive to the guidelines of Aldrich and Waldinger (1990) and Braadbaart (1995), and avoided the pitfalls implicit in the assumptions outlined above. We thus adopted a combination of the application of inductive science and paradigm interplay and bridging (Schultz and Hatch, 1996). In the following, we expand on our approach to this research.

A continuing challenge to researchers working in multi-country fieldwork is the opaque nature of networks that we noted above (Forsgren and Johanson, 1992). This opaqueness is a result of the invisible nature of relationships, and requires insiders, or a 'fifth column' of deeply embedded observers to expose what is happening. Thus, to learn about network coordination, researchers need to interact with the players in the network. But those relational contracts that make up the network are very difficult to study because of their secret nature. The nearest that the researcher can observe are the traces which trusting bonds leave in the behaviour of other players in the network, including such core concepts as trust, reciprocity, opportunism, and forbearance.

The approach that we have adopted relies in part upon uncovering the 'traces' left by relational contracts upon the background. These traces take the form of subjective behaviour, opinions, and attitudes of the players themselves. Given the opaque nature of these relationships, this provides us with a viable alternative to attempting to expose the contracts themselves. This 'tracing of the telltale signs' approach presented challenges in design, but these paid off by having high ($\geq$ 95 per cent) response rates to personal requests for interviews in the garment industry (see also Pyatt, 1995b for application to other industries), and resulted in adequate sample sizes for our research.

Of course, this approach also imposed limitations on our conclusions. Some of these delimitations are related to the challenges just mentioned and some are generic in this field of research. These include systems delimitations in the network approach, cultural dimensions, indiginization, network structure dimensions, and analytical issues.

Using the guidelines of Aldrich and Waldinger (1990), and Braadbaart (1995) as a benchmark, however, it has been possible to justify this approach from the broader literature, addressing four points as follows:

1. *Qualitative studies are the methodological norm in directly related fields.* Drawing upon Bettis (1991) and Hambrick (1990), Parkhe (1993, p. 231) expressed the opinion that methods using 'hard' data sources, such as the 'over-use' of large-scale mail surveys and ready-made databases (Bettis, 1991, p. 316, quoted in Parkhe, 1993) are 'unlikely to capture the core concepts' involved in motives for coordinations in international business. Also, Hambrick (1990, quoted in Parkhe, 1993) has advised against multi-variate number crunching. Studies that are primarily qualitative in methodology should use constructs, laws of interaction, and system states from which to build propositions in preparation of the research model (Dubin, 1982).
2. *Unobservable entities such as trust are a feature of this and other Asian economic culture studies.* See Clegg, Higgins and Speybey (1990), Fukuyama (1995), and Peyfrefitte (1996) for elaboration of this issue. Basically, the unobservable entities cannot be ignored. Instead, they need to be drawn out of the prevailing background and understood within their context.
3. *Organizational researchers face a variety of paradigms with which to theorize.* This is especially true for studies involving cultural issues. Schultz and Hatch (1996), for example, argue that culture researchers need to face this issue, regardless of whether or not paradigmatic assumptions are dealt with explicitly.
4. *The relationship between ethnicity and entrepreneurship highlighted in studies of the Sojourners.* This issue is pertinent when investigating the trading perspectives of Chinese manufacturers towards Asians, as we did in this research.

The solution that we have adopted to overcome the opaque nature of networks and to address the issues we have listed above is based on the standpoint of 'illumination' (Herbert, 1990, p. 36). In this respect, we have adopted the specific approach of triangulation (Jick, 1979), where observations measured quantitatively are used in combination with a subjective interpretation of social life. By adopting this approach, the effects of relational contracts can be traced, and some clarity found in the opaque images non-players obtain of business networks.

In particular, our research employed participant observation as discussed by Layder (1993) in the manner advocated by Strauss, Bucher, Enrlich, Schatzman and Sabshin (1964). The objective of this type of research is to produce findings not arrived at by means of statistical procedures or other means of quantification. As a result, we were able to gain an understanding of the emerging phenomenon of global tribes through access to the underlying reasons and motivations for country-net partnerships and entry mode choices.

In summary, our research approach employed a triangulation of qualitative and quantitative data in a study of Southeast Asian Strategic Network Studies in Hong Kong and Thailand. This approach enabled us to plumb the underlying ethnology of the phenomena under investigation, to relate these findings to our numerical data, and to interplay the approaches in the manner suggested by Schultz and Hatch (1996). Further, this approach allows us to explain how country-nets of Chinese family firms relate internally, with other Chinese businesses, and with non-Chinese. Although we report only limited quantitative results in this article, other specific quantitative data analysis methods employed in our overall research programme included content analysis, linear regression, two-way contingency tables, chi-square analysis, external and internal validation processes, and research auditing (see Pyatt, 1999, for details).

RESULTS AND ANALYSIS

Qualitative Interview Results

The outstanding finding from our interviews with twenty Thailand and twenty Hong Kong business leaders in the garment industry was the strength of personal networking in the business dynamics of Chinese business enterprises. The absolute centrality of this process was not something that we anticipated, but came to light during the course of our interviews. In particular, the Thai interviews suggest that clan linkages play an vital role in network entry and positioning, while the Hong Kong investigations highlighted the critical interweaving of the personal and the business network.

In the context of our research, the productive power of transnational networks was partially determined by the availability of garment export quotas in areas such as the Mekong region, and based upon the dynamic extension of personal networks beyond the business network. Thus, we were able to uncover a ten-step process of Chinese network expansion: (1) expand personal network beyond industry network; (2) search internationally for import quotas; (3) search regionally for lower labour cost capacity; (4) prioritize relationships, barriers, and market potential; (5) buy production in quota country; (6) set up new business network in quota country; (7) reposition established network into quota country; (8) set up production in quota country; (9) review transfer of production from other country; and (10) return to step 1. The process provides a picture of the revolving network expansion process of owner managers. The important point is the expansion of personal networks for the purposes of reducing costs of exchange and production.

The network power expansion we describe above entails 'spinning the web' of personal contacts. The model depicts the Sojourners' method for extending domain overlap and having something to offer in a network. This is achieved by extending their personal network into all the stakeholders involved in supporting their business network expansion plans. This differs fundamentally from the models found in rational interpretations of networks in textbooks such as Jarillo (1988) and Lorange and Roos (1992), and is more akin to personal networks found in entrepreneurial and sociological studies (e.g., Easton and Araujo, 1993).

The productive power expansion process we found clearly applies specifically to types of secondary production such as garments, where the ability to manufacture is dependent upon the import quotas allocated to that country by the major importers such as the European Union and North America. Nevertheless, it appears to be in general use by transnational corporations in the Asia-Pacific region. Outside this region there may also be other aspects that also apply generically into what Kao (1993) calls the 'world wide web' of the Overseas Chinese.

Finally, we note that, in the pragmatics of the real world, players may use more or fewer steps than is indicated in the model. Also the 'spinning of the web' steps might require a number of attempts with different people in the real world. There may, for example, need to be 'repairs' to the web of contacts brought about through dynamic movement in the players' own networks and those of their trading partners. For example, customs or party officials who become strands in the web are not always to be relied upon in the long term, so that their replacements have to be identified well ahead of the time they are needed.

Delineation of Architectures

Within the context of the network expansion model described above, we were able to delineate clearly different relational network characteristics. Applied to the 'country-nets of a global tribe', in this chapter, the term 'architecture' relates to the 'distinguishable characteristics' (see Kotkin, 1992) of the relationships of the Sojourners in Thailand and Hong Kong.

The results of our field interviews suggest that three distinguishable architectures typify the Hong Kong and Thailand garment manufacturers (see Pyatt, 1999 for further details), delineated by the nature of the relationships within the networks, and their propensity for local versus international and transnational expansion. We have called these three forms: (1) 'Country-net', (2) 'International', and (3) 'Transnational' architectures respectively. Further, we have identified six stages of development of the architectures. The model that comprises the three architectures and their stages is set out Table 5.1.

We acknowledge that linkages possibly exist between the three architectures, and that some firms will be in transition between these forms. Further, certain architecture characteristics are likely to be strongly interrelated in

Table 5.1   Staged development of three distinguishable architectures

Stage	Country-net architecture	International architecture	Transnational architecture
1.	Chinese management attributes, and spinning of personal networks for business.	Chinese management attributes, and spinning of personal networks for business.	Chinese management attributes, and spinning of personal networks for business.
2.	Trade coordination based on the entrepreneurial-clan. (Avoid non-Chinese Asians. Distant with other Chinese and Westerners.)	Trading coordination based on open trading preferences. (Avoidance of non-Chinese Asians. Comfortable with other Chinese and Westerners.)	Trading coordinations based upon proactive buying and selling, long-term strategies, forbearance based networking and corporate memory.
3.	Management values are the underlying attributes: (i) Reciprocity (ii) Relationships (iii) Long-term Interactions	Traditional values are still present, yet social capital is developed as an attribute from increased interface with suppliers and customers outside the ethnic group. Attributes are: (i) Rationality (ii) Business trust	Traditional values and social capital as in the other architectures, yet human capital a highly developed attribute: (i) Organization (ii) Law-abiding (iii) Knowledge (iv) Technology (v) Education

Table 5.1   (continued)

Stage	Country-net architecture	International architecture	Transnational architecture
4.	Limited vertical integration.	Limited vertical integration, but possibly production offshore.	Extensive vertical integration, and multiple offshore manufacturing.
5.	Ethnic networks. Attributes: (i) Ownership (ii) Investment (iii) Production	National networks. Attributes: (i) Ownership (ii) Investment (iii) Production (iv) Distribution	Transnational networks. Attributes: (i) Ownership (ii) Investment (iii) Production (iv) Distribution
6.	The country-net architecture may not be able to develop past this point.	Slow adoption of advanced data-communications systems.	Strategic dependence upon advanced data-communications systems.

reality, so that some combinations, hybrids, and plural or intermediary forms are more likely to develop than others are. Indeed, the variety of feasible architectures that have the potential to develop in Southeast Asia is not small, and reflects the variety of economic cultures in networks. Finally, we acknowledge that the three architectures that we observed in our two-country fieldwork are only a sample, and may be unique. We suggest, nonetheless, that equivalents are likely to be found amongst other global tribes.

Quantitative Survey Data Results

Table 5.2 presents a summary of business relationship preferences for the Hong Kong and Thailand respondents, based on the survey data. The results represent a cross-tabulation of relationships developed from the combined valid responses from the Hong Kong and Thailand respondents. The data reveal two configurations of networks of trading relationships: 47 per cent of respondents preferred to deal with local Chinese ('Country-net architecture'), while 23 per cent of respondents preferred to deal with Westerners ('International architecture').

Results of the survey data, and supported by the interviews, also showed that, although the dominant pattern was to prefer to trade with fellow Chinese within the country, there was a small proportion of respondents in each

Table 5.2 Summary of country-net preferences of the Thailand and Hong Kong Sojourners (combined sample)

	Least prefer non-Chinese Asians	Least prefer Westerners	Other	Total	Per cent
Prefer Westerners (international architecture)	47	–	–	47	23.4
Prefer local Chinese (country-net architecture)	52	43	–	95	47.3
Other preferences	–	–	59	59	29.3
Valid response[a]	99	43	59	201	100

Notes: [a] Thailand, n = 78; Hong Kong, n = 123.

country who preferred to trade internationally. This proportion was different in Thailand and Hong Kong. In Thailand, only 2 per cent of respondents expressed this preference, while the proportion in Hong Kong was 6 per cent. This difference was statistically significant ($p < .001$), and supports our prediction that Hong Kong firms would be more internationally oriented. In particular, while these entrepreneurial respondents constitute only small percentages of the whole sample, we argue that they constitute a powerful group because of their extensive value-added chain. This is clearly consistent with what we concluded in our discussion of qualitative results.

In summary, our results point to the existence of three distinguishable architectures amongst the Sojourners: 'Country-net', 'International', and 'Transnational'. These architectures are characterized by distinguishable stages of development (Table 5.1) and different preferences for doing business with local Chinese, non-Chinese, and Westerners (Table 5.2).

Six Stages of Development

In this section, we discuss in more detail the six stages of the three architectures in the model described in Table 5.1, based largely on the field interviews. Firstly, the respondents in each architecture share the same Mainland China roots. This common heritage of dispersion is expressed in Stage 1. In this stage, all three architectures share the Chinese management attributes and human resource policies that we discussed earlier. All three were in the initial stages developed through the spinning of personal networks in the ways that were clearly evident in our case interviews.

Stages 2 and 3 of our model of country-net and international architectures are based on our interviews and are supported by the survey results. Our data indicate that the Sojourners tend to avoid doing business with non-Chinese Asians and are distant with other country Chinese and with Westerners (see Table 5.2). In addition, it was apparent from our interview data that the transnational firms in Stages 2 and 3 exhibit trading coordinations based upon proactive buying and selling; they also exhibit long-term strategies, and had developed levels of forbearance with networks of suppliers and customers in a number of economies and cultures. In particular, these ethnic Chinese transnational firms manifested a clear corporate memory; they knew what strategic choices brought them to their current market position and who their best contacts were. Still, we noted that the human capital, social capital, and management values of the Sojourners differed between Thailand and Hong Kong, reflecting the demographic and economic differences between the two locations.

As we expected, the majority of the country-net architecture and international architecture firms were found to reside in Thailand, so it is reasonable to associate survey results on Thailand trading partner attributes with those architectures that are not transnational. Conversely, the majority of the transnational architecture firms are found to reside in Hong Kong, so it is reasonable to associate survey results on Hong Kong trading partner attributes with those architectures that are transnational. Stage 4 of our model reflects the changing structure of firms as they develop their strategies from the country-net form, through the international form, and into the transnational forms associated with each country-net. Finally, Stages 5 and 6 of our model are directly related to the literature we discussed earlier in this chapter.

Three Distinguishing Architectures

In Table 5.3, we summarize the distinguishing features of the three architectures. Essentially, the country-net architecture corresponds to the traditional Chinese family business or *quan-xi*. The international and transnational architectures are more modern organizational forms that have emerged as Asia has entered into the industrialized global economy. Still, all three architectural forms maintain the essential Chineseness that we noted earlier in the chapter, and this makes them unique from their Western counterparts. In the following sections, we discuss each of the architectures, and place them in the context of post-modern theories of organization.

Country-net architecture. The basic feature of a country-net architecture is its short valued-added chain. As an embodiment of the CFB, it typically includes strong traditional values, family-oriented human resource policies,

Table 5.3   Summary comparison of distinguishable architectures

	Country-net architecture	*International architecture*	*Transnational architecture*
Internal network structure	Strong (family-based).	Strong (family-based).	Medium-strong (family-based, but with managerial systems).
External network structure	Limited.	Extended.	Extensive, including retail distribution and franchising.
Locus of production	Domestic.	Cross-border.	Offshore.
Main focus of relationships	Centred around clan lineage.	International.	Transnational and international.

and limited vertical integration inside ethnic networks. Direct control of distribution by members in this chain is unlikely. A family-based internal network structure characterizes the firms who are most likely to be the typical players in this foundation form of architecture. Finally, if the firm is limited in resources and/or is suspicious of foreign trade, then it may not be able to advance beyond this architecture.

International architecture. Features of the international architecture include a longer value-added chain than that adopted by the country-net architecture. Although this will be similar to the short value-added chain in its basic design and composition by *quan-xi* firms, it will extend outside the domestic country market, involve agents for major brands, and may adopt offshore (cross-border) manufacture. *Quan-xi-qiye* firms are more competitive than *quan-xi* organizational forms, and may be found more frequently in this architecture than in the country-net architecture and also, perhaps, in some 'quasi-corporations', which we define as corporations having the appearance of Western organizational forms, but still existing within a traditional Chinese economic infrastructure. Direct control of distribution in the form of retail outlets, brand development, and perhaps franchising are likely to be seen developing incrementally in this architecture. Even in medium-size firms aspiring to develop an international architecture this may be coupled with the use of advanced electronic data communications systems with selected suppliers and customers. Family contacts are still the dominant underlying mode of relationship, however, and determine human resource policies. Once established, international architectures assist a firm to develop a degree of autonomy from the economic culture of the host economy.

Radical changes in architecture (for example from country-net to international) are more likely to be brought about from the transfer of human capital from outside the country-net than from changes in the host economy.

Transnational architecture. There are certain distinguishable features of the advanced transnational architecture that some firms adopt which can assist our understanding of the ways in which the ethnic Chinese transnational network comes about and is sustained. This is achieved by firms who will typically be quasi-corporations; distinguishable by multi-country sourcing and production, and international marketing that is likely to include direct, or semi-direct, distribution in three or more economies. It should be noted, however, that the traditional families in all cases we studied were unwilling to relinquish control of the firm, even though by now it may be a stock exchange listed company. Internal networks are encompassed by the family, but may be extended into professional managers, whose employment will be necessary if it is further to expand offshore. Cross-border and cross-cultural manufacture from factories in emerging economies is a normal feature of this architecture. The strategic use of advanced data-communications systems aspired to in the international architecture becomes a standard component of the transnational architecture and is also a competitively important feature of its configuration. Human resource policies in these organizational forms include management systems, but still retain elements of the family-oriented approach to human resources associated with the other forms.

DISCUSSION

Early in this chapter, we pointed out that, if competitive price provides the exchange mechanism of markets, and administrative regulations that of hierarchies, then trust is what controls opaque networks of relational contracts. Understanding the boundaries of trust, reciprocity, and forbearance in the different architectures has been an underlying aim of this study. A number of interesting factors have come to light in our exploration of the architectures and boundaries of trust in the Chinese relational networks in Hong Kong and Thailand. With two noticeable exceptions, only country-net architectures were identified in Thailand. In Hong Kong, all three architectures (country-net, international and trans-national architectures) were observed. Boundaries of trust also differed between the Thailand respondents and the Hong Kong respondents.

Results revealed three patterns of trust and forbearance that we characterized as three distinguishing architectures. At this point, we interpret the three architectures more specifically in terms of different forms of CFB organization.

1. The traditional *quan-xi* CFB form, characterized by strong family and regional ties, high levels of trust, long-term interactions, and implicit reciprocity. These firms also exhibit little vertical integration, and the limitations usually associated with the *quan-xi* form. We have termed this 'country-net' architecture. These firms have a definite preference for working with local Chinese, and least prefer to work with either Westerners or non-Chinese Asians.

2. A more open form, that we refer to as the 'international' architecture, is similar to the Chinese *quan-xi-qiye* organizational form, and is characterized by a more competitive hierarchy than the traditional *quan-xi*. These firms employ more open trading preferences, although they remain uncomfortable dealing with non-Chinese Asians. They also rely more on social capital developed through increased interactions with suppliers and customers outside of the local Chinese ethnic group. Rationality and business trust has replaced the values of long-term relationships and reciprocity evident in the more traditional form.

3. Finally, we identified a 'transnational' architecture, more akin to what is found in Western corporations, and quite distinct from the traditional CFB. We term these organizations 'quasi-corporations'. While they 'look and feel' like their Western counterparts, these organizations still retain their central Chinese values, including an emphasis on the spinning of personal networks for business, both within and without the firm. At the same time, however, human capital is viewed as a highly valued attribute, with trading based on proactive buying and selling, long-term strategies, forbearance based networking, and corporate memory. Key values in these firms are respect for laws and procedures, education, knowledge, technology, and education. They also extensively employ modern communication technology, vertical integration, and multiple offshore manufacturing facilities. Finally, these organizations prefer to work with Westerners and local Chinese, rather than with other Chinese or non-Chinese Asians.

In addition, our results showed that, as we expected, the more traditional 'country-net architecture' was the dominant organizational form of Chinese business located in Thailand. Conversely, the 'transnational' architecture was just almost exclusively located in Hong Kong.

SUMMARY AND CONCLUSIONS

The purpose of this chapter has been to uncover the distinguishing characteristics of the opaque business relationships of the Sojourners. Amongst other matters, our research has uncovered relationships at the country, international, and transnational levels. The shape of the individual net relationships of firms will be determined by partner preferences, coordinations, and management attributes. Although it is not suggested that the three 'Q-form' network configurations adopted by the Sojourners in our study are universally applicable, we suggest that their competencies may have important implications for future collaborative and competitive business forms.

The neo-feudal features of the Q-forms share a number of features with *keiretsu* and *chaebol* that Donleavy (1995) has described as post-modern (in that they have evolved in response to prevailing values). Using the Donleavy definition, these Chinese Q-forms include family or clan management and human resource policies, the Confucian work ethic, close relationships with government, and informal systems. Indeed, we argue that these organizational forms may be interpreted as a form of post-modern firm. The particular post-modern aspect of Confucian firms that we focus on is their ability to disentangle cultural and relational components from the transactional and pragmatic (Donleavy, 1995).

We have seen that a network of relational contracts in and around a firm (its architecture) can form a distinctive capability, which when applied to an industry and market can be a source of competitive advantage for the firm (Kay, 1993). Therefore, if the distinguishing characteristics of the business relationships of the Sojourners are distinctive capabilities, an implication of our findings would be that the Q-forms of Chinese organization result in competitive advantages over other forms of management within the *Nanyang* context, and perhaps more widely. A detailed study of these potential competitive advantages is a complex task, however, and beyond the scope of the present study. Therefore, an important step for future research is to investigate whether the distinguishing characteristics of the Sojourners' webs are indeed distinctive and lead to competitive advantages.

In conclusion, we note that it is necessary neither to underestimate nor to exaggerate the scope and domain of the Chinese Q-form architectures. Our research fits within the growing body of literature dealing with the phenomenon of globalization in the contemporary world of the twenty-first century. Further, the intra-Asian linkages of the global tribe in Southeast Asia, although identifiable, are complex geographically and relationally. Finally, it must also be noted that the Chinese Sojourners in the *Nanyang* and China Coast are not universally connected. Chinese traders in one country have no more affinity with Chinese traders in another country than their counterparts of British ethnic origins in Canada have affinity with their counterparts in South Africa or Australia. Yet there are strong linkages carried out by a leading entrepreneurial elite heading up those firms with transnational architectures. The elite constitute a pro-active minority who need to trade beyond kinship. It clearly behoves us to learn more about how these elites operate, and then to use this knowledge to further our understanding of organizations in the Asia-Pacific region and beyond.

Note

1. The Chinese word *pang* can be translated as speech-group solidarities (Mackie, 1992a; Chen, 1995). The major speech-groups (dialect-groups) referred to in this chapter are the Cantonese, the Chiu-chow, and the Fukienese.

References

Alchian, A. and Demsetz, H. (1972) 'Production, Information Costs, and Economic Organization', *American Economic Review*, 62, pp. 777–95.
Aldrich, H. E. and Waldinger, R. (1990) 'Ethnicity and Entrepreneurship', *Annual Review of Sociology*, 16, pp. 111–35.
Alter, C. and Hage, J. (1993) *Organizations Working Together* (Newbury Park, CA: Sage).
Asia Inc. (1996).
Bettis, R. A. (1991) 'Strategic Management and the Straitjacket: An Editorial Essay', *Organization Science*, 2, pp. 315–19.
Bleeke, J. and Ernst, D. (1993) *Collaborating to Compete: Using Strategic Alliances and Acquisitions in the Global Marketplace* (New York: Wiley).
Boisot, M. (1987) *Information and Organizations: The Manager as Anthropologist* (London: Fontana Paperbacks).
Bond, M. H. (1991) *Beyond the Chinese Face: Insights from Psychology* (Hong Kong: Oxford University Press).
Braadbaart, O. (1995) 'Sources of Ethnic Advantage in Brown', in R. Ampalavanar (ed.), *Chinese Business Enterprise in Asia* (London: Routledge) pp. 177–96.
Buckley, P. J. and Casson, M. (1988) *The Future of the Multinational Enterprise* (Basingstoke: Macmillan).
Calton, J. and Lad, L. (1995) 'Social Contracting as a Trust-Building Process of Network Governance', *Business Ethics Quarterly*, 5, pp. 271–95.
Cauley de la Sierra, M. (1995) *Managing Global Alliances: Key Steps for Successful Collaboration* (Wokingham, UK: Addison Wesley Publishing).
Chen, M. (1995) *Asian Management Systems: Chinese, Japanese, and Korean Styles of Business* (London: International Thomson Business Press).
Clegg, S. W., Higgins, W. and Speybey, T. (1990) 'Post-Confucianism, Social Democracy and Economic Culture', in S. W. Clegg, G. Redding and M. Cartner (eds), *Capitalism in Contrasting Cultures* (Berlin: Walter de Gruyter) pp. 31–78.
Clegg, S. W., Redding, G. and Cartner, M. (1990) *Capitalism in Contrasting Cultures* (Berlin: Walter de Gruyter).
Conry, E. J. (1995) 'A Critique of Social Contracts for Business', *Business Ethics Quarterly*, 5, pp. 187–212.

Dannhaeuser, N. (1981) 'Evolution and Devolution of Downward Channel Integration in the Philippines', *Economic Development and Cultural Change*, 29, pp. 577–95.

Donleavy, G. (1995) 'Feudalism, Ethics and Postmodern Company Life', in S. Stewart and G. Donleavy (eds), *Whose Business Values? Some Asian and Cross-Cultural Perspectives* (Hong Kong: Hong Kong University Press).

Dubin, R. (1982) 'Management: Meanings, Methods and Moxie', *Academy of Management Review*, 7, pp. 372–9.

Easton, G. and Araujo, L. (1993) 'Language, Metaphors and Networks', *Advances in International Marketing*, 5, pp. 67–85.

Enright, M., Scott, E. and Dodwell, D. (1997) *The Hong Kong Advantage* (Hong Kong: Oxford University Press).

Ford, I. D. (1990) *Understanding Business Markets* (London: Academic Press).

Forsgren, M. and Johanson, J. (1992) *Managing Networks in International Business* (Philadelphia, PA: Gordon & Breach Science Publishers).

Fox, A. (1974) *Beyond Contract: Work, Power and Trust Relations* (London: Faber & Faber).

Fukuyama, F. (1995) *Trust: The Social Virtues and the Creation of Prosperity* (New York: The Free Press).

Granovetter, M. (1985) 'Economic Action and Social Structure: The Problem of Embeddedness', *American Journal of Sociology*, 91, pp. 481–501.

Hambrick, D. C. (1990) 'The Adolescence of Strategic Management, 1980–1985', in J. Frederickson (ed.), *Perspectives on Strategic Management* (Cambridge, MA: Ballinger) pp. 230–51.

Hamilton, G., Chen, E. and Wong, S. L. (eds) (1991) *Business Networks and Economic Development in East and Southeast Asia* (Hong Kong: University of Hong Kong Press).

Hamilton, G. G., Zeile, W. and Kim, W. J. (1990) 'The Network Structures of East Asian Economies', in S. W. Clegg, G. Redding and M. Cartner (eds), *Capitalism in Contrasting Cultures* (Berlin: Walter de Gruyter) pp. 105–29.

Henderson, A. (1998) *Asia Falling? Making Sense of the Asian Currency Crisis and Its Aftermath* (New York: McGraw-Hill).

Herbert, M. (1990) *Planning a Research Project: A Guide for Practitioners and Trainees in the Helping Professions* (London: Cassell).

Jacobs, N. (1985) *The Korean Road to Modernization and Development* (Urbana, IL.: University of Illinois Press).

Jarillo, J. C. (1988) 'On Strategic Networks', *Strategic Management Journal*, 9, pp. 31–41.

Jick, T. D. (1979) 'Mixing Qualitative and Quantitative Methods. Triangulation in Action', *Administrative Science Quarterly*, 24, pp. 602–11.

Johanson, J. and Mattson, L. (1987) 'Inter-Organizational Relations in Industrial Systems: A Network Approach Compared With the Transactions-Cost Approach', *International Studies of Management and Organization*, 17(1), pp. 34–48.

Kao, J. (1993) 'The Worldwide Web of Chinese Business', *Harvard Business Review*, 71, pp. 24–34.

Kay, J. A. (1993) *Foundations of Corporate Success* (New York: Oxford University Press).

Klein, B. (1983) 'Contractual Costs and Residual Claims', *Journal of Law and Economics*, 26, pp. 367–74.

Kotkin, J. (1992) *Tribes: How Race, Religion and Identity Define Success in the New Global Economy* (Beverly Hills, CA: Sage).

Kuhn, T. S. (1962) *The Structure of Scientific Revolutions* (Chicago: University of Chicago Press).

Larson, A. (1992) 'Network Dyads in Entrepreneurial Settings: A Study of the Governance of Exchange Relationships', *Administrative Science Quarterly*, 37, pp. 76–104.

Layder, D. (1993) *New Strategies in Social Research* (London: Polity Press).

Lim, L. Y. C. and Gosling, L. A. P. (1983) 'The Chinese in Southeast Asia', *Maruzen Asia*, 1, pp. 5–6.

Limerick, D. and Cunnington, B. (1993) *Managing the New Organization* (Sydney: Professional Publishing).

Liu, T. and Faure, D. (1996) *Unity and Diversity: Local Cultures and Identities in China* (Hong Kong: Hong Kong University press).

Lorange, P. and Roos, J. (1992) *Strategic Alliances: Formation, Implementation and Evolution* (Cambridge, MA: Blackwell).

Macaulay, S. (1963) 'Non-Contractual Relations in Business: A Preliminary Study', *American Sociological Review*, 28, pp. 55–67.

Mackie, J. A. (1992a) 'Changing Patterns of Chinese Big Business in Southeast Asia', in R. McVey (ed.), *Southeast Asian Capitalists* (New York: Cornell University Southeast Asia Program).

Mackie, J. A. (1992b) 'Overseas Chinese Entrepreneurship', *Asia-Pacific Economic Literature*, 6(1), pp. 41–64.

Macneil, I. R. (1980) *The New Social Contract: An Inquiry into Modern Contractual Relations* (New Haven: Yale University Press).

McLuhan, M. and McLuhan E. (1989) *Laws of Media: The New Science* (Toronto: University of Toronto Press).

Numazaki, I. (1991) 'The Role of Personal Networks in the Making of Taiwan's *guang-xi-qiye*' [Related Enterprises], in G. Hamilton, E. Chen and S. L. Wong (eds), *Business Networks and Economic Development in East and Southeast Asia* (Hong Kong: University of Hong Kong Press) pp. 77–93.

Ohmae, K. (1995) *The Evolving Global Economy: Making Sense of the New World Order* (Boston: Harvard Business School Press).

Ouchi, W. G. (1980) 'Markets, Bureaucracies and Clans', *Administrative Science Quarterly*, 25, pp. 129–41.

Parkhe, A. (1993) 'Messy Research, Methodological Predispositions and Theory Development in International Joint Ventures', *Academy of Management Review*, 18, pp. 227–68.

Patten, C. (1997) 'Beyond the Myths', *The Economist*, January 4, pp. 19–21.

Peyrefitte, A. (1996) *La societe de confidance: Essai les origines et la nature de developement* (Paris: Editions Odile Jacob).

Powell, W. (1990) 'Neither Market nor Hierarchy: Network Forms of Organization', *Research in Organizational Behavior*, 12, pp. 295–336.

Pyatt. T. R. (1995a) 'Business Networks and Dyad Studies: Theory and Practice in Southeast Asia', *Journal of Far Eastern Business*, 1(4), pp. 1–14.

Pyatt, T. R. (1995b) 'The Domain of a Soviet-Type Command Network: An Embedded Case Study of Eight Industrial Networks in Vietnam', *Journal of Business and Industrial Marketing*, 10(1), pp. 44–63.

Pyatt, T. R. (1996) 'Chinese Business Networks and Entrepreneurial-clans in Thailand', *Asia Pacific Business Review*, 3(2), pp. 1–25.

104   *Transitions and Traditions in Chinese Family Businesses*

Pyatt, R. (1999) 'The Transnational Network of the Southeast Asian Chinese: Country-Net Architectures and Cross-Cultural Partnerships', Unpublished PhD Dissertation (Brisbane, Queensland: The University of Queensland).
Pyatt, T. R. and Trimarchi, M. (1998) 'Inter-organizational interaction in intra-Asia business: A four-country study', *Asia Pacific Business Review*, 4(4), pp. 36–52.
Redding, S. G. (1990) *The spirit of Chinese capitalism* (Berlin: Walter de Gruytes).
Redding, S. G. (1991) 'Weak Organizations and Strong Linkages: Managerial Ideology and Chinese Family Business Networks', in G. Hamilton, E. Chen and S. L. Wong (eds), *Business Networks and Economic Development in East and Southeast Asia* (Hong Kong: University of Hong Kong Press) pp. 30–48.
Redding, S. G. (1995) 'Overseas Chinese Networks: Understanding the Enigma', *Long Range Planning*, 28, pp. 61–8.
Rohwer, J. (1998) *Asia Rising: The Economic Miracle in East and Southeast Asia and Why the West Will Profit* (New York: Touchstone Books).
Schultz, M. and Hatch M. J. (1996) 'Living with Multiple Paradigms: The Case of Paradigm Interplay in Organizational Culture Studies', *Academy of Management Review*, 21, pp. 529–57.
Semkow, B. W. (1992) *Taiwan's Financial Markets and Institutions: The Legal and Financial Issues of Deregulation and Internalization* (London: Quorum Books).
Strauss, A., Bucher, R., Ehrlich, D., Schatzman, L. and Sabshin, M. (1964) *Psychiatric Ideologies and Institutions* (Glencoe, Illinois: Free Press).
Thompson, G. T., Francis, J., Levacic, R. and Mitchell, J. (1991) *Markets, Hierarchies and Networks: The Coordination of Social Life* (London: Sage).
Thorelli, H. B. (1986) 'Networks: Between Markets and Hierarchies', *Strategic Management Journal*, 7, pp. 37–52.
Wang, G. (1994) 'Hong Kong as the Home of China Coast Chinese: A Historical Perspective', The 1994 Hong Kong Lectures, Rayson Huang Theatre, University of Hong Kong, Pokfulam, 26th November.
Whitley, R. D. (1992) *Business Systems in East Asia: Firms, Markets and Societies* (London: Sage).
Wickberg, E. (1965) *The Chinese in Philippine Life* (Newhaven, CT: Yale University Press).
Wilson, D. T. and Mummalaneni, V. (1986) 'Bonding and Commitment in Buyer–Seller Relationships: A Preliminary Conceptualization', *Industrial Marketing and Purchasing*, 1(3), pp. 44–58.
Wong, S. (1997) 'Chinese Trust and Prosperity: The Role of Chinese Family Enterprise in Economic Development', the inaugural T. T. Tsui Annual Lecture in Asia-Pacific Business, University of Hong Kong, 3 February.
Zucker, L. G. (1986) 'Production of Trust: Institutional Sources of Economic Structure, 1840–1920', *Research in Organizational Behavior*, 8, pp. 53–111.

6 Thai Business Culture: Hierarchy and Groups, Initiative and Motivation

Niti Dubey-Villinger

INTRODUCTION

Thai management and business culture is receiving more attention as a focus of research by scholars and practitioners (Cooper, 1994; Holmes and Tangtongtavy, 1997). Indeed, there is a growing awareness of the role of culture in the international management or cross-border setting (Hofstede, 1980; Adler, 1992). While there is some disagreement in some circles about the relative importance of culture in relation to actual management practices (Appold *et al.*, 1998), whether differences might indeed be attributable to cultural differences, it is clear that managers often attribute differences in behaviour and attitudes in terms of a cultural label. The objective of this investigation is to examine Thai management and business culture from the views of foreign, expatriate managers and Thai managers alike. In addition to a survey of academic research and practitioner publications, several foreign and Thai managers at leading corporations situated in Thailand were interviewed for their perspectives on Thai management and business culture. What follows is an overview of these findings.

Thai management and business culture is unique in certain respects. Yet it retains elements of other Asian cultural practices. On the one hand, one is constantly reminded of the noted Thai propensity for *sanuk* (literally, 'fun') or the carefree attitude which characterizes *mai pen rai* ('never mind/don't worry'). Foreigners are quick to recite experiences where each has been observed. On the other hand, certain elements of Thai culture are similar to those observed in other Asian traditions. Group orientation, the emphasis on hierarchy and personal connections or networks have also been attributed to East Asian societies (Japan, China, for example). While the focus of this investigation does not explicitly view the roots of Thai culture as they may have evolved from outside Asian influences, there does seem to be a connection in terms of certain formalized cultural practices which are evident in Thailand. *Quan-xi*, which refers to a special relationship among two persons or two parties in a network in Chinese, is an example of one of these practices, though a similar term has not been explicitly included in the Thai (cultural) vocabulary.

The investigation is broadly divided into two categories which define Thai attitudes towards work and the relationships that form in one's work environment. The first addresses the issue of hierarchical constructs (group dynamics and networks) among people in an organization; the second, individual motivation and initiative (individual behaviour). This article will consider these 'Thai traits' as important lenses with which to view Thai management and business culture.

HIERARCHY AND GROUPS

Avoidance of conflict. Avoidance of differences. Avoid issues. Don't bring it up. You don't go into the conflict. You avoid it. You hate to lose face. You don't want anyone to feel uncomfortable. (Foreign expatriate manager)

When foreigners first arrive in Thailand, they are usually confronted with a barrage of advice in the form of 'dos and don'ts' with respect to Thai society. Business guides, relocation services and cross-cultural trainers provide details of what is considered appropriate behaviour in the Thai setting. Foreigners are taught that Thailand is a hierarchical society (Holmes and Tangtongtavy, 1997). In particular, there exists a strong social structure in the society, which guides how relationships and transactions are conducted. At the top of the hierarchy lies the revered Royal Family and its members, followed by titled citizens. This group is followed by those having attained power and influence either in terms of business or political means. Broadly, this category includes the large business families, prominent civil servants and military leaders. Following this category one finds professional bureaucrats and managerial staff and other commercial workers. Thai society acknowledges and accepts this structure and is particularly adherent to the structure in terms of actual practices and behaviour.

This social hierarchy is the basis for what should ideally guide one's dealings with Thais in terms of proper decorum and the accordance of respect. Some have argued that the roots for this deference to certain members of society is based on a strong agriculturally based society where the ranking of citizens was determined by ownership of land (Holmes and Tangtongtavy, 1997; also Phongpaichit and Baker, 1999). It is perhaps this value of financial power which succeeding generations of Thais transferred to business leaders and political leaders, the former gaining their status by sheer financial strength, the latter obtaining wealth through political and/or nepotistic means (see Backman, 1999). The Royal Family remains at the top of the hierarchical pyramid; others have 'migrated' to their relative high positions on the basis of wealth and power.

In addition to the historical basis of societal hierarchy, Thais also grapple with the notion of hierarchy which is implicitly drawn from two diverging yet related sources: *karma* and *karuna*. Both are derived from Buddhist philosophy. *Karma* is the view that everything is predetermined or destined and one's position in society is of a static nature. One is therefore born into a social class and remains in that class till death. Essentially, social mobility is neither available nor subsequently pursued. Ranks reward the 'moral and ethical excellence accumulated in previous lives' (Hall, 1996, p. 19). *Karma* is also considered by some to be an alibi for the acceptance of many social ills in Thai society (Ungpakorn, 1999):

> A boss should be forgiving of a subordinate who has made a big mistake. A teacher should be generous with time and effort in order to help his students. A rich person should be generous with tips to servants and donations to beggars. (Holmes and Tangtongtavy, 1997, p. 31)

Karuna, or what Holmes and Tangtongtavy (1997) term *mettaa karunaa*, refers to the quality of being 'merciful and kind' in one's dealings. This quality is best exemplified through harmonious relationships, which is another aspect of Thai management and business culture. In particular, the quality of *metta karunaa* applies to the relationship between a person of higher stature or position with someone in a lower position where the superior person behaves 'benevolently' towards him. This to some extent reflects upon the caretaker or reciprocal role of master to servant which characterizes feudal society (Phongpaichit and Baker, 1999).

Foreign managers do not explicitly discuss or even think about *karma* or *karuna* in addressing their views of Thais and hierarchy. What foreigners do notice is the Thai propensity for and awareness of hierarchy in social and business constructs. An awareness of hierarchy is an important thing to keep in mind when working in Thailand. According to one foreign manager, power distance in the Thai management setting is 'huge':

> The Thais are very hierarchical. They are not only aware of hierarchy when dealing with foreigners, but also when dealing with each other. Hierarchy clearly plays a strong role in their dealings in the company. (Foreign expatriate manager)

An awareness of hierarchy is readily observed in symbolic practices, which are not infrequent. For example, Western managers are startled to find when they first arrive at their jobs that subordinate Thai workers literally bow at their presence. This is a tradition steeped in Thai culture – superiors are accorded respect and this is acknowledged by the symbolic bow or *wai* upon interaction. Some foreign managers are surprised that this custom of bowing is not limited to introductions. In traditional companies, even those with foreign managers, Thais tirelessly continue to accord their Western colleagues – notably their superiors – with symbolic gestures like a deep *wai*. One manager noted, 'even as I walk down the hallway, my Thai colleagues [subordinates] will literally bow down to me in deference ... sometimes even avoiding eye contact'. The practice of *wai* is not dissimilar to greetings observed in Japan, for example, or even China. The degree to which this practice is encouraged or expected depends upon the penetration of Thai management and business culture in relation to other influences (e.g., corporate culture, policy, etc.) in an organizational setting. The lower-ranking individual is expected to keep his or her head below that of the superior. One foreign manager noted that this practice is more common among Thais as a group than in interactions with foreigners.

Thais are especially aware of proper dress, behaviour and decorum, which, in sum, indicate a person's status within the organization. They are said to reveal great deference for rank, which is revealed by proper gestures and subdued behaviour and practices. An expatriate manager at a bank observed that while senior managers wear suits with jackets to meetings, their subordinates wear only shirts and ties *minus* jackets to signify their rank as juniors. This is an example of the unwritten code of practice expected of employees at certain organizations.

There are also several words in the Thai language which deal generally with what is considered appropriate behaviour. For example, the term for humility is *on nom thom ton*. This literally means to 'lower oneself'. This might be reflected in the following example, as iterated by a foreign manager. An employee would let a boss explain something even if he or she already knows what is being explained. The employee would allow the boss to look authoritative and knowledgeable even when he or she knows what is being discussed. It is another example of maintaining harmonious relationships by letting the other person feel that they are right or correct. Thais also have a word for politeness, *supab*, which is an important feature of maintaining relationships. This is very much connected with hierarchy and how people are to be addressed in society, for example. There is even a term in the Thai vocabulary for 'appropriate behaviour' which refers to the right behaviour at the right place and the right time.

Related to the issue of deference to superiors in a hierarchy, is the issue of communication. Foreign managers, in their discussion of 'Thai traits', note a problem which cannot necessarily be attributed exclusively to language. Communication, or the lack of effective communication, is seen as an important obstacle to effective management. While there is clearly a communication gap in terms of language in many companies, there exists a greater communication deficiency in terms of direct, open expression of one's thoughts. Perhaps arising out of hierarchy, many Thais are said to be ineffective, even scared, when communicating their true feelings or views. A strong awareness of hierarchy might indicate that Thais are afraid of making their intentions known to superiors. A predilection for harmonious relationships or conflict avoidance would further support this frequent observation by Western managers:

Ours is the society where people, from their childhood learn to suppress their resentment and openly say 'mai pen rai' or 'it doesn't matter' while, in fact, it does. (Manusphaibool, 1994)

Holmes and Tangtongtavy (1997) note that communication issues arise out of the hierarchical nature of Thai society. Because of a 'power distance gap', they believe communication is a top-down affair in organizations:

Thai tradition has encouraged junior family members and young students to absorb rather than initiate, to 'get it right' rather than to question or express opinions, especially dissenting ones. The result of this pattern is that most Thais – even at rather senior levels – have not had extensive practice in expressing themselves in an assertive way, in either Thai or English. (Holmes and Tangtongtavy, 1997, p. 35)

Assertiveness is discouraged in Thai culture from the formative years of childhood. Furthermore, a strongly hierarchical oriented society will not encourage potentially inflammatory disruptions which individual assertiveness might promote. The maintenance of harmonious relationships is of utmost importance for a society, which is guided by philosophical principles on the one hand, and societal *uber*structure, on the other:

We Thais often feel that unless a problem is very serious we should not disturb the boss. Again, on a walk around, the boss should both approach and be approachable. (Thai senior manager)

There is an interesting twist to the discussion of hierarchy in Thailand. In particular, there is a historical basis for what constitutes the status quo among superiors and their employees. On the one hand, the hierarchical difference is clearly acknowledged and accepted. On the other hand, it is understood by Thais (often only Thais) that there are certain norms and practices associated with being an employer or superior. Often, it is implicitly acknowledged that a relationship of reciprocity exists between the two parties; that the one with power in the relationship holds certain duties and responsibilities associated with that power. In other words, the one with power holds certain responsibilities in terms of caring for subordinates and as is often the case, to know exactly what their needs and concerns are. In essence, the superior party is the concerned caretaker. Foreign managers in Thailand superficially observe the trappings of hierarchy in certain behaviours like shyness or lack of communication, but they often do not understand that there are certain practices which Thais may expect on the part of their superiors:

> Huge power distance. Management is extremely hierarchical. More junior people don't speak up. When they know that person doesn't want to hear something [referring to powerful family patriarchs] they will say something wrong even consciously making false statements to appease seniors. (Foreign manager describing power distance in Thai companies)

> When problems occur, Thais have a tendency to beat about the bush. This is not easy for an impatient manager but encouraging a full explanation will be far more productive than screaming at a Thai subordinate to get to the point. (Thai senior manager)

Thais are not strongly averse to authority or authority figures. But, according to some managers, Thais will gravitate towards group orientation against a figure of authority when the dignity or the interests of one member of the group are being undermined. In this regard, they are said to be extremely loyal to one another and to a superior provided that the superior is behaving as he or she should. Group oriented behaviour is also said to be observed in common work situations. Manusphaibool (1994) has made the observation that Thais like to work together in groups and show an inclination to work with people of their own age group. Given the strongly hierarchical nature of Thai organizations, coupled with the fact that many prominent Thai organizations are family managed, the point regarding age is understandable. Seniority based upon age is likely to be reflected in career progression so one may not find significant diversity within the organization as far as age is concerned at the managerial levels:

The great majority of Thais are happiest, and usually most productive, when working in some form of group. (Cooper, 1994, p. 182)

A number of managers have made the observation that Thai colleagues enjoy working (harmoniously) in groups. This may be a problem for a supervisor if the nature of the tasks assigned require individual and self-motivated effort on the part of an employee. Furthermore, the tendency of working in a group formation may mean that individuals are reluctant to 'outshine' one another. This may promote uniformity in what each member of the group provides (what each member believes should be provided) and no real opportunity for one member to excel. Of course, this has implications for harmonious relationships but also for what constitutes the final product. Foreign managers at companies have to ask themselves if the group approach to work is feasible for the tasks they require:

Career oriented people here are as competitive as in the West. (Foreign manager)

The issue of competition, especially among employees within an organization, arouses a host of varied opinions. On the one hand, foreign managers observe the inclination towards group orientation and harmony on the part of Thai employees. Yet, on the other hand, these managers are aware of competitive careers and the competition associated with career progression, most notably in foreign companies operating in Thailand. Cooper (1994, p. 39) holds a different view: 'Competition, in spite of the superficially free-wheeling capitalism that seems to characterize the Thai business world, is a word and action to be avoided. Don't talk of friendly competition, only friendly cooperation.'

Group orientation is also reflected in other daily management settings. One manager has made the observation that during the acts of leisure at work – as reflected in the sharing of meals for example – Thais prefer not to be alone. Social interaction and group formation are the preferred means of operation. Exclusion or isolation is unwelcome. It is interesting to note, however, that as a cultural group, Thais are said to be more individualistic than other Asian groups (see Hofstede, 1980).

Managers interviewed for this chapter made several interesting comments with respect to the issue of group orientation. Several managers, for example, discussed the overall tendency for Thais in his organization to unite in the name of gossip. Though this might seem like a trivial matter in the discussion of management, this is an important aspect of interaction for Thais. This is an accepted and acceptable part of their interaction and will determine how individuals are viewed in the organization. In a sense, it may be a reaction to the lack of vertical communication in an organization – rich horizontal communication exists though it may not necessarily focus on work itself. Cooper (1994, p. 90) also addresses this issue in his guide to doing business in Thailand. He does not view gossip as a natural outcome of social interaction but rather a negative feature of the Thais which undermines their 'surface harmony'. He asserts, 'gossip is greatest within a peer group and criticism is usually reserved for individuals outside of one's own group'. Foreigners, due to their 'difference', are natural targets for such gossip. He further states that gossip is a feature in all levels of the organization. 'Businessmen, politicians, government servants and influential persons who have developed a group-based mutual trust relationship are certainly no exception.'

The tendency to form groups has another potential implication: the formation of networks. *Quan-xi* is a term which characterizes group and network formation in reference to Chinese business practices. Some have argued that examples of the most extreme forms of personal networking might be observed in the Thai business landscape (Cooper, 1994; Phongpaichit and Baker, 1999; Backman, 1999). One example at the more extreme end of personal networking would be in Western terms defined as nepotism, or the favouring of familial or personal contacts for appointments, promotions or contracts. Cooper (1994) sees nepotism as an essential part of Thai business practice and is an area which cannot be avoided (see also Backman, 1999). Managers may be hesitant to discuss this aspect of business for a number of reasons. Depending upon their level in the organizational hierarchy, they may not truly be aware of its existence in practice. Or, they may not be willing to acknowledge it as a feature of their organizations for fear of repercussions.

Creating goodwill is the reason often given for practices which favour personal contacts over strangers. There is an implied 'calculation' among relationships where favours are rewarded with favours. A manager may remember a kind act or favour offered in the past by a personal friend or contact. He or she will try to find a situation where this favour can be returned. In the West this might be considered inappropriate, even discouraged as practice. Perhaps 'unprofessional' is how this practice might be coined in the West. In the Thai environment, even if it is officially discouraged, the practice of rewarding favours with favours to personal contacts is widely acknowledged and accepted. The term *quan-xi* itself – originally Chinese – might be known only to those in the Chinese business community in Thailand. Its practice, however, is known to all.

INITIATIVE AND MOTIVATION

Monotonous jobs, hard work, and high-pressure tasks do not appeal to Thais. (Hall, 1996, p. 19)

The difference is, expatriates like to finish work first and enjoy themselves afterwards. Thais want both at the same time. (Manusphaibool, 1994)

A major goal for the majority of the people in Thailand is enjoying life. The aforementioned 'Thai trait' *mai pen rai* describes a carefree attitude towards life. When events do not matter, as they often may not for a person engaged with *sanuk* or fun, fulfilling tasks, especially in the confines of a profit-oriented organization, might require additional incentive(s). Foreign managers and Thai managers alike have noted a number of issues pertaining to initiative and motivation on the part of Thai colleagues.

It is important to remember that a strongly articulated view of Thais persists, especially at the lower levels of an organization, as comprising 'a hardworking, reliable workforce'. The Thai government in particular markets its workforce to potential suitors with accolades from a very satisfied foundation of foreign investor companies which operate in the country. Foreign managers marvel at the speed with which tasks are completed, under supervision, by their Thai workers. In comparison with workers from other neighbouring countries, Thais are considered to be especially resilient and reliant. On the surface, everything seems to be fine. When examining the situation more carefully, both Thais and Western managers acknowledge several issues pertaining to initiative and motivation on the part of Thais. These issues cover all positions in the organizational hierarchy, but are more likely to be relevant to a typical 'organization man' in a typical Thai organization.

Manusphaibool (1994) is critical of Thai work habits and even goes as far as to say that Thais cannot be enticed by incentives to work harder. This view is clearly not shared by everyone. Foreign managers consulted here have differing views but they agree that initiative and motivation might be dealt with through the right incentives and proper cross-cultural understanding. According to one prominent cross-cultural trainer, Henry Holmes, it is important to recognize that from a cultural point of view, Thais are not encouraged to 'dare', to make mistakes, to take initiatives (Holmes and Tangtongtavy, 1997). He further argues that when action is to be taken at work, employees believe (based upon tradition) that it is the boss who is to initiate it because that is what the boss is paid to do. Those with power or control or authority are to do the initiating.

Motivation is another facet of initiative. There are several ways to motivate employees. Some are applicable across cultures – money, for example – but there are some motivation factors that appeal particularly to Thais. These include company image and prestige (Holmes and Tangtongtavy, 1997). Money is considered an important motivating factor (ibid). Salary raises and bonuses are important incentives for increasing one's motivation at work. There are other incentives along this line too. Some have suggested convenience at work as a strong incentive. Incentives may also be provided through refreshments and snacks, as was suggested by a number of managers. Thais apparently enjoy working around snacks and food. As strange as this may sound to outsiders, this is not only an incentive but also another example of fostering social harmony and group formation in the guise of ritualized practices. Security, specifically job security, is another motivation factor (Holmes and Tangtongtavy, 1997). In the tumultuous economic environment which has characterized Thailand in recent years, job security is very important to Thai employees. Many Thais furthermore feel loyalty to their employers. Given the hierarchical nature of Thai society itself, titles become very important and valued. Thus, the prestige of certain job titles – irrespective of the actual responsibility incurred – is another motivating factor for employees.

Arising from hierarchy within Thai society, and coupled with its group orientation, Thais are said to display *kreng jai* or an attitude where one restrains self-interest or desire in order to maintain harmony. This is an important consideration when viewing initiative and motivation carefully. There are several ways where this quality is reflected in working life. On a basic level, one displays *kreng jai* in complying with the wishes of others or their requests (Holmes and Tangtongtavy, 1997). This is viewed positively in the organization. However, as is more often the case, *kreng jai* is also viewed somewhat negatively by foreign managers who observe, for example, that:

- Thai employees do not communicate their disagreement or dissatisfaction with how business is being conducted in their job/company;
- Employees do not assert their true feelings or opinions about a matter;
- They do not wish to participate in the evaluation of a situation/problem or even of a colleague;
- They cannot admit that they do not understand something or that they have made a mistake.

Connected with the preceding issues is the notion of 'saving face' which is ascribed to a large share of Asian societies. Essentially, one avoids situations where someone might be potentially embarrassed or appear disadvantaged in some way, called *sia nah* in Thai. 'Saving face' is the notion that you create a situation or response where no one appears to be disadvantaged or at fault in any way. Thus, harmony is maintained. This again is a positive outcome. On the other side, continuously striving to maintain harmonious situations might require that the needs and interests of individual parties are stifled. An individual may feel constrained by having to do what is considered acceptable by other members of the group. Hence, their actions and true wishes are restricted. Harmony is achieved at personal cost.

Initiative and motivation are two major areas of discussion for both foreign and local managers. It is recognized that initiative is an area which needs further development on the part of Thai employees and managers. A language barrier or a lack of confidence in expressing oneself in a foreign language may further impact the degree of initiative one shows in daily business actions. In both foreign and locally managed companies, initiative is one of the most cited problems facing senior managers in Thailand, particularly those at foreign companies.

The previous section's discussion of hierarchy plays an important role in the discussion of initiative. A strongly hierarchical society, where 'top-down' control is highly centralized in many organizations, is likely to inhibit self-expression and initiative. Cultural factors, furthermore, indicate that in Thailand, the average employee expects that his seniors take responsibility for decisions, to take initiative when necessary.

CONCLUSION

There are other distinguishing Thai-specific issues which were noted by managers but were not discussed in this chapter. For example, one foreign manager noted the Thai predilection for the belief in the supernatural. Thais, especially those of Chinese origin, believe in fortune-telling and use these beliefs in their decision-making process at even the largest of Thai companies. Some Chinese Thais are even said to employ 'face readers' to assess the character of their managers. *Feng shui*, another Chinese import, is also used by Chinese Thais in the design of their buildings and offices.

For the most part, comments about defining cultural traits or characteristics of Thai culture as it pertains to management focus on hierarchy and the need for maintaining harmonious relationships. The Thai vocabulary has several words which deal with these issues. One foreign manager who spent several years working for a large foreign manufacturing company in Thailand noted that building trust was an important feature of relationships in Thailand. This is demonstrated through the following Thai ideas: *hai kiet* and *a-wu so*. The former refers to demonstrating a belief in someone where trust is built up privately. A junior person does not contradict or correct the senior in public. Trust is built up privately. Related to this point is the second concept that deals with seniority and rank. In essence, *a-wu so* refers to respecting the senior person – always. In essence, trusting their judgement or wisdom.

In sum, Thai management or business culture does present specific characteristics which are uniquely Thai and specific to the culture. Both foreign and local managers have stressed a number of points about Thai culture as it relates to the management or business situation. The most significant observations have been connected with hierarchy and group orientation through harmonious relationships. Initiative issues also feature prominently in the discussion and can be said to be related to hierarchy and group orientation. Thai society is also influenced by Chinese culture, perhaps owing to its visible Chinese community, and shares a number of 'Asian characteristics' with reference to decorum and formality in the conduct of relationships.

References

Adler, Nancy J. (1992) *International Dimensions of Organizational Behavior*, 2nd edn (Boston: Wadsworth).
Appold, Stephen J., Siengthai, Sununtha and Kasarda, John D. (1998) 'The Employment of Women Managers and Professionals in an Emerging Economy: Gender Inequality as an Organizational Practice', *Administrative Science Quarterly*, 43, pp. 538–65.
Backman, Michael (1999) *Asian Eclipse: Exposing the Dark Side of Business in Asia* (Singapore: John Wiley & Sons).
Cooper, Robert (1994) *Thais Mean Business* (Singapore: Times Books International).
Hall, Denise (1996) *Business Prospects in Thailand* (Singapore: Prentice Hall).
Hofstede, Geert (1980) *Culture's Consequences* (London: Sage).
Holmes, Henry and Tangtongtavy, Suchada (1997) *Working with the Thais* (Bangkok: White Lotus).
Manusphaibool, Supachai (1994) 'Cross Cultural Problems in the Management of Human Resource in Thailand', in *Legal, Socio-cultural Problems in the Management of Human Resource in Thai Industries* (Bangkok: Board of Investment).
Phongpaichit, Pasuk and Baker, Chris (1999) *Thailand Economy and Politics* (New York: Oxford University Press).
Ungpakorn, Ji G. (1999) *Thailand: Class Struggle in an Era of Economic Crisis* (Bangkok and Hong Kong: Asia Monitor Resources Centre and Workers Democracy Book Club).

7 Career Planning and Development of Managers in Thailand

Vinda Chainuvati and Cherlyn S. Granrose

This chapter describes the career system in Thailand during the 1990s. Using 'A Model of Organizational Careers in National Contexts', proposed by Granrose (1995), as a framework to guide and shape this research, we examine career-related factors at three levels of analysis: the nation, the organization and the individual.

NATIONAL CHARACTERISTICS OF THAILAND THAT INFLUENCE CAREERS

Nations have two characteristics which make them especially useful units for career research: (a) particular geographic locations with generally recognized physical boundaries; and (b) specific political-legal systems which normally regulate economic activity within this geo-physical space (Granrose, 1995, p. 8). The national level of analysis includes factors that shape individual career opportunities such as a nation's political history, religion and values important to the national culture, economic policy, labour force participation, and the education system.

Geography, Population and Legal Environment

Thailand is situated at the heart of Southeast Asia in a strategic position for regional offices of international companies expanding their markets into Southeast Asia. 'In 1998 the population in Thailand was 60.9 million. In the year 2000, the population is estimated to be about 64 million people' (Thailand Board of Investment, 1998). The dominant ethnic group is Thai, forming more than 80 per cent of the total population. The Chinese are the biggest minority. Thailand's work force is 32 million, of which the majority is under 30 years old (Thailand Board of Investment, 1998). This demographic profile means many career opportunities for today's adults but increasing competition for education leading to good jobs among maturing youth.

Education has a strong influence on Thai career opportunities. In 1996 compulsory schooling was increased to nine years, beginning at the age of 7. The government has put more emphasis on education in the Eighth National Economic and Social Development Plan (1997–2002), stating the high priority of Human Resources in Thailand. For example, Thailand has established a goal to promote literacy for all people aged 14–50 by the end of 2001 (Thailand Board of Investment, 1998).

Access to tertiary education is limited because the government regulates the entrance examination to control the number of young people admitted to higher education each year. Access to postgraduate education is even more limited; however in times of economic prosperity, many companies in Thailand encourage their employees to study part-time for an MBA by providing financial assistance.

In order to support industrial growth and employee welfare, Thailand has reformed the labour and employment laws in recent years. Special national statutory limitations and protections set by the Labour Ministry play an important role in defining the limits of employment contracts between firms and labour organizations. Many labour practices, such as mandatory severance packages, workers' compensation, workers' hours, and overtime are specified by law.

Thai employees rarely use unions to improve their working conditions or to increase their benefits. Less than 3 per cent of the industrialized workers are unionized (Fairclough, 1992; Vause and Chandravithun, 1992). There are two explanations for the low level of unionization in Thailand. First, the employer–employee relationship is more likely to be paternalistic, and employees tend to accept the power of management. Second, employees have little bargaining power in the workplace and they do not perceive unions to be an effective means to gain power.

At the time of this study, the rapid economic growth created many employment opportunities that could not be filled by the number of available Thai managers. Many multinational companies wanted to assign expatriate managers from their home offices to Thailand in order to help alleviate the managerial shortage. However, a control on immigration through The Alien Work Permit Act limits the number of expatriate managers in Thailand (Vause and Chandravithun, 1992). In times of economic hardship such as the last years of the 1990s, one way the nation may choose to protect jobs for Thai managers is to tighten issuance of these permits.

Cultural Values Related to Employment

Thailand was able to avoid European colonization and thus was able to preserve much of its tradition of Buddhism (Fieg, 1989). Buddhism plays a vital role in creating the Thai national identity and in framing the Thai philosophy of life. For example, the teaching of 'Karma' refers to the belief that the status of one's life at present is a consequence of one's merit in past life. This supports the hierarchical arrangement of society and of organizations.

When Komin (1990) surveyed cultural and work-related values in Thai organizations, he identified nine cultural values that influence Thai workers in both government and private organizations. These included: Ego (face saving and criticism avoidance), Grateful (paternalistic) relationships, Smooth interpersonal relationships, Flexibility, Education-competence, Interdependence, Fun/pleasure, and Achievement/task orientation. The strong positive evaluation of maintaining harmonious social relationships in Thai society has been confirmed by studies of the most commonly used conflict management styles in Thailand. In order of most common to least common, these included: accommodation, followed by compromize, avoidance, and collaboration (Kuriavikitkul, 1994). The importance of face is also salient for ethnic Chinese in Thailand (Redding and Ng, 1982). Accommodation and face-saving enhance the role of group harmony and help to support the hierarchical system of careers in Thailand. These cultural values have a great influence on the career goals many Thais select and on the career choices they make.

Changing Economic Conditions

At the time of the primary data collection for this research, in the first half of the decade of the 1990s, Thailand was experiencing an economic miracle. Like other countries in Asia, Thailand enjoyed a strong economic growth, with an average Gross Domestic Product (GDP) growth rate of 8 per cent per year. Foreign trade in Thailand increased by 24 per cent each year between 1987 and 1992. This was due primarily to the expansion of foreign direct investment and international trade with the US and Japan (Apibunyanuch, 1993). The situation has changed dramatically since mid-1997. GDP growth rate declined from from +6 per cent (1996) to −2 per cent (1997) and −10 per cent in 1998 and the currency devalued from Baht 26 to Baht 40 per dollar. During 1999 the GDP stabilized and may have shown a slight increase due to currency devaluation but few firms were hiring new employees and emphasis on cost-saving remained high.

Many reasons contributed to the downturn in economic growth, including over-borrowing of net capital which led to failure to repay loans and non-productive investments. Moreover, disappointing exports, financial sector problems, inadequate bank regulation, and lack of transparency in government policies also contributed to the economic crisis (Posner, 1998). The findings and analyses of the research reported in this chapter reflect a situation of economic expansion, not a situation of economic downturn. Thus, readers should interpret these findings with caution. The anticipated impact on Thai managers' careers caused by the contraction of the economy will be discussed at the end of this chapter.

ORGANIZATIONAL CHARACTERISTICS THAT INFLUENCE CAREERS IN THAILAND

The second level of career analysis is the organization, including organizational constraints, different patterns of jobs, and varieties of positions (Granrose, 1995). Home office nationality, human resource policies and practices, organizational design, and the relative value of different positions and functions play major roles in defining the career opportunities available to individuals inside their current organization.

The data on organizational factors in US firms operating in Thailand were collected by interviews with country CEOs or top-level human resource managers. In the Thai firms, organizational level data were collected from a sample of human resource managers from an association of human resource managers where each manager was employed in a different firm. To be included in this study, the firm had to be a representative of one of the following industries: insurance, petrochemical, manufacturing of durable goods, or manufacturing of non-durable goods.

Career Practices of Two US Firms in Thailand

Organization A is a multinational manufacturing company with its home office located in the US. In Thailand, its head office is based in Bangkok, while its production facility is located in the outskirts of Bangkok. Approximately 450 employees work for this company in Thailand, of which 20 are managers and three are non-Thais. Organization A has five departments and four levels of management. Regional and home offices conduct human resource planning. At the regional level, human resource planning is tied to the company's strategic planning only in a general sense by inclusion in its annual plan.

According to the country manager, new managers are usually hired from outside through recruiting companies or by word of mouth. The main reason for using outside hires is that the people within the company have inadequate experience to fill upper-level management positions. The entry qualifications for management positions are previous work experience with a multinational company, technical knowledge, assertiveness, and English proficiency. Transferring middle managers from other regional countries is theoretically possible, but has never happened.

The career planning activities available to employees are conducted during performance reviews and training courses. Some informal coaching also occurs. The main criteria for promotion include a track record of good job performance, good interpersonal skills, and a good understanding of the business. The country manager or the plant manager makes promotion decisions, with approval from the regional office.

There are two points when managers are likely to leave the company. The first is during the first 6 months as they assess whether or not they like their work in this firm. The second point is in their second year if the jobs do not match their personal expectations or if they are offered a higher salary elsewhere. The managerial turnover is high, about 30 per cent annually. Therefore, the key human resource difficulty is retention. The company does not use any particular retention strategies to counteract this problem.

Organization B is a multinational insurance company with its home office in the US. Human resource planning in this organization in Thailand fits with the home office 3–5 year strategic plan. Due to the shortage of managerial personnel, Organization B usually gets new managers by outside hire. The qualifications of entry managers are service orientation (e.g., willing to meet people), 3–5 years of experience, a college degree, and English communication abilities. The company provides a number of career management activities that are available formally (i.e., performance review and training workshops) and informally (i.e., career counselling, career testing, job or task rotation, coaching or mentors, and job or organizational information).

Generally, a manager stays in the same position for 3–5 years before getting a promotion. The main criterion for promotion is performance, and a promotion decision is made by joint agreement between the immediate supervisor and the country manager.

The major human resource problem in this firm is its ability to match the market salary levels because the local office does not have the authority to make these decisions. Thus, a problem of high turnover exists. Organizational retention strategies include providing good working conditions, promoting teamwork, stating its superiority to competing organizations, setting performance goals and rewarding good performance. Another human resource difficulty is the large gap between Thai managers and US executives in terms of experience, maturity, and managerial skills. Providing coaching and challenging assignments are considered by managers in the firm to be successful approaches to address this problem.

Organizational Career Practices of Thai Firms

Half of the 42 Thai companies were in manufacturing, and the other half were either in the insurance/finance or petrochemical industries. The size of the firms varied from 50 to over 500 employees. Many Thai firms did not have a dedicated Human Resource Department, particularly in the small-sized firms. In these cases, Human Resource functions and activities were handled by the Finance Department or by the Administration Department.

Generally, in Thai firms the concept of career management and planning is not fully developed. The Thai managers who were responsible for the Human Resource function were asked 'What kind of formal human resource planning does this organization have?' Only 30 per cent replied that their organizations had effective human resource planning. In addition, only 26 per cent of the respondents perceived that their organizations had career planning for employees. Career management activities tended to be available only on an informal basis; the career planning strategies they reported included performance reviews, leadership or skill training, providing organization information or career information, career counselling, and job rotation.

In comparison to Thai line managers employed in US firms, Thai firm line managers were more likely to report that coaching and mentors were available, though only informally. This suggests that a more supportive climate and personal relationships are used for career management in Thai firms. In contrast, more Thai managers of US firms than employees of Thai firms reported that they had formal performance reviews.

About half of the human resource managers in Thai firms indicated that to fill management positions their firms used many different kinds of strategies. The remainder reported that their firms were almost equally divided between using outside hires and promotion from within. Substantial hiring at higher levels occurred for two reasons. First, internal employees could not be developed fast enough to catch up with business demands. Second, firms faced a problem of high turnover since many managers were leaving in response to higher salary offers by competitors. During the booming economy the increase in management salaries was more than 11 per cent above the inflation rate so this was a problem for all Thai firms('Labor Letter', *Wall Street Journal*, 1994). The main criterion for promotion perceived by Thai HR managers in Thai firms was good performance, followed by seniority and political influence. Upper management played a major role in deciding who should be promoted, as reported by 60 per cent of the respondents.

Respondents also were asked to rate how much their organizations used each of a list of tactics to influence them to meet the organization's goals (responses could vary from 1 = very unlikely, 5 = very likely). The top organizational influence tactics perceived by the managers in Thai firms were promoting teamwork and offering good pay and fringe benefits, whereas Thai managers working for US firms reported their organizations were most likely to use information-sharing, teamwork, career opportunity, and broader job experience to influence them. The Thai firms were more likely to influence their managers by using authority based on family connection or status (M-Thai = 3.49, M-US = 1.82, p < .05) and threatening to punish or withholding rewards for nonconformity (M-Thai = 3.04, M-US = 1.93, p < .05). In contrast, US firms were more likely to refer to management culture or organizational mission to influence employees (M-US = 3.37, M-Thai = 2.86, p < .05).

INDIVIDUAL CAREERS IN THAILAND

Characteristics of the externally observable careers of individuals include educational preparation for a career as well as patterns of job history within and across organizations. In addition, individual internal careers include subjective aspects such as the way a persons thinks about his or her work experiences – desires, career aspirations and expectations as well as evaluations (Granrose, 1995).

Methodology

The data collected for organizational level and individual level analyses are part of the International Career Project. For details of data collection procedures, see the book reporting the methods of data collection in other phases in this project (Granrose, 1997). In Thailand, two Thai scholars and two graduate students from Thammasat University contributed a non-US perspective, taking Thai culture into consideration in evaluating and translating the survey. Thai scholars conducted the interviews with Thai managers employed in Thai firms in the Thai language. Interviews with employees of US firms were conducted in English but all respondents were given the choice of whether or not to have a translator present and all asked the translator to leave.

The human resource managers from the US firms operating in Thailand were requested to provide 10 or more names of line managers who were representatives of various departments, organizational levels, and performance levels in the firms. The Thai managers working for Thai firms were located through the members of the Thai organization of human resources so human resource managers were over-sampled in the Thai managers working for Thai firms. A total of 84 line managers in Thailand participated in this study. Twenty-nine of the participants were working for US firms in Thailand. All of the respondents were Thai and 56 of the 84 managers were male. More than 63 per cent were married and they had an average of 1.78 children. The sample was composed mostly of managers near the top of their organizations, with an average age of 48-years-old and an average number of years of employment of 11 years, most with the present firm.

Subjective Careers of Thai Managers

In general, Thai managers had thought a great deal about their careers. They had specific (35 per cent) or very specific plans (37 per cent) for their future work life. Most of them had either medium (2–5 years) or long-term (6 years or more) plans for their future.

The managers were asked to describe not only their career plans but also major aids or blocks to being able to make their plans work. The most-often cited obstacle to career advancement was their own skills and performance (21 per cent), and many particularly mentioned English language skills in interviews. However, skills and performance were also the second most frequently cited factor for career enhancement (21 per cent). Similarly, superiors were listed as the most significant assistance (26 per cent) and the second most frequently cited obstacle (16 per cent) to career advancement. For example, some respondents said 'My boss teaches me the knowledge and skills to do the job' and 'My boss has been a great support to me', but another reported 'My main career block is (my) boss's unfairness because he is so powerful.' Factors related to the organizations, such as company policies, number of available jobs, and organizational structure, were not found to play a significant role in terms of career obstacles. This is probably due to the availability of many job and promotion opportunities at the time of this study, but this might be perceived differently in conditions of economic downturn.

It was interesting to find that 'my spouse' was listed as a key assistance to career advancement by 12 per cent of respondents. Male managers particularly reported that their spouses supported their careers. For example, many wives were willing to adapt themselves to their husband's careers. Co-workers also were listed as a career help (12 per cent). This confirms the influence of social relationships in the Thai society.

In this study, respondents indicated a moderate satisfaction with their careers (M = 3.40, 1 = very dissatisfied, 5 = very satisfied) and with life in general

(M = 3.76). In addition, the managers considered work to be very important or significant in their lives (M = 4.37).

Career Goals

The survey asked managers to identify the importance of each of 23 career goals (1 = of little importance, 5 = extremely important). The results comparing responses from the Thai managers working in Thai and US firms are summarized in Table 7.1.

The top five career goals of managers employed in Thai firms were friendship, promotions, security, contribution to family, and well-being. To find friendship among the highest ranked goals was not surprising due to the collectivist Thai culture (Hofstede, 1983) but this finding differed from

Table 7.1   The importance of career goals in Thai managers

Goals	Thai firms		US firms	
	Mean	*S.D.*	*Mean*	*S.D.*
Income	4.27	0.69	4.00	0.72
Variety	3.75	0.85	3.43	0.69
Autonomy	3.89	0.95	3.96	0.76
Achievement	4.02	0.87	4.29	0.76
Residence	3.33	1.18	3.41	1.08
Contributing to my organization	4.26	0.94	4.46	0.58
Contributing to society	3.85	0.96	3.96	0.84
Contributing to my family	4.34	0.76	4.04	0.92
Security	4.40	0.69	3.93	0.81**
Good working conditions	3.85	0.89	3.68	0.90
Keeping busy	3.36	1.21	3.54	0.96
Prestige	3.77	1.00	3.93	0.81
Fringe benefits	3.89	0.91	3.64	0.78
Meaningful work	3.71	0.49	4.57	0.59**
Growth	4.00	0.58	4.52	0.67
Well being	4.29	0.76	3.91	0.79
Power	2.80	0.96	3.50	0.75**
Skills	3.94	1.00	4.21	0.92
Creativity	2.77	1.04	3.96	1.00***
Fun	3.35	0.93	4.07	0.86**
Working hours	2.81	1.14	3.00	1.15
Friendship	4.48	0.70	4.21	0.74
Promotions	4.43	0.75	4.41	0.69

Note: Significant differences between managers employed by Thai firms and managers employed by US firms: * = p < . 05, ** = p < .01, ***p = < .001.

responses to the same question in all other Asian locations (Granrose, 1997). Brown and Ladawan (1979) have suggested that friendly and pleasant relationships are highly regarded and expected in the Thai work setting. Promotion has a high value because of the status associated with it in a hierarchical system. Well-being in the Thai sense means having a decent life and pleasant working atmosphere. This reflects strong cultural values of maintaining an 'easy-going attitude'.

The highest ranked career goals for Thai managers working in US firms were meaningful work, followed by growth, contribution to the organization, promotion, and achievement. This is similar to Fieg's (1989) description of the expectations of Thai managers working for US firms. Fieg stated: 'A Thai coming to work for an American firm would tend to be somewhat materialistic, interested in upward mobility, eager to learn new techniques and practices..., and generally somewhat above average in daring and self-confidence in order to cope with the demands of working in an alien cultural environment' (p. 70). Additionally, he suggests that a Thai manager might feel proud to work for an American firm because it proves that he or she must be very competent.

There are significant differences in career goals between those who work for Thai firms and those who work for US firms in Thailand. Thai managers working for US firms considered intrinsic values, such as meaningful work, creativity, and fun or enjoyment, more important than those working for Thai firms. However, obtaining skills was also considered very important to US firm managers. Generally, US firms tended to promote creativity and they even may include creativity as an important aspect in performance evaluation. As a result, US firms may attract employees who value creativity.

US firm managers placed a lower value on security than those in Thai firms. According to Fieg (1989) and Mead, Jones and Chansarkar (1997), Thai managers may regard employment with multinational companies as a necessary apprenticeship to be taken before starting their own companies or moving to work with new companies. So they do not worry as much about job security as those employed in Thai firms. This was confirmed by several interview comments in the present study. One respondent said: 'My final career plan is to have my own business three years from now. I joined this company so I can learn more and gain experience.' Responses to the question 'How easy would it be for you to obtain an equal or better job in a different organization, if you wanted to?' indicated that managers working for US firms reported significantly higher perceptions of opportunities to find employment in a different organization. Additionally, US firm managers expected to continue working for the current organizations for a shorter period of time (M = 6 years) than Thai firm managers (M = 8.7 years), although these averages do not reflect the HR manager's experience that many managers leave after two years when Thai managers work in a US firm.

Career Tactics and Satisfaction

Respondents were asked to rate how likely they were to use each of 35 tactics to reach their career goals or have the kind of work life they wanted (1 = very unlikely, 5 = very likely). The results of the mean scores of each career tactic are represented in Table 7.2.

The strategies most commonly used by both Thai and US firm managers were: working hard, learning more about the business, getting more education or training, and gaining rapport with subordinates. Getting help from God, leaving it to fate, and threatening to leave were the least commonly used strategies for both groups.

There were a number of differences in the career tactics that Thai managers employed in Thai firms and in US firms would use. Thai managers employed in US firms were more likely to work hard, learn more about the business, and try to do their current job well. This may result from the performance review system practised in US firms. In Thai firms, a performance review may be done but it is not viewed as the only determinant to career advancement or promotions. Other factors, such as seniority, politics and social relationships, also play a key role. Consistently, the highest-rated career tactic among Thai firm managers was building rapport with subordinates. Additionally, they were more likely to use the tactics of becoming indispensable, creating a new job, counting on others to recognize their accomplishments, and exchanging favours.

Career satisfaction was measured by answers to the following question: 'How satisfied are you that this organization provides you with each of the following opportunities or rewards?' This was followed by the same list rated as career goals. The managers working for Thai and US firms showed no significant differences in satisfaction with their organization (see Table 7.3). It is not clear whether this lack of significant differences reflected perceived similarity between firms or a general predisposition to rate satisfaction measures as moderately high because of cultural values.

Results of the current study indicated that managers working for US firms were more committed to their occupations than to their organizations (see Table 7.4).

This may suggest that Thai managers who were employed in US firms were more willing to meet the demanding and intensive work in order to obtain skills and experience in preparation to move to another company, but did not consider their current work to be their real occupation or final company.

128   *Career Planning and Managers in Thailand*

Table 7.2   Career tactics used by Thai managers

Career tactics	Thai firms		US firms	
	Mean	S.D.	Mean	S.D.
Work hard	4.02	0.89	4.48	0.69*
Ask for help	2.02	1.08	2.03	0.87
Make an action plan	3.73	1.08	3.62	1.27
Get help from friends	2.94	0.94	2.69	1.31
Offer loyalty to my organization	3.65	0.95	3.97	0.94
Offer loyalty to my superior	3.35	1.03	3.72	1.00
Learn more	4.26	0.76	4.76	0.44**
Get more education	4.32	0.70	4.48	0.87
Develop rapport with subordinates	4.40	0.69	4.38	0.73
Do better than my peers	3.27	1.00	3.62	0.98
Become indispensable	4.32	0.78	3.00	1.13***
Work long hours	3.27	0.95	3.55	0.78
Gain access to information	4.04	0.95	3.69	0.97
Conform to what is expected	3.58	0.64	3.90	0.82
Get help from my family	2.24	0.89	2.00	1.20
Get help from God	1.29	0.64	1.41	0.87
Change family plans	2.12	0.99	2.38	1.29
Transfer to a different job	3.04	1.17	2.55	1.18
Transfer to a different organization	2.63	1.11	2.55	1.12
Get a second job	2.41	0.96	1.83	1.07*
Create a new job	3.85	0.92	2.52	1.18***
Get more control over my job	3.81	0.89	3.31	1.11*
Do my job well	3.25	1.71	4.58	0.50**
My way of thinking	3.38	0.91	3.11	1.17
Build networks	3.67	0.73	3.76	0.79
Start my own business	2.67	1.40	2.59	1.52
Let others recognize me	3.23	1.02	2.52	1.18**
Leave it to fate	1.29	0.67	1.38	0.73
Tell my boss my career plans	2.65	1.00	2.93	1.03
Seek career guidance	2.80	1.11	2.86	1.22
Do noticeable things	3.00	0.93	3.34	0.97
Do what my boss wants	3.60	0.91	3.59	0.95
Act humble toward superiors	3.33	1.04	3.28	0.92
Assertively ask	2.57	1.10	3.07	1.10*
Exchange favours	3.79	1.04	3.00	1.31**
Threaten to leave	1.28	0.89	1.38	0.56

Note: Significant differences between managers employed by Thai firms and manager employed by US firms: * = p < . 05, ** = p < .01, *** = p < .001.

Table 7.3   Career satisfaction in Thai managers

	Thai firms		US firms	
	Mean	*S.D.*	*Mean*	*S.D.*
Income	3.33	0.89	3.51	1.24
Variety	3.17	0.87	3.03	0.93
Autonomy	3.36	1.08	3.39	0.95
Achievement	3.36	0.97	3.42	0.95
Residence	3.21	1.02	3.44	0.97
Contribution to my organization	3.25	0.95	3.47	1.08
Contribution to society	3.00	0.96	3.32	1.02
Contribution to my family	3.43	0.98	3.32	0.72
Security	3.43	0.99	3.50	0.92
Working conditions	3.28	0.89	3.37	0.88
Keeping busy	3.11	0.85	3.51	0.89
Prestige	3.26	0.81	3.10	0.68
Fringe benefits	3.26	1.04	3.14	0.97
Meaningful work	3.00	0.57	3.52	1.03
Growth	2.85	0.89	3.56	1.12
Well being	2.85	1.06	3.40	0.59
Power	3.21	0.60	3.14	0.93
Skills	3.37	1.06	3.60	0.95
Creativity	3.30	1.11	3.39	0.99
Fun	3.25	0.92	2.96	0.88
Working hours	3.03	0.73	3.35	1.09
Friendship	3.26	1.02	3.32	1.05
Promotions	3.26	1.00	3.14	0.93

Notes: 1 = very dissatisfied, 5 = very satisfied. Significant differences between managers employed by Thai firms and managers employed by US firms: * = $p < .05$, ** = $p < .01$, ***$p = < .001$.

The Thai firm-employed managers also seemed to have a misfit between the occupation each person preferred and his or her occupation at the time of the survey. We asked respondents if they would like to change their occupation. A majority of Thais employed in Thai firms listed an alternative occupation in response to this question.

IMPLICATIONS FOR CAREERS AND MANAGEMENT DEVELOPMENT

Although this was not a representative national sample, and thus we must be careful of over-generalizations, this study provides some understanding of

Table 7.4   Thai organizational, job, and occupational commitment

Commitment	Thai firms Mean	US firms Mean
This organization means a lot to me	3.71	3.93
I am not part of this organization family	2.90	2.00**
I do not belong to this organization	3.88	2.03***
The most important things in my life involve my job	1.96	3.48**
My job is only a small part of me	3.67	2.03***
My occupation reflects my personality	2.27	3.24***
I want a career in my occupation	1.02	1.20***
I wish I had chosen a different occupation	4.08	2.57*

Note: 1 = strongly disagree, 5 = strongly agree; Significant differences between managers employed by Thai firms and managers employed by US firms: * = p < 0 .05, ** = p < 0.01, *** = p < 0.001.

common human resource planning and practices in Thailand, and individual career plans of Thai managers as these managers experienced a growing economy. Three major points emerge as implications for careers and management development that are unlikely to change with changing economic conditions. First, a gap exists between individual career plans and human resource planning in Thai organizations. Thai managers have carefully thought about and planned their careers using a medium- to long-term perspective. However, organizational human resource planning is not fully implemented to serve these managers. Thus, it is time for organizations to put more focus on career-related HR policies and ensure their effective implementation if they want to keep their top managers who want to be eligible for good jobs in Thai and in international firms. This is a challenge because organizations are not likely to realize the importance of effective HR practices when they are occupied with producing goods and services to meet the demand of an expanding market. Perhaps it is even less likely to occur in hard economic times when organizations are concerned about survival.

Second, since the Thai national culture has influential nationally shared work values (Sorod, 1991), international companies may want to consider modifying their organizational or management policies to become more effective within the Thai culture. For example, international companies may want to integrate a more benevolent paternalistic culture into their organizational culture in order to accommodate the strong value of hierarchy and harmonious relationships among Thai employees. Organizational tactics may have to be adjusted to focus more on long-term family aspects of fringe benefits such as providing health and group life insurance and financial assistance to employees' children. This may create higher motivation, satisfaction, and commitment among Thai workers who value not only friendships but also value making a contribution to their families. Although Thai managers who choose to work for US firms may favour some Western business practices, they still expect that the companies should be sensitive to the Thai culture because the business is operated in Thailand.

Third, to be able to compete and survive in a slow economy, Thai firms will need to put more emphasis on a performance-driven organizational culture. How to do this while maintaining the importance of relationships and reducing reliance on competition may be a major challenge for Thai firms. They may want to review their HR policies and pay more attention to giving rewards for performance in order to encourage higher levels of performance of their employees. They also may be able to achieve this by implementing more formal career management programmes, for example mentoring programmes and education sponsorship. In addition, due to a common misfit between an employee's self-concept and their occupation in Thai firms, the selection, recruiting, and placement policies of Thai firms should be revisited to see if adjustments in job assignments could be used to motivate employees to contribute to firm performance.

The change in the Thai national economic situation due to the severe current economic downturn affects all aspects of Thai employment. It especially affects those in financial services, real estate development, and manufacturing. In contrast to the high demands for employment occurring during the data collection of this report, workers now encounter a buyer's market and have much less bargaining power. This trend may continue for some time, despite the fact that Thailand has started to show positive signs of gradual recovery resulting from recent government efforts (Goad, 1998). A large survey in Thailand (Watson Wyatt, 1998) shows that cost-cutting tactics will continue to be used by companies operating in Thailand, including both foreign-owned and Thai-owned companies. Specifically, pay cuts (45 per cent), work relocations, and control of headcount (29 per cent) are strategies many companies are beginning to implement. Downsizing trends are increasing – 40 per cent of the companies surveyed respond that they will downsize in the future or are in the process of doing so. Most companies in Thailand plan to choose who should be laid-off in a elective manner rather than using across-the-board layoffs. The most commonly used criteria for retaining employees are competencies (23 per cent) and performance level (20 per cent) (Watson Wyatt, 1998). In addition, more and more companies will employ performance pay in order to retain fewer and better employees. Organizations will need to maintain good communications, such as clearly communicating their lay-off criteria, so that the organization is able to maintain high morale among its workers.

As a result of these layoffs, it is anticipated that changes in career goals toward security and stability may become more common. For example, giving a higher priority to job security and better long-term potential may outweigh the high evaluation of overpriced salaries common in the past (O'Shea, 1998). Many people are willing to accept a large pay cut in order to work for a multinational company in more secure and better long-term jobs. To thrive in this situation, employees have to ensure that their career tactics are effective in enhancing organizational performance. These career tactics may include working hard, learning more, getting more education and training. It is especially important for employees to keep up with new technology skills in the slow economy. In this employers' market, voluntary turnover will be less than before. People are willing to move only if it is good for the long-term, such as moving from a start-up to an established company.

Economic changes do not alter all career goals, however. There were some consistent findings between this study and the earlier study on work values conducted by Komin (1990). Generally, Thai managers in both studies put high a value on social interaction. In addition, goals related to achievement values (achievement, growth, promotions) were rated as moderately important in both studies. Salary was also an important career goal. In this study Thai managers wanted fast promotion, more opportunities to grow on the job, and a high salary. This may be because external factors (salary, and status in the organizational hierarchy) are instrumental for access to wealth, and wealth is an important determinant of one's place in Thai society. Convenient working hours, residence location, and keeping busy were among the lowest-ranked career goals for Thai managers.

Another more recent study investigating the career aspirations among managerial elite in Thailand (Mead, Jones and Chansarkar, 1997) found that future entrepreneurs had slightly different career goals. Specifically, short-term objectives, such as salary and promotion, were subordinated to long-term success goals for this sample. The respondents' long-term objective (a time horizon of 10 years) was to run their own business. However, the Mead *et al.* findings should be interpreted with caution as most of the respondents claimed to have a family business background and were graduates from Thailand's most prestigious and expensive management school. Thus, they may not represent most Thai managers in general and only partly matched the sample of managers in the present study.

In sum, in the face of the new economic and environmental situation, it can be anticipated that the careers of managers in Thailand will have to make some changes. Future career research investigating these changes deserves attention both by academia and professionals. In the meantime, managers can expect that managerial employees will continue to value good interpersonal relationships, and being able to take care of their families. They can expect that Thai mangers are willing to work hard and get further education to achieve these goals if the firm can demonstrate a connection between this hard work and personal long-term career objectives.

References

Apibunyanuch, P. (1993) 'TNCs and Impacts on Industrialization in Thailand', *Regional Development Dialogue*, 14, pp. 94–117.

Brown, S. E. and Ladawan, T. (1979) 'Perceived Satisfaction with Leadership as Related to Subordinate Managerial Philosophies', *Perceptual and Motor Skills*, 48, pp. 355–9.

Chow, I. (1995) 'Career Planning and Development for Hong Kong Chinese Managers', *Journal of Asian Business*, 11(3), pp. 27–54.

Fairclough, G. (1992) 'Thailand – Back to Work: Organized Labour Seeks to Restore', *Far Eastern Economic Review*, 155 (5 Nov.), (44) pp. 21–2.

Fieg, J. (1989) *A Common Core: Thais and Americans* (New York: Intercultural Press).

Goad, G. P. (1998) 'Recovery in worst-hit Asian economies will take more time, economists say', *Wall Street Journal* (Eastern edition), 27 March, p. B7A.

Granrose, C. S. (1992) 'Careers of Asian Managers in U.S. Firms in Thailand, Singapore, and Malaysia', *Journal of Southeast Asian Business*, 8(2), pp. 58–70.

Granrose, C. S. (1995) 'A Model of Organizational Careers in National Contexts', *Journal of Southeast Asian Business*, 11(3), pp. 5–25.

Granrose, C. S. (1997) *The Careers of Managers in East Asia* (Westport, CT: Quorum).

Hofstede, G. (1983) *Culture's consequences: International differences in work-related values* (Newport Beach, CA: Sage).

Komin, S. (1990) 'Culture and Work-Related Values in Thai Organizations', *International Journal of Psychology*, 25, pp. 681–704.

Kuriavikitkul, W. (1994) 'Conflict management, job satisfaction, intent to stay, and specific demographic variables of professional nurses in Thailand', *Dissertation Abstract International*, 55(12), p. 5285.

'Labour Letter': Asian managers' pay (1994) *Wall Street Journal* (Eastern edition), 17 May, p. A1.

Mead, J., Jones, C. J. and Chansarkar, B. (1997) 'The Managerial Elite in Thailand: Their Long- and Short-Term Career Aspirations', *International Journal of Management*, 14(3), pp. 387–94.

Morrison, A. M. and Von Glinow, M. A. (1990) 'Women and Minorities in Management', *American Psychologist*, 45, pp. 200–8.

O'Shea, L. (1998) 'The Hardest Job of All', *Asian Business*, 34(2), pp. 56–8.

Posner, M. (1998) 'Asian Economy in Decline', *Credit Management*, pp. 24–8.

Redding, S. G. and Ng, M. (1982) 'The Role of Face in the Organizational Perceptions of Chinese Managers', *Organization Studies*, 3(3), pp. 201–19.

Sorod, B. (1991) 'The influence of national and organizational cultures on managerial values, attitudes, and performance (national cultures)', Dissertation Abstract International Item: AAG9129283.

Thailand Board of Investment (1998) 'Thailand: Demographics' [on-line]: www.boi.go.th/thailand/index.html

Vause, G. W. and Chandravithun, N. (1992) 'Thailand's Labour and Employment Law: Balancing the Demands of a Newly Industrializing State', *Northwestern Journal of International Law & Business*, 13(2), pp. 398–403.

Watson Wyatt Company (1998) *Retrenchment in Thailand*, Bangkok, July.

Woodall, P. (1998) 'Survey: East Asian Economy: Tiger Adrift', *The Economist*, 346, pp. S3–S5.

8 Training in Thailand: Trends and Cases from the Service Industries

Niti Dubey-Villinger

INTRODUCTION

The purpose of this chapter is to provide an overview of training and development trends in Thailand with a focus on the service industries. A number of cases are described as examples of practices in leading organizations. The emphasis of this chapter is on major training or development needs in Thai service organizations and the strategies employed in meeting these needs. An overview of the types of training employed and methods utilized is discussed, with implications for the future. The article begins with a discussion of the state of training in Thailand using government initiatives and training companies as examples.

Numerous companies offer specialized and general management training in Thailand. The government also offers several training and development programmes for a wide range of students. The main difference between the two groups is that while private companies target employed professionals at private sector organizations in Thailand, especially those approaching positions of managerial responsibility, governmental initiatives target semi-skilled and low-skilled labour including those still unemployed. There may be areas of overlap in some cases but the trend indicates that private companies take the lead in developing training in areas of demand for their client organizations. In Thailand, these areas have included general management and cross-cultural skills, sales management skills and language training. There are numerous companies offering such training and development in the business community in Thailand and two such companies are highlighted below.

PRIVATE COMPANIES AND CONSULTANCIES: MANAGEMENT, CROSS-CULTURAL AND SALES TRAINING

A number of companies offer management development and training in Thailand targeting both the expatriate and Thai management communities. These companies focus on training along the following areas:

- General management training
- Cross-cultural management and language training
- Sales management and negotiations training
- Specialty training such as recruitment, computer-based training

Cross-cultural management training is a broad area of training which includes human resources management as well as language proficiency training. The American Management Association International (AMAI) and a company called Cross-Cultural Management (CCM), for example, offer extensive courses in this area targeting managers in both Thai and Western organizations. These companies offer tailor-made programmes for potential clients, though the thrust of their offerings centre around management skills and cross-cultural issues respectively.

The AMAI offers a variety of programmes (featuring Thai-language programmes) including: Management Skills and Techniques for New Supervisors, Improving Managerial Skills of the New or Prospective Manager, Fundamental Selling Techniques for the New or Prospective Salesperson, Principles of Professional Selling, Managing the Sales Force, Strategies for Developing Effective Presentation Skills, Building Better Negotiating Skills, Strategic Planning and The Fundamentals of Human Resource Management.

CCM is an older company founded by Henry Holmes, a seasoned expatriate who is known in the Bangkok business community for his observations on Thai management culture (see Holmes and Tangtongtavy, 1997). CCM offers five main training areas: The Skills of Cross-Cultural Management in Thailand, The Keys to Assertiveness and Accountability, Making Effective Presentations, Communication and Team-building, and Building Your Company Culture in Thailand. Michelin Siam and Procter & Gamble are among its larger corporate clients.

CCM targets three groups of clients: (1) high potential Thais (who lack extensive overseas experience); (2) expatriate executives (both newcomers to Thailand as well as experienced executives in Thailand); and (3) expatriate spouses 'whose adjustment to Thailand is considered critical for family satisfaction'. This third group is often not discussed as a potential target for training though spouse adjustment in the international assignments of managers is viewed with increasing importance. CCM training strives to provide comprehensive training wherein expatriates and Thais learn essential skills for effective management and team building (Table 8.1)

According to CCM, their cross-cultural training is most effective when there are equally balanced groups of Thais and expatriates from any given company participating in the course.

Table 8.1   Skills for effective management and team-building

Skills for expatriates	Skills for Thais
Getting timely, reliable information	Approaching expatriates directly
Understanding and utilizing important values such as *kreng jai*, *hai kiad*, and others	Understanding major values of successful expatriate executives: accountability, assertiveness, and others
Interpreting Thai behaviour correctly	Using assertion effectively: initiating, contradicting and convincing
Motivating Thais	Interpreting foreign behaviour correctly
Issuing instructions that work	Contributing effectively in meetings
Conducting effective meetings	Techniques of giving and receiving feedback/criticism
Major dos and don'ts	Gaining career advancement in a multinational company
Understanding Thai expectations of a manager	Ability to separate personal and professional relationships
Ways of changing old patterns for new ones	
Managing domestic staff more effectively	

The Thai Management Association also offers a variety of courses in presentation skills training, project management and a compensation workshop for interested parties. Other training companies specialize in language training, computer-based training, quality management training and what is now increasingly in demand in Thailand, 'train the trainer' programmes which promote the effective development of trainers and executives/supervisors in their training roles.

GOVERNMENTAL/PUBLIC INSTITUTIONS AND TRAINING: AN EMPHASIS ON LOW-SKILLED AND SEMI-SKILLED LABOUR

The Thai government, recognizing the need for and importance of a skilled labour force, has planned and implemented several training programmes for the Thai workforce. Many of these programmes target low-skilled and semi-skilled labour. Initiatives such as the Thai Skills Development Project (1997–2001), a joint effort of the Ministry of Labour and Social Welfare and the Asian Development Bank, focus upon improving the quality and relevance of the skills development system in Thailand. Its primary objectives include the expansion and improvement of training capacity in the country and enhancing the institutional capacity of the Department of Skills Development (DSD) in the Ministry of Labour and Social Welfare. This specific project has utilized both domestic and international consultants (and contracted staff). These include: technical advisors, career guidance specialists, computer-based training specialists, financial analysts, management training specialists, marketing specialists, among others.

The DSD has a primary role in developing labour skills by providing pre-employment and upgrading training to the labour force 'in order to facilitate the country's development'. Women, youth and farmers are targeted for the training, as are the unemployed, skilled and semi-skilled workers.

The DSD states that skill development in Thailand emerges from a combination of formal and informal vocational training and educational practices. The resulting practice of the Ministry of Labour and Social Welfare is to devote a lion's share of its programmes to:

1. Establishing and monitoring human resource needs which correspond to the national economic reform plans, within, particularly, the industrial infrastructure, business, services and agricultural sectors;
2. Developing the potential and raising the standard of the labour force to meet the needs of both the domestic and international markets;
3. Encouraging the private sector to participate in skill development;
4. Increasing cooperation in skill development at national and international levels;
5. Developing information systems in skill development.

The main participants for the trainings offered by DSD are non-skilled and semi-skilled workers with primary (compulsory education of six years) to secondary school (up to six additional years) education. Other governmental bodies and private vocational institutes also offer training. These include: the Ministry of Defence; the Ministry of the Interior; the Ministry of Industry; and the Ministry of Agriculture and Cooperatives.

The DSD estimates that 75 per cent of the present labour force of 33 million workers are unskilled workers with an average of 5.1 years of education. TDRI, the Thailand Development Research Institute, found in its projection of the labour force a greater demand for workers with medium and higher educational levels than what is currently available in the primary-education-dominated labour force. This is in line with the aforementioned findings of the Thailand Skills Development Project. One policy move to address this deficiency has been to increase the compulsory education of workers from the current system of six years to nine years.

The DSD has formulated its own strategy to increase the education of the labour force. Through its work with the Ministry of Education (DOVE – Department of Vocational Education which is the largest training programme in the country), DSD provides basic education to two major groups of workers, the first comprising of those having completed some basic education, the latter consisting of those not having finishing basic education. DOVE provides courses in polytechnics and the Industrial and Community Education College. DSD and its twelve regional training institutes have created and implemented a professional training system. Courses are divided into the following training areas: pre-employment training; skill upgrading training (for those with basic education); and general personnel development training courses.

Pre-employment training consists of curricula along the following areas: machining; welding; automotive; electricity; electronics; construction; drawing; the arts industries; and business/services areas. Theory is offered with practical, on-the-job experience. Skill upgrading training is available along all the preceding areas with a more detailed selection of subjects through three to six day courses. Personnel development training courses follow a similar line.

In conjunction with this professional training system, the DSD has encouraged the participation of the private sector in stimulating the achievement of its labour force objectives. The private sector is to benefit from skill development. For example, employers who register as professional trainers are exempt, under the Vocational Training Promotion Act 1994, from labour and private institution law and are allowed to deduct additional expenses from income tax (50 per cent deduction of training expenses).

In addition, the DSD is encouraging the private sector to become more responsible in skill development by improving the law under the Act Promoting Professional Training 1994 in two main areas: (1) requiring employers to develop the skills of some of their employees or contribute to the Skill Development Fund; and (2) offering loans to businesses to help them provide skill development for their employees. The Skill Development Fund also offers loans at a very low interest rate (1 per cent) to new entrants to the labour market, laid-off workers and those wishing to upgrade their skills. Those eligible for the loan must be poor Thai nationals, aged 15–45, who will use the loan for training expenses. Following the economic crisis of 1997, this Fund has enabled many to continue their professional development.

When progress in education is considered on a historical basis, Thailand can be viewed as a success story. Thailand has made substantial progress in

140   *Training in Thailand*

Table 8.2   Adult literacy rates for selected Asian countries (per cent)

Country	1960	1970	1980	1990
Thailand	67.7	78.6	86.0	93.0
Hong Kong	70.4	77.3a	90.0b	n.a.
India	27.8c	34.1a	36.0d	48.0
Indonesia	39.0c	56.6a	62.0e	74.0
Malaysia	52.8f	58.5	60.0	78.0
Philippines	71.9	82.6	75.0b	90.0
Singapore	n.a.	68.9	83.0	n.a.
South Korea	70.6	87.6	93.0	96.0
Sri Lanka	75.0f	77.6a	85.0b	88.0

Note: a = 1971, b = 1979, c = 1961, d = 1981, e = 1978, f = 1962.
Sources: Adapted from Sussangkarn and Chalamwong, 1994, p. 4; IBRD, *World Tables 1983*, and *World Development Report 1991, 1994*.

this area during the last few decades. Primary school enrolment has been substantial and Thailand experienced universal enrolment (Sussangkarn and Chalamwong, 1994) during the 1980s. Considering its population explosion during the 1960s and 1970s, this is a commendable accomplishment. In particular, when adult literacy rates are evaluated in a regional comparison, Thailand's 1990 rate of 93 per cent was just short of those found in more developed countries like South Korea (96 per cent), for example (Table 8.2). The National Plans subsequently reflect the need for *continued* human resources development in Thailand where a skilled and semi-skilled labour force is to satisfy the demands of a rapidly industrializing market.

THE SERVICE INDUSTRIES

The hospitality industry is an important feature of Thailand's economy. The industry plays an important role in the country's development. Training, it is expected, will play an important role in the development of hospitality organizations. The following cases highlight the state of training in the Thai hospitality sector and how the industry has addressed the need for training in a number of innovative ways like the development of training schools at individual hotels.

The section will also discuss the main training needs of organizations in other service industries, notably financial and professional services. These two examples, although different in terms of the content of their training requirements, reveal that international industry trends play an important role in the effective maintainance of standards as well as keeping organizations in line with developments along several fronts such as information technology, for example. Language training, which is a subject addressed by the professional services case, is an area which was also recognized as being an essential part of training in the hospitality sector.

Training in the Hospitality Industry

In the United States, labour and human resources are said to be the primary challenges facing the hotel industry in the year 2000 and beyond (Worcester, 1999). The industry is experiencing a shortage of workers with some estimating over 800,000 available jobs (Worcester, 1999; also Surati, 1999). Respondents to the Hotel and Motel Management's 1999 Independent Management Company survey indicated that attracting, retaining and training employees was their primary objective. Strauss (1999) also notes that hospitality executives stress the importance of leadership skills, benefit of internships, management skills and diversity training as areas which 'employees wish educators would teach'. The importance of industry experience in addition to classroom study was also emphasized.

According to Theibert (1996), companies have now started to offer their own courses or are engaging in the degree-granting business largely due to a lack of adequately trained employees in the skill areas they require. The hotel industry specifically requires employees with specialization in more than one area with a higher degree of sophistication (ibid, 1996). To some extent, it has been suggested that people get diverse experience and do not remain in one area of business like marketing or human resources, for example (Strauss, 1999). Some companies are even forming partnerships with universities and colleges to educate and train employees. According to Theibert (1996), building customized curricula in alliance with colleges might lead to higher productivity and higher skilled jobs.

Branded hospitality chains seek a strong service-oriented culture in the behaviour of their employees in the delivery of service (Gross-Turner, 1999). 'As a result, HR strategy becomes a critical factor, as does the regional manager's involvement with the HR practices which emanate from that strategy.' Gross-Turner (1999, p. 49) in his investigation of branded hotel-chains in the United Kingdom found that the overall concept of recruitment and selection of multi-unit managers is a combination of task-oriented and people-oriented approaches (Wright and Storey, 1997):

This surfaces as an intention to recruit and select an individual who has the capabilities to carry out the job, but who will also fit into the culture and

the team. Where the culture is particularly strong, as in some of the internationally franchised branded restaurant chains, the recruitment and
selection methods are specifically formulated in order to bring to the fore
the candidates who most readily display the characteristics and personality
desired. The personality was particularly important where the technical
skills were extremely simple and could be acquired in a short space of time.

(Gross-Turner (*op cit*))

Gross-Turner (1999) found that managers were mainly promoted from
within in the companies he studied – their promotion being based upon a
proven track record and endorsed by personal recommendations, appraisals
and personal credibility.

There is a general view that there needs to be more emphasis on training
(Kapner, 1996) in the hospitality industry. On the other hand, some consider
training unnecessary and believe people development, perhaps in learning to
unlearn old behaviour is the key to new, improved behaviours (Sullivan, 1998).

Service is considered a special element of Thai hospitality culture. This
view has also been attributed to other Southeast Asian cultures (Dutton,
1998) but remains a crucial distinguishing feature of Thailand's hospitality
management. Several hotels hope to achieve this objective and operate their
own training schools or centres to fulfil the growing demand for training personnel in this area. The Evergreen Group, the Oriental Hotel and the Dusit
Thani College are three such organizations.

Evergreen Laurel Institute of Hotel Management:
A New School for Teaching Service Skills

The Evergreen Group, headquartered in Taiwan, operates a chain of mid-
sized hotels around Asia. Their operation in Bangkok, a property with 160
rooms, recently launched its own training institute, the Evergreen Laurel
Institute of Hotel Management (ELI) to provide people who do not have
upper high school education or university/college training with the opportunity of gaining a professional qualification, the Professional Diploma in Management of Hotel Operations, through their six-month intensive programme.
The school was developed along the lines of the general manager's vision to
provide education to those without the resources to pursue training via other
formal means. The programme is comprised of both theoretical and on-the-
job training. Courses include:

1. Introduction to Hospitality Industry
2. Hospitality Sales and Marketing

3. Management of Hospitality Human Resources and Training
4. Managing Change and Organizational Development
5. Integrated Marketing Communications
6. Professional English (International Hotel and Restaurant)
7. Front Office Seminar
8. Food and Beverage Seminar
9. Management of Hospitality Service Quality: Be my guest programme
10. Project I (How to manage the boutique hotel or specialty restaurant)

When comparing the curriculum with an established hotel management programme, such as one found in the US in an undergraduate course, one finds ELI's mix of courses more 'operational' in nature than the theoretical foundations of a formal hotel school. For example, Cornell's School of Hotel Administration, though an undergraduate programme (normally a four-year course), requires courses in the following areas:

- Management Operation
- Human-Resources Management
- Financial Management
- Food and Beverage Management
- Marketing and Tourism
- Marketing Elective
- Property Asset Management
- Communication
- Operations Management and Information Technology
- Law
- Economics
- Macroeconomics
- Assorted electives

The differences highlight the nature, orientation and objectives of the two programmes. One emphasizes opportunity for those lacking formal qualifications, the other, a more rigorous and some might argue thorough programme for those wishing to have a more managerial career in the hospitality industry. The Cornell programme requires financial management, operations management and information technology in addition to courses in marketing. A course at the Hawaii Pacific University, also for undergraduates, pinpoints the importance of information technology in the industry.

In comparison to a Western hotel school, ELI believes that it follows the Thai tradition of excellence in service. While the hotel previously sent employees to the United States for study, there was a view that Thailand's recognition for service orientation would mean additional training in that area would be redundant or unnecessary. In other words, 'Why go to the West for training?' was an underlying premize in the minds of some management staff. Indeed, one manager described the focus of Thai hospitality schools as being quality of service (orientation) or 'how to exceed customer expectations'. In comparison, the focus of Western schools, such as those present in the United States, is on managerial skills. In terms of areas for further development, one ELI manager pointed to the need for improvement in sales and marketing training. A priority was defined in terms of 'creating new strategies in this area'.

ELI uses a combination of internal staff trainers with outside consultants for conducting its courses. Marketing Communications, Human Resources and Training Management are areas which employ outside consultants. On-the-job training is obtained by work in housekeeping, front office, food/beverage and catering.

In addition to training students under the aegis of ELI's professional diploma programme, the Institute also participates in a number of 'community relations activities'. Their 'Leadership trainee programme for hospitality educators' is a three-month course for university (and other) hospitality educators to further improve their knowledge of the industry. A management trainee course, comprised of a six to nine month tenure with the Institute and hotel, is available to students. A similar internship programme is also available to students under the 'student trainee programme' which requires 400 hours of on-the-job work. The hotel also participates in the 'Hotel Trainers Club', a local trainers alliance group, which is a forum for the exchange of information and networking.

As discussed in the previous section, ELI management are looking for people with experience, the 'right experience' in terms of hiring for their hotel. While recruits to their Institute do not necessarily search for employment at the Evergreen Hotel, their training prepares them for careers in similar organizations. The company believes in a philosophy of training and instilling new ideas.

The Oriental Hotel: A Two-Tier Approach to Training

The Oriental Hotel has consistently been regarded as a leading world class in terms of service. Like other established hotels in the country, the hotel operates a training school for hotel employees, primarily operations staff with the following minimum qualifications:

- Age between 17 and 25
- High School Diploma
- 'Clearly understands and accepts the concept of apprenticeship school'
- Service orientation
- 'Good personality'
- English proficiency

The school is called OHAP and stands for the Oriental Hotel Apprenticeship Programme. When candidates meet OHAP's minimum qualifications, they can proceed to any of the following courses offered: restaurant operations; bartending; assorted cookery courses; butler and housekeeping operations; and the front office officer course.

The school was established in response 'to the demand for hotel personnel in the rank-and-file and lower middle management categories'. In terms of orientation, the school emphasizes practical training under the umbrella of the Oriental standard. While theory is not completely ignored, it is kept to a minimum or rudimentary level. The thrust of the programme is on practical, hands-on training.

English and English conversation courses are required as fundamental subjects in the programmes. Additional subjects are geared towards the specific qualifications of each individual programme. OHAP participation does not guarantee employment at the Oriental Hotel. But it does provide a marketable label for a career in the industry in Thailand (and even abroad).

While the focus of OHAP training is geared towards fulfilling the categories described above, namely in the areas of operational staff and lower middle management, additional training is offered to supervisory and managerial staff members of the hotel as well as to the typically higher-qualified front office staff members. Front office staff at the hotel are provided with language training in English and learn about teamwork and team-building skills with both internal and external trainers. All staff become familiar with Oriental's 'legendary' 'Service and Training Operation Manual' which was prepared by training staff and department heads. This manual familiarizes staff with the hotel's standards for quality and service.

Employees, primarily department heads and managers, also take an assortment of classes ranging from management and leadership skills to communications and recently a course on 'creative/innovative thinking'. According to one training manager at the hotel, the training concentrates on skill development, knowledge, personality and Thai culture. Specifically, in Thai culture, for example, emphasis is placed with providing service in a uniquely Thai manner.

Expatriate managers at the hotel are not excluded from courses. While they have limited contact with hotel guests, they are provided with training in the area of cross-cultural management.

Language proficiency, primarily in English, and computer-based training is also provided to employees of the hotel. On-the-job training is directed at operational staff in the areas of restaurant operations, housekeeping, reservations desk and engineering, according to the training manager. Staff also receive coaching from department trainers. Some staff choose to participate in OHIP, the Oriental Hotel Internship Programme, a two-year training programme for the development of supervisors at the hotel.

The hotel's human resources department consists of the personnel and training departments. Trainers conduct both internal and in-house training and arrange external training with consultants for all levels of staff. The focus of their training is primarily Thai staff, as mentioned above. The training staff meets on a weekly basis to discuss training methods. They agree upon further actions, how to organize their work and to assess the suitability of instructors (their competency, preparatory skills, organizational abilities, etc.). Following upon a number of training experiences in the past, the suitability of instructors is of primary importance to the training department. Occasionally, a problem may lie with students. Students sometimes do not concentrate properly, for example, and classes have to be reorganized or moulded to suit their abilities and ways of thinking. Some courses have been very successful – the training manager at the hotel cited a computer-training programme which was particularly successful in terms of stimulating learning. Another class on speech power and development also elicited favourable responses from students and managers.

The training manager at the hotel feels that a mixture of training methods is necessary to generate desired results. The lecture method is not the only route for training. The key to effectiveness during the entire process of facilitating learning is communication, according to this training manager.

The Dusit Thani College: A Formal Approach to Hospitality Management

The Dusit Thani College is a private, undergraduate college dedicated to the education of hospitality industry personnel. The college is owned by the Dusit Group of hotels, a leading Thai hotel company. According to the Rector of the College, Khun Veera Paspattanapanich, the objective of starting the school was to 'produce quality staff' for the industry. Students who choose to enrol in the BBA (Bachelor of Business Administration) programme can choose from four majors: Hotel management, Kitchen and Restaurant management, Tourism management and Management majors. All students enrolled in the programme are Thai.

Classroom learning by dedicated full-time teachers is supplemented with field training (a minimum of 1,000 hours) at hotels, travel agencies, airlines and tour operators. Occasionally, lecturers from the field are invited to teach students at the College. Khun Veera believes that classroom learning is an effective way for promoting learning. She believes that on-the-job training is effective for practical skills, but theory, as taught in the classroom, is needed for effective learning. Research, making presentations, sharing ideas and exchanging knowledge are important ways of learning which occur in the classroom.

Frequent evaluation of their courses, particularly when courses are conducted for other diverse organizations, including recently a health care provider, for example, has indicated that their training, especially in the customer service area, is effective. Repeat business furthermore validates its effectiveness in Khun Veera's view. The Tourism Authority of Thailand (TAT) has, in addition, subsidized training programmes for the College. This has enabled other organizations to benefit from the expertiz of the school. Given Thailand's location in the Mekong area, organizations from neighbouring countries are said to have also benefited.

The increasing competition in training in the hospitality industry in Thailand is viewed by the College as a good development. Although it is difficult to find good teachers – indeed, occasionally teachers are imported temporarily from other countries – the competition generated by the various suppliers of these training courses has meant that participating students, and the organizations which support them (especially the international hotel chains), are able to regularly upgrade their skills, an important consideration in the hospitality industry. Furthermore, in the view of the College, competition prevents them from 'becoming too lazy'. The College also sees itself as increasingly becoming a place where 'training of trainers' will transpire, reflecting a growing need of the marketplace.

Tourism Authority of Thailand: Promoting Thai Hospitality and Service

Training for the hospitality industry is also conducted by the government tourism agency in Thailand, or TAT, Tourism Authority of Thailand. Vocational training is provided primarily to semi-skilled staff, persons considered by the agency as being 'stakeholders in the tourist industry'. This includes hotel, restaurant staff, local guides, boat drivers, people selling merchandise, even taxi drivers. The thrust of their training, conducted for Thais, are small and medium sized (up to 200 rooms) hotel establishments, restaurants and shops. TAT conducts trainings in the Thai language (while other travel organizations conduct similar training in English in Thailand for reasonable fees). As with other hospitality organizations, TAT will emphasize skills development and training on 'train the trainers' programmes starting in 2001 to satisfy the growing need in the marketplace for skills in this area. There is a growing need for qualified teaching staff in the country and TAT is making an effort to develop staff in areas most impacting the tourism sector.

The effectiveness of their training has been evaluated not just by owners or managers of the aforementioned establishments, but also by actual 'customers', tourists and guests patronizing these organizations. In general, their training is viewed as effective though continual improvement is viewed as a necessity for meeting the requirements of the marketplace. On a positive note, organizations have been satisfied with the way the training has been conducted – largely onsite at the establishments concerned. Although the Technical and Training division of TAT maintains a library and documents department (with multimedia and video-based training) for use with clients, their onsite presence is valued by participants. In addition, their teachers are highly qualified, many holding postgraduate degrees. TAT also has a Technical Cooperation Division which features a 'tourist guide training section'. In the future, however, training in this area will be outsourced to universities (Thai history, psychology, food and handicrafts), as resources will be limited in this particular area.

Financial and Professional Services Companies

DBS Thai Danu Bank: Keeping Up with International Developments

The Chairman of DBS Thai Danu Bank, Pakorn Thavisin, commenting upon the state of affairs in corporate Thailand, where family connections feature prominently in the careers of many managers, believes that in the near future, Thai companies will have to accept change in terms of 'world class standards of practices'. There will be a need for:

- Junior and middle/senior management to understand world-class standards of practice;
- Understanding the nature of competition; Thai banking is essentially a protected industry which must adapt to change;
- Understanding neighbours (countries like Singapore, Malaysia, Vietnam) and other competitors.

There are several implications of this on training. First of all, there needs to be an emphasis on changing legal and institutional issues pertaining to banking/financial services, he states. In particular, banks need to adapt to international or IMF standards. Secondly, banks will have to keep up with new developments, like electronic banking, for example.

The financial crisis of 1997–8 has meant that the human resources, and especially the training group within the company has become leaner. Specialized training is outsourced and competition for training is keen among staff. Currently, many banks in Thailand, which had operated their own training centres, now contract out training. Thai Danu, for example, previously offered a three-month mini-MBA course to branch managers which exposed them to courses like business ethics, operations and financial analysis. Due to external factors, the training was phased out. Some training is now conducted in cooperation with other banks in the country, but some is still being conducted internally, notably seminars on new systems (IT-related) and operational training in a number of areas. Training is still required in important areas to the bank – risk management, foreign exchange, among others.

Bank staff members are also encouraged to take an external basic banking training course which, upon successful completion of the exam, is fully reimbursed by the bank. Basic management training does not exist, perhaps because the bank has not been able to 'locate a professional company [which conducts this] yet', Khun Pakorn states. The bank does, however, also utilize other associations, organizations and institutes that offer training in areas like financial analysis.

Training methods vary, some being in-class training, some on-the-job training. Khun Pakorn is of the view that independent learning does not work too well in Thailand, as Thais like being organized into groups and classes. Thais like the interdependent nature of group work, which works as an effective stimulus for learning.

The recent merger of his bank Thai Danu with the Singaporean DBS Bank had several implications on training. One was the need for training in the area of communication and English language skills. Secondly, the marketing area was viewed as a primary target for training and development. In particular, the marketing of new products and services (credit cards, electronic banking, etc.) requires training of staff unfamiliar with presenting these diverse and often new offerings to the end customer.

On the whole, Khun Pakorn is satisfied with how bank staff have successfully absorbed new learning and skills from the bank's various training opportunities though there are times when cooperation and coordination have not been optimal. Furthermore, there are certain initiative issues concerning Thai employees, in his view. Thai culture is still very much 'top-down' – employees still prefer to be told to do things rather than to pursue matters themselves.

International Management Consulting Firm: Emphasizing a Global Standard

Given its strategic location as a headquarters for many large and medium sized Thai companies, Bangkok is host to a number of leading international firms offering general and specialized management consulting services. One such firm, which wishes to remain anonymous, is an organization with strong Asian presence, including a number of offices in Southeast Asia. A partner of this firm, an expatriate with two years of experience in Thailand, discussed his company's training and development needs and approach, focusing on its Thai employees. The main training and development needs can be distinguished by type of staff, professional (consulting) vs. support personnel (e.g., administrators, secretarial staff, graphic design experts, researchers and other specialists), and by the type of training required – e.g., managerial (which includes leadership, management and communication training) vs. specific functional training.

Regarding general managerial training, professional staff, or the consultants in the company, have development needs in the areas of leadership, initiative and assertiveness, as well as communication and presentation skills. They also need to learn to behave in a less hierarchical manner with each other and with expatriates. For support personnel, development is also required in the leadership/initiative and assertiveness areas.

In terms of functional training, there are several development needs. For professional staff, general problem solving and consulting skills need to be developed. This includes various functional skills covering strategic, financial, organizational and operations issues. Training in the functional areas for support personnel varies by job, e.g., research and information services, IT support, etc.

The consultancy partner suggested the area which required most development, in his view, considering his prior overseas experiences, was the issue of assertiveness and open communications, across all levels of employees. He continued and pinpointed another key training need that has been emerging more recently in areas dealing with the 'new' economy – areas such as electronic commerce and the establishment of dynamic networks of business partnerships. 'These new economy changes will have to be more and more reflected in training', he said. This is clearly a priority for the firm in order to meet the demands of its increasing client base in Thailand.

The firm utilizes several types of trainings in parallel – internal, external and on-the-job coaching – to achieve its objectives.

- *Internal training*: the company uses experienced consultants and functional experts from the Asian region as well as from its overseas offices to conduct different types of training:

- General problem solving and consulting skills for professional staff: these courses are very 'interactive', 'real-life case based' and are conducted by senior consultants and partners of the firm.
- Communication, interaction and social skills, including project team leadership: again, very interactive training based on detailed feedback for the candidates, conducted with internal faculty and supplemented by external trainers such as psychologists.
- In addition, there are various functional courses, which are conducted to address areas like strategy, financial valuation, organization design, e-business building, market research, etc., covering aspects relevant to the firm's client service. These are also conducted by highly experienced practitioners from within the firm who ensure the practical nature of the training and the immediate applicability by the trained consultants in their client work.
- Furthermore, there are 'special needs' courses that are flexibly established to address any emerging areas for skill development, e.g., interviewer training conducted for those who are involved in recruiting new staff.
- *External training*: primarily English-language training, the language of operation for the firm. English is a requirement for employment in the company and all levels of staff are given additional training in this area if necessary. Typically this is more an issue for the support personnel than for the professional consulting staff, who have generally enjoyed a part of their education (typically MBA degrees) overseas.
- *On-the-job training*: the key development model, however, is the 'apprenticeship' or coaching on consulting assignments. Project teams are formed in the firm to ensure a good mix of experience and competency on the job. More senior members of the team bring their expertize and train and coach junior members in the course of their joint consulting work. Regular feedback and debriefing sessions form an important part of this process. There also exists a vast storehouse of information in the company's intranet with innumerable online know-how documents prepared by consultants and specialists around the world for use by consultants when required. Specialists and experts are also readily available by phone and through knowledge-building and enhancing efforts. These efforts are enhanced with regular conferences having global expert participants from the company in attendance.

A large part of the success of the firm's training efforts appears to be the fact that senior members of the professional consulting staff are dedicated as faculty to the firm's training, and that courses are very interactive and case-based rather than being offered and presented by way of standard lecture format. The quality of the firm's training, on the part of the trainees as well as the senior staff, has been rated as good and highly effective.

An important side-effect of the training is that a more clearly defined identity of the company emerges in the minds of the participants through the networking and social interaction aspects of these events. This 'identity building' process, as an indirect outcome of the training, is considered very important.

While the staff serves local clients in Thailand, they are dispersing global know-how and competency. Hence, they are representing the one 'global firm'. In a way, there are trainers being trained here, as the trained consultants use their acquired know-how to support their clients.

CONCLUSIONS

The demand for training/development is strong in Thailand. Both the public and private sectors, with supporting 'suppliers', have offered training in several key areas addressing the particular needs of the Thai environment. The Thai government has identified training and human resources development as priorities for the future. Training by the public sector has focused primarily on the semi-skilled and low-skilled areas of the labour force, including those unemployed or displaced from the labour force. Private companies offering general training have targeted more educated and skilled staff. Their offering focuses largely on managerial (leadership and communication) and cross-cultural training with specific expertize also in the information technology areas.

Given Thailand's strong tourism orientation, the chapter has as one focus, training in the hospitality sector. The selected cases from this sector reveal that the need for specialized training, focusing especially on practical skills, resulted in: (1) the growth of company hospitality schools for the training of semi-skilled as well as skilled staff; (2) development of apprenticeship/internship programmes; and (3) external training in areas requiring further development such as language, communication and marketing/sales training.

The investigation's financial and professional service cases had foreign 'parents' but retained a largely local staff. Though these companies employ skilled and educated staff, their main training and development needs were found to be in the area(s) which were most impacted by global trends in their (sector) areas, notably, online banking and electronic commerce. Furthermore, on the social skills side, assertiveness training and learning to be less hierarchical are also seen as development needs.

Training and development is viewed as effective when based on more interactive training approaches, possibly involving on-the-job training. In all cases, it was believed that using the standard lecture method alone is ineffective in terms of facilitating learning relating to practical skills. Continual training, especially in keeping with trends in the sectors concerned, was deemed necessary and valuable for the development of staff and the maintenance of international standards. Culturally rooted behaviours were identified by some managers, especially in cross-border organizations, as playing a role in developing the topics and strategies for training and the possible outcomes.

References

Dutton, Gail (1998) 'Case Study: A Language for All Seasons', *Management Review*, 87(11), p. 46.
Gross-Turner, Steven (1999) 'The Role of the Multi-Unit Manager in Branded Hospitality Chains', *Human Resource Management Journal*, 9(4), pp. 39–57.
Holmes, Henry and Tangtongtavy, Suchada (1997) *Working with the Thais* (Bangkok: White Lotus).
Kapner, Suzanne (1996) 'Educators focus on training, trends at the 50th anniversary of CHRIE', *Nation's Restaurant News*, 23 September, pp. 88–9.
Strauss, Karyn (1999) 'Industry execs, educators discuss merits of training at CHRIE confab', *Nation's Restaurant News*, 13 September, pp. 48–9.
Sullivan, Jim (1998) 'Why training doesn't work . . . and what operators better do about it', *Nation's Restaurant News*, 20 July, pp. 54–5.
Surati, Ramesh (1999) 'Education Becomes Cornerstone in AAHOA's Strategy', *Hotel and Motel Management*, 13 December, p. 18.
Sussangkarn, Chalongphob and Chalamwong, Yongyuth (1994) *Development Strategies and Their Impacts on Labour Market and Migration: Thai Case Study* (Bangkok: Thailand Development Research Institute).
Theibert, Philip R. (1996) 'Train and Degree Them – Anywhere', *Personnel Journal*, 75(2), p. 28.
Worcester, Barbara A. (1999) 'The People Problem', *Hotel and Motel Management*, 1 March, pp. 38–9.
Wright, M. and Storey, J. (1997) 'Recruitment and Selection', in *Human Resource Management – A Contemporary Perspective*, ed. I Beardwell and L. Holden (London).

9 The Future of China's Human Resource Management in its Asia-Pacific Context: A Critical Perspective

Malcolm Warner

INTRODUCTION

Discussing the future of Chinese HR in its Asia-Pacific regional dimension is a challenging task. To start with we look at the broader Chinese IR (Industrial Relations)/HRM system in its pre-reform and post-reform stages. We next attempt to place it in its regional context. We then attempt to see if it is likely to 'converge' or 'diverge' from HR patterns both internationally and within the region. This is a challenging task but one that will reveal possibly important insights into its present and potential strengths and weaknesses.

After the 'Liberation' in 1949 when the Chinese Communist Party took power, state-owned enterprises (SOEs) dominated Chinese industrial production and its HR (Warner, 1995) over a period ranging from the early 1950s to the late 1980s. Such work-units (*danwei*), as they were called, embodied the so-called 'iron rice-bowl' (*tie fan wan*) which ensured 'jobs for life' and 'cradle to grave' welfare for many urban industrial SOE workers. Walder (1986) has described this relationship as 'institutional dependency', to which we will return later. In the last two decades, a wider range of ownership has been introduced, such as wholly Foreign-Funded Enterprises (FFEs) most notably Joint-Venture firms (JVs) whereby state enterprises have linked up with foreign business partners. A vast new non-state sector of both quasi-private Town and Village Enterprises (TVEs) has sprung up, as well as fully privately-owned firms. Once SOEs dominated employment in industry in the PRC; now they do not. The Chinese economic horizon has widened considerably and the structure of its industry has diversified immeasurably since the early days of the Open Door reforms in the late 1970s. As we move into the twenty-first century, China has emerged from not only a final stages of a 'command-economy' but also the early phases of a 'transitional' one. We may call it a 'mature transitional economy'.

An important feature of the change-process in the Chinese economy leading to the latest phases of transition has been the enterprise and labour reforms that have largely occurred in the 1980s and 1990s, aimed at phasing-out the 'iron rice bowl'; the latter was generally believed by economists to be associated with poor people-management and to bolster factor-immobility and inefficiency (Warner, 1995). Managers were thus allowed more autonomy, particularly to hire and fire; decision-making was to become more decentralized in not only personnel but also marketing and purchasing domains. Already, many JVs quickly incorporated such practices in their own management systems. Most foreign-funded, as well as Town and Village and privately-owned enterprises had much more autonomy in their people-management compared with their state-owned equivalents. Today, even SOEs are evolving in this direction but it will take some time given their institutional and organizational inertia, before they are as 'flexible' as the others mentioned above. The future decades are likely to see an acceleration of this trend.

Many personnel reforms involving the introduction of labour contracts, performance-related rewards systems and contributory social insurance were introduced (see Ng and Warner, 1998). Separate specific governmental regulations governed the JVs and FFEs initially set up but later wider reforms have been implemented that have been applicable to both state and non-state enterprises. The new 1994 labour legislation, amongst other reforms, for example, was intended to cover Chinese firms across the board. A new labour-management relations system has been put in place. The new labour legislation placed fixed-term labour contracts, collective contracts and agreements, redundancies, dispute arbitration, amongst other issues, on a formal codified legal basis. There may now be over 300,000 such collective contracts signed, according to ACFTU (All-China Federation of Trade Unions) sources. Some scholars have even speculated on such reported widespread diffusion of this practice whether China is now evolving a system of 'collective bargaining', based on collective contracts (see Warner and Ng, 1999). In so far as China has an HR system in a sense comparable with Western or other Asian ones, it was now embedded in a more market-driven framework. This may also have led to an evolution of people-management in the PRC from personnel administration (*renshi guanli*) as typical of most SOEs, to human resource management (*renshi ziyuan guanli*) as seen in the leading-edge JVs (see Warner, 1995; Ng and Warner, 1998). But one must be cautious here in seeing this form of HRM as typical of Chinese practice. Many academic papers written on this subject tend towards wishful thinking and exaggerate the degree to which HRM is

Table 9.1   The evolution of the Chinese IR/HRM systems

Pre-reform model	Post-reform model
State ownership	Diffused ownership
Resource-constrained	Market-driven
Technical criteria	Allocative efficiency
Economic cadres	Professional managers
Iron rice bowl	Labour market
Jobs for life	Employment contracts
Work assignment	Job choice
Personnel administration	Human resource management
Egalitarian pay and perks	Performance-related rewards
Enterprise-based training	Outside-courses
Company flats	Rented housing-market
In-house social services	External social provision
Free medical care	Contributory medical insurance
Central trade union role	Weaker union influence
Top-down union structure	Firm-based union structure
High institutional dependency	Low institutional dependency

implanted, often using it as a synonym for PA (Personnel Administration), or IR more broadly.

The contrast between the pre-reform and reformed systems of people-management, whether IR or HRM, is set out in Table 9.1. We can see the transition from the 'iron rice-bowl' and associated characteristics to the new market-based one.

COMPARING THE CHINESE HR SYSTEM WITH ITS ASIAN COUNTERPARTS

We next attempt to place the description of the Chinese system outlined above in its Asia-Pacific dimension.Some writers indeed refer to the 'Asian model' in the HR field (see Ng and Warner, 1998); it is seen as basically 'non-adversarial' in nature (although South Korea may be an exception). The Asia-Pacific countries are generally seen as low in their unionization (although this level varies) or that their unions are government-sponsored and often rather 'tame'. Strikes are perceived to be less common than in the West or constrained by either by culture, ideology or law. According to scholars such as Dore (1973) and Thurley (1988), the Asian model is said to reduce the 'we–they' relationship and may help negate conflicts between capital and labour. Other writers (Deery and Mitchell, 1993, p. 16) are uncertain and argue that some cultural influences may be present in one sector but not in others in the same country. Although Chinese HR may be said to have once been 'exceptional', it is also less so in that it is broadly 'Asian' in the sense of being 'non-adversarial' (see Ng and Warner, 1998). Not all Asian HR systems are neatly harmonious and conflict-management is handled in a variety of ways in the respective national contexts, however (see Leung and Tjosvold, 1998).

As Rowley (1997, p. 1) puts it: 'Asia provides a paragon of practices around which companies searching for "success" and the "one best way" can converge.' The Asian way was identifiable and transplantable. There are common features in many Asian-Pacific Rim economies in these respects and in others, although the specific institutional forms may have varied from one country to another (see Hamilton, 1995). But the Asian model 'was stretched thin' (Godement, 1999, p. 15). It was probably naïve, in retrospect, to have imagined a homogeneous bloc of countries, institutions and practices. The Asia-Pacific people-management or HRM model has, further, been put forward as an 'alternative' to the Western standard industrial relations and HRM templates which have emerged in the post-war years, although we would not argue here that across Asia or even in the West these systems and sub-systems have much more than a family resemblance. Yet the Chinese HR system has relatively more of the Asian model than its Western counter-parts.

Problems

An attempt to evaluate where Asia-Pacific HR systems, including that of the PRC, are going has been made by the present writer and a colleague (see Ng and Warner, 1999) based on 'the late-development effect'. It breaks down the whole into two sectors, namely the advanced economies and sectors on the one hand and the less developed countries on the other. Yet there remain problems with compressing so much into a basic dichotomy. The region is so widely defined and so varied. Geographical factors feature so strongly, with the PRC pre-eminent so clearly in terms of land-mass and population. The economies of the region have on the other hand been economically and industrially dominated by another nation, namely Japan. The 'little Dragon' economies in turn also stand apart from many others in terms of the level of economic development they have achieved. Whether the Asian so-called 'miracle' will be able to be sustained into the twenty-first century is of course moot. Even if Asian economies grow at respectable rates of growth, they may not pick up the pace of the 1990s. China has had a floundering growth-rate for the last ten years and it was down to only just over 7 per cent per annum for 1999, if official statistics are to be believed. But even this level is well above the average for, say EU economies.

Additionally, many cultural traditions criss-cross the Asia-Pacific Rim; Confucianism has been one that has been much discussed in recent years (see Redding, 1990) as associated with economic dynamism (although in the past, the opposite had been argued by other scholars particularly in the immediate post-war period). Certainly, there are common values in Asian societies, regardless of their political complexion. The importance of respect for seniority, the search for harmony, the role of relationship and connections (*guanxi*) are no doubt important in the Chinese context. Whether, on the other hand, the Chinese HR system is critically determined by this cultural legacy is moot.

Political factors also form patterns; there were for instance the British, Dutch and Japanese colonial legacies. More recently, Marxist-Leninism in both Soviet and modified versions was a formative force in many parts of Asia, most notably in the PRC (as well as in North Korea and North Vietnam). Since the onset of the economic reforms in China, this is less the case, as the market-driven reform policies of Deng Xiaoping took root. The future of Chinese HR may be less 'politicized' in future for this reason, although the Chinese trade unions, the All-China Federation of Trade Unions (ACFTU) will still remain tied to the Party. It role may have of necessity to be less centralized in a market-driven economy with a burgeoning non-state sector, as we shall see in more detail later in this chapter.

AN ANALYTICAL FRAMEWORK

We now attempt to devise an analytical framework to see how far Asian people-management systems may becoming more or less like each other. One possible way of analysing this problem of convergence/divergence in general terms is to construct a fourfold analytical framework of logical possibilities (adapted and developed from an earlier version: see Warner, 2000). The four categories below sum up what is possible as outcomes (see Table 9.2). We will apply this framework both broadly and to the PRC specifically.

The Possibilities

1. 'Hard convergence'
2. 'Soft convergence'
3. 'Soft divergence'
4. 'Hard divergence'

Table 9.2   Fourfold analytical framework

	Convergence	Divergence
Hard	1*	4****
Soft	2**	3***

Key:
* Relatively most improbable
** Most probable
*** Equally probable
**** Absolutely most improbable

The Probabilities

(1) Taking what we imagine to be the most relatively improbable scenario first: 'hard convergence' seems an unlikely prospect for the Asia-Pacific HR systems and the Chinese one in particular, unless one fully accepts the classic 'convergence' argument as articulated by Kerr *et al.* (1973) and successors. If spreading industrialization and technological change makes for comparable superstructures, it would follow that we would see common IR/HRM systems all over. Globalization, in the latest modified version of the convergence hypothesis, may be seen to lead to international economic competition presenting common problems and comparable organizational solutions for enterprises wherever they were located. Deregulation and privatization would also follow in their train. We do not find this scenario likely, given our research in the field over many years. To argue however that all Asian IR/ HRM systems, including the Chinese one, have or are likely to converge seems to be too bold an assertion to justify, given the empirical evidence available. On the surface, there may have been apparently common economic, social and political problems across the region as devaluations led to bankruptcies and downsizing, but it is vital to underline that the specifics have varied greatly from economy to economy (see Godement, 1999). In this context, we must assert once again that the 'devil', as always, is in the details. It is therefore unlikely that the Chinese case, in the context discussed here, will be a case of 'hard convergence'.

(2) On the other hand, we may be able to more convincingly argue that 'soft convergence' may be a somewhat more plausible and more likely outcome both for the region as a whole and for China in particular. Here, we would only need to posit some 'family resemblance' (see Warner and Ng, 1999, for a discussion on the prospects of collective agreements in the PRC,

for example). It may of course be possible to see common features in, say, the sectors dominated by the MNCs or where there are joint ventures in the PRC or indeed elsewhere. It could be argued that soft (alternatively, one may call it relative) convergence might be achieved by the implementation of International Labour Organization (ILO) standards, for instance. By this, the local practices may converge with the external templates. Some kind of 'soft convergence' might occur where a regulatory framework of labour-markets was laid down by law. Even if the State was 'in retreat', at least in terms of ownership, stronger labour legislation, in principle, might be enforced. Another way may be where the local 'deviant' form may relatively converge with the local form that is more aligned with the external one that conforms more with international, mainly Western-style, HR practice, say where Chinese SOEs begin to copy joint ventures or foreign wholly-owned firms. This prospect seems more likely for the Chinese HR system but with important caveats, as we shall now see below.

(3) 'Soft divergence' may be equally persuasive as an option, with diversity more or less weighing in the balance for the following reason. The Chinese system, and indeed many other Asian systems, always saw themselves as distinct, the former probably more than the others. The phrase 'with Chinese characteristics' is often used. We would here posit that national/local differences remain relatively more or less stable (see Hofstede, 1980) but not indefinitely so. We would posit here that differences would remain relatively strong due to strong institutional and organizational inertia.

Looking at a specific HR/IR example: common, international bench- marks in terms of labour protection for instance might be implemented in the broad but with differences of detailed implementation. Here, the 'deviant', relatively divergent forms may prevail in one form or another. The local firms may adapt to some degree but still retain their 'core'. It is clear from existing evidence that the Chinese IR system remains one with 'Chinese characteristics'.

(4) Looking now at the other extreme case: 'hard divergence' may also be the least plausible outcome and the absolutely most improbable scenario, as it would be hard to argue that countries are tending towards becoming more and more different, even taking into account the so-called Chinese (or indeed Japanese) 'exceptionalism'. Few observers would argue that 'exceptionalism' is on the increase in Asia or elsewhere. Structural reform may be advocated by international agencies and banks across the board. Some, however, may be moving in one direction, whereas others may be gravitating in another. Some countries may become more or less responsive to International Monetary Fund or World Bank programmes, for instance. Others may try to go their own ways. But there are common paths which are suggested by those pushing for 'globalization'. While there are still distinctive policies, there is very little

data to suggest that the PRC is becoming absolutely 'divergent' in its economic characteristics and in particular its people-management systems. In no convincing way is China becoming increasingly and absolutely dissimilar from its Asian counterparts in its economic and its people-management characteristics.

DISCUSSION

Not only have we to take into account the commonly experienced 'late development effect' in the Asia-Pacific region but also the recent economic and organizational turbulence in looking at how the Chinese HR system has evolved. The former endowed several advantages on the countries involved (they could, for instance, learn from the mistakes of the West and later Japan *vis-à-vis* the industrialization process), but the latter presents more difficulties as the so-called Asian crisis was not only unexpected but offered no templates as to how to cope with the implications of the down turn. Knee-jerk reactions in the case of many countries in terms of reacting by mass 'lay-offs' in enterprises experiencing financial and trading difficulties might be one reaction but its implications in the long term are unclear. China has also responded by taking World Bank criticisms of its SOEs seriously, for example; it has similarly cut jobs and welfare.

Not only were large numbers of workers reduced to 'bread-line' conditions in many Asia-Pacific countries during the recent 'Asian crisis' but also many members of the middle class and 'new rich' were pauperized. Where there were 'jobs for life' in some sectors – often State jobs but in some countries private, say in Japan, South Korea, Taiwan and so on – these were to now be under a cloud. Deflation and job insecurity now go hand in hand not only in those countries but also in the PRC. Workers, including formerly protected Chinese ones, now fear for their jobs and have stopped spending. Prices have moved downwards and inventories of unsold goods have mounted. Deregulation, too, has meant more income has to be spent on what were formerly 'free' or highly subsidized goods and services. China has experienced a number of the above consequences of downturn and downsizing. If anything, this is likely to increase as key Chinese SOEs downsize further and many Sino-foreign JVs trim their workforces to become more competitive.

The evidence of 'hard convergence' is nonetheless clearly confounded by the continuing visibility of institutional, legal and structural diversity in the region. There was hardly any evidence to support the classic convergence hypothesis, looking at the accumulating evidence from a wide range of sources. It is hard to argue that Asian HRM is fast converging to a common model and this in line with Western practice. Speaking more broadly, reform of the corporate dinosaurs took different forms in different national contexts, ranging from 'corporatization' of China's SOEs, to revitalization of Japan's keiretsu, to restructuring of its South Korean chaebols and so on. Even the MNCs in joint ventures reacted differently across the region, although business restructuring as a reactive strategy has been a common theme across the Asia-Pacific region. The Chinese HR responses have been highly specific.

Yet there were common IR/HR themes to be found, as we set out below; these affected Chinese reforms in people-management as much as changes elsewhere. Some were linked to long-term changes but others were short-term reactions to recent economic pressures for competitive advantage. Matched against evidence in other comparisons, we can see how 'soft convergence' of IR/HR practices in the Asian context has occurred. Other data may even indicate a degree of 'soft divergence', where differentiation is maintained as between what happens in one national context as compared with another (even within the same corporation).

'Hard divergence' does not seem to be the case either. One cannot say that all examples of Asian IR/HRM are becoming more and more varied. Whilst there may be a trend in a country-wide system towards adaptation with 'national characteristics', it may possibly indicate 'soft' rather than 'hard' divergence. Turning the Kerr *et al.* (1973) 'convergence thesis' on its head finds very few supporters. The 'societal effect' argument (Maurice *et al.*, 1980) in its turn does not require the effect to become stronger, merely to maintain differentiation. We would argue that 'soft divergence' would cover this.

Economic, legal, political and social institutional backgrounds do in this regard remain influential in many countries. The institutional framework broadly speaking and the labour law background in particular remain distinctive in most Asia-Pacific countries (see Deery and Mitchell, 1993). Three models prevail: first, the British model, in Hong Kong, Malaysia and Singapore; second, the American system still influences Japan, the Philippines and South Korea; Taiwan and Thailand being less easy to fit in as they have non-Western colonial backgrounds but may have some resemblance to US practices (ibid, pp. 9–10). A persuasive illustration comes from the Greater China context. Although the PRC and Hong Kong Special Administrative Region (SAR) share many common cultural features, they have very different labour law systems, for instance. Each is in the process of evolution but they remain distinct. They may be edging to some forms of institutional convergence very slowly in the long term but the creation of the 'one country, two systems' SAR formula recognized the special nature of the Hong Kong institutional and organizational models.

We can posit here that the convergence/divergence process works rather slowly at the macro-, namely institutional, level than at the micro-, namely organizational, one. Thus, we may have a refinement of our four categories. Specifically, soft convergence way occur less at the former level than the latter, for example. Nationwide institutions do normally change more slowly than sub-sets of firms at organizational level. If there is a dualistic industrial structure and concomitant industrial and labour relations regime, we may have change where the sub-sets of firms are more flexible than elsewhere. Where there are enterprise-based IR/HRM sub-systems, how they change will be based less on what has been set out at national level than *vis-à-vis* the firm or sector involved.

Shared cultural factors in the Asia-Pacific region may indicate another dimension of convergence/divergence, namely in terms of values held. Again, in this context, these may result in *behavioural* in addition to *cultural* convergence/divergence. These may not necessarily be the same thing as a common set of cultural influences and may not result in similar behavioural outcomes. As we have suggested above, there is a strong shared cultural inheritance between most Asia-Pacific nations in terms of the Confucian influence (see Redding, 1990). If not a determinant in all cases, it is often a constraint. This shared influence may only be a common theme if looked at in the broad; examining it in its national contexts may reveal very distinct forms of Confucianism. Its manifestation in, say, officially atheistic China may be very different from its role in, say, publicly Shintoist Japan. Again, Deery and Mitchell (1993, p. 15) point out that paternalism in the work environment may be 'institutionalized' in some national systems, as they suggest is the case in Japan, but may be 'personalized', in their phrase, in settings like the Malaysian.

There may also be common features in Asian IR/HRM systems, such as the prominent role of the state across nations across the region but even here there have been different rates of change across the region. China has still its ubiquitous state-sponsored trade unions, namely those belonging to the All China Federation of Trade Unions (ACFTU), but as the state sector has attenuated, its often almost 100 per cent unionization level in most SOEs has become less characteristic, with sometimes no unions apparent in smaller joint ventures or rural firms. The average for China we estimated as 65 per cent union density in urban industrial sectors; much lower elsewhere and about 15 per cent if the whole workforce both urban and rural is taken into account. The trade unions in China are however less and less dominant, as their strengths were in the state-owned and related sectors. Now the non-state sectors are becoming the main employers of urban and rural industrial labour. There is a new Labour Law in the PRC since 1994 (see Warner, 1996) but the slowdown in economic growth and reform of the state-owned enterprises has led to a weakening of the workers' job security and labour-market strength. The 'iron rice-bowl' system is now in terminal decline.

Will the Chinese HR system in its new guise now follow the Japanese model? The latter, one of the most original in the region, is now in the throes of transformation. The former 'three pillars' model (lifetime employment, seniority wages and company unions) has now come into question. Lifetime employment which was *de rigueur* for those working in large firms for many years is now being eroded, as in China; seniority is being weakened (as we have seen) as in the Chinese case; 'enterprise unionism' is still ongoing (the analogy is weaker in the PRC context) but is even tamer in the tougher economic climate of the late 1990s. The Japanese system faces many obstacles, not the least the high cost of redundancies: it is estimated that the average cost to a large firm is around US$ 200,000 per employee (*The Economist*, 26 June 1999), allegedly five times the 'going rate' in comparable European MNCs. The high costs of downsizing may slow down its pace but this is not certain.

In future years, the industrial landscape of Japan will change beyond recognition. Many big Japanese companies with household names have already embarked on major restructuring programmes. By the end of 1998, unemployment in Japan had risen to around 4.4 per cent and was still growing. Within six months, it had risen to 5 per cent and probably double for young workers; the percentage of temporary and part-time workers rose to over 7 per cent (*Japan Labour Bulletin*, August 1999). Whilst Japanese unions are not as yet in significant decline, like many of their counterparts elsewhere, they do face challenges such as having to recruit members in newer service-sectors to compensate for losses in older manufacturing ones (Whittaker, 1998). But this may not be able to keep pace with their loss of members, as in many other countries.

There have been many 'myths' which have grown up around the Japanese model; one important one relates to job-protection, which was only relatively partial in its scope. In the post-war years, large firms clearly did evolve a distinctive system. But 'jobs for life' were never comprehensively institutionalized in the Japanese HR system (as in the Chinese state-owned industries) even if job-security was strong (Sano, 1995); many writers believed *major* change in the corporate lifetime employment system, where it was found, was not yet likely (Selmer, 2000). By the end of the 1990s, the corporate 'chickens were coming home to roost'. As the economic upturn failed to appear, serious steps were finally being taken to downsize large Japanese corporations as we have noted, although not as trenchantly as in South Korea. Even so, unemployment rose significantly in both countries, as it also did in Hong Kong, to over 5 per cent.

China embarked on downsizing its inflated state-owned industry payrolls. The jobless rate is hard to estimate in China, as the official rate of 3.5 per cent in 1998 has been estimated by the trade unions there as twice as much in reality; it is likely to be even double this figure once over, say closer to 15 per cent in many urban areas, if unofficial estimates are correct. This is especially true of the north-east 'rust-belt' of China known as the *dongbei*. Professor Hu Angang, a Chinese Academy of Social Science (CASS) labour economist, has cited figures to show that between 1993 and 1997, laid-off workers rose from 3 million to 15 million (with two in three from the SOEs). He estimated around 10–15 million more coming on to the dole by the end of 1999. The highest reported joblessness cited is in Liaoning Province with over 22.4 per cent, followed by Hunan with 21.3 per cent; at city level, Chongqing at 18 per cent and Tianjin with 17 per cent, both with noteworthily high levels of unemployment (see Documentation section of *The China Quarterly*, no. 160, December 1999, p. 1106).

In the Asia-Pacific region as a whole, the jobless rate was highest in Indonesia (estimated at over 20 per cent in the cities and possibly double this in the countryside) but lowest in Taiwan, at just under 3 per cent. Since 1998, unemployment has come down in some economies where there has been a partial economic recovery from the Asia crisis but it has been rising in other locations such as the PRC. This latter malaise because of the absolute numbers involved does not augur well for the social and political scenario of the future in Asia-Pacific. Unemployment and indeed other economic statistics from official sources must be viewed with caution in any event.

How to characterize the main drift of change in broad-brush terms? Once, Japanese experience was offered as a guide as to where the more industrialized parts of Asia were moving. However, much water has flowed under the conceptual bridges.

What is now less likely than many previously conjectured is that the Japanese model will be *the* template for Asia-Pacific IR/HRM, or for China in particular. 'Japanization' so-called may be hard to implant outside Japan, other than superficially or at best in subsidiaries of Japanese MNCs. A recent study (Taylor, 1999) questions whether Japanese plants in the PRC actually used specific practices associated with Japanization and its accompanying production methods. One further important question here is however about the degree to which the HRM model itself is based on Japanese practices (and not everyone would agree with this thesis, looking in part at least to its US origins); if a great deal, then the spread of HRM might imply 'Japanization'; if not, then its diffusion may mean something else. Japanese HRM has common characteristics with international HR practices but has also featured specific features such as the so-called lifetime employment, seniority and so on, for many of the workers involved.

Others might see HRM as essentially of Western provenance and imported along with MNC investment into the Asia-Pacific region, as indeed elsewhere in emerging economies. This is another version of the 'convergence' thesis, 'soft' possibly in this domain. In this context, the expansion of Western MNCs in China may in some measure point to an eventual spread of their version of HRM there, if less slowly outside the JV or FFE sectors. But MNCs, and frequently the Asian ones, have often combined their own HR practices in their JVs in China with residual 'iron rice-bowl' ones. The outcome here has been 'hybrid' HRM of different kinds, all with some 'Chinese characteristics'.

The Chinese HR system will no doubt take on more and more HRM practices (if rather loosely defined) *grosso modo*; this will inevitably involve more flexible, individually based employment contracts, more performance-driven rewards systems and less enterprise-subsidized welfare services. Collective contracts too are now relatively widespread, at least in larger firms, both SOE and JV (see Warner and Ng, 1999). As the 1994 Labour Law provisions which incorporate such principles are more widely enforced and implemented, such notions may diffuse across the HR system more widely, but it will take time. It would be unwise to exaggerate the degree to which this has taken place already but there are more than 'straws in the wind'. As to the future, it will take some decades and much systemic change before a convincing level of collective bargaining is truly achieved.

CONCLUDING REMARKS

How then to place the future of Chinese reformed HR in its Asia Pacific regional context? We may now try to summarize the central argument of this chapter and the main points adduced to support it.

The most important feature of the Asia-Pacific region is its sheer variety. The economic systems in the region range from those emerging from communist planned economies to more openly liberalized market-driven ones. The political systems differ greatly, as do the social arrangements. There is probably more cultural variation than acknowledged by many writers in the field. There is thus a fair degree of residual diversity in the Asia-Pacific region. The degree of state involvement in the Chinese HR case for example still remains 'medium-to-high' and the system remains 'distinctive', if no longer that 'exceptional'.

The SOEs, it must be conceded, are no longer the dominant influence in Chinese HR. In the last two decades, as we have seen, many changes have taken place (see Table 9.1); for example, a wider range of ownership other than that of the state is now *de rigueur*, such as wholly Foreign-Funded Enterprises (FFEs) and most notably Joint-Venture firms (JVs) where state enterprises are in alliances with foreign businesses. A vast new non-state sector of quasi-private Town and Village Enterprises (TVEs) has also sprung up, as well as fully privately-owned firms. Once, SOEs set the pattern for HR in Chinese industry in the PRC; now they do not. The future labour-management model therefore will have to cope with the new non-state sectors; the larger MNC-influenced firms may help implement HRM but the spread of myriad smaller, particularly Overseas Chinese-funded JVs and additionally domestic TVEs may lead to what we may call an 'HR-vacuum' (for details, see Chan, 1995; 1998). In such small firms (and sometimes some above this size), there will continue to be either no trade union presence to speak of, or at best weak ACFTU unions. However, as far as medium- and large-sized firms are concerned, the future of Chinese HR lies in a move from the left-hand column to the right-hand one in Table 9.1.

On the other hand, if there is a common direction in which IR/HR systems in Asia-Pacific, including the Chinese, are moving, *it is most likely to be towards adaptation to business restructuring, deregulation and liberalization vis-à-vis the challenges of globalization.* Downsizing is now a common experience in Asia-Pacific economies. But all countries are not moving at the same pace and there is much variation. In this context, we have found a reasonable amount of evidence of 'soft convergence', particularly in the Chinese HR case but in many instances it has been constrained (see Rowley, 1997) by a fair measure of accompanying 'soft' divergence.

References

Chan, A. (1995) 'The Emerging Patterns of Industrial Relations in China and the Rise of the Two Labour Movements', *China Information: A Quarterly Journal*, 9(1), pp. 36–59.

Chan, A. (1998) 'Labour Relations in Foreign-Owned Ventures: Chinese Trade Unions and the Prospects for Collective Bargaining', in G. O'Leary (ed.), *Adjusting to Capitalism: Chinese Workers and the State* (Armonk, NY and London: M. E. Sharpe), pp. 122–49.

Child, J. (1994) *Management in China During the Era of Reform* (Cambridge: CUP).

Deery, S. J. and Mitchell, R. J. (eds) (1993) *Labour Law and Industrial Relations in Asia: Eight Country Studies* (Melbourne: Longman Cheshire).

Dore, R. (1973) *British Factory–Japanese Factory* (London: Allen & Unwin).

Frenkel, S. (ed.) (1993) *Organized Labour in the Asia-Pacific Region* (Ithaca, NY: Cornell University ILR Press).

Godement, F. (1999) *The Downsizing of Asia* (London: Routledge).

168   *China's HRM in its Asia-Pacific Context*

Hamilton, G. G. (1995) 'Overseas Chinese Capitalism', in W. Tu (ed.), *The Confucian Dimensions of Industrial East Asia* (Cambridge, Mass: Harvard University Press).

Hofstede, G. (1980) *Culture's Consequences: International Differences in Work-Related Values* (Beverley Hills and London: Sage).

Kerr, C., Dunlop, J. T., Harbison, F. H. and Myers, C. (1973) *Industrialism and Industrial Man* (Harmondsworth, Middlesex: Penguin Books).

Leung, K. and Tjosvold, D. (eds) (1998) *Conflict Management in the Asia Pacific: Assumptions and Approaches in Different Cultures* (Singapore and New York: John Wiley).

Mann, J. (1997) *Beijing Jeep: A Case Study of Western Business in China* (Boulder, Colorado and London: Westview).

Maurice, M., Sorge, A. and Warner, M. (1980) 'Societal Differences in Organizing Manufacturing Units: A Comparison of France, West Germany and Great Britain', *Organization Studies*, 1(1), pp. 59–86.

Ng, S-H. and Warner, M. (1998) *China's Trade Unions and Management* (London: Macmillan; and New York: St. Martins Press).

Ng, S-H. and Warner, M. (1999) 'Human Resource Management in Asia', in B. Morton and P. Joynt (eds), *The Global HR Manager* (London: IPD) pp. 233–57.

Redding, G. (1990) *The Spirit of Chinese Capitalism* (Berlin: de Gruyter).

Rowley, C. (1997) 'Introduction: Comparisons and Perspectives on HRM in the Asia Pacific', Special Issue: 'Human Resource Management in the Asia Pacific Region Questioned', *Asia Pacific Business Review*, 3(4), pp. 1–18.

Sano, Y. (1995) *Human Resource Management in Japan* (Tokyo: Keio University Press).

Selmer, J. (2000) 'Human Resource Management in Asia', in M. Warner (ed.), *Management in Asia Pacific*, vol. 2 of the *Regional Encyclopedia of Business and Management* (4 vols) (London: Thomson Learning) pp. 101–14.

Taylor, B. (1999) 'Japanese Manufacturing Style in China? Production Practices in Japanese Manufacturing Plants', *New Technology, Work and Employment*, 14(2), pp. 129–42.

Thurley, K. (1988) 'Trade Unionism in Asian Countries', in Y. C. Yao, David A. Levin, S-H. Ng and E. Sinn (eds), *Labour Movement in A Changing Society: The Experience of Hong Kong* (Hong Kong: Centre for Asian Studies, University of Hong Kong).

Walder, M. (1986) *Communist Neo-Traditionalism: Work and Authority in Chinese Industry* (Berkeley, CA: University of California Press).

Warner, M. (1993) 'Human Resource Management "with Chinese Characteristics"', *International Journal of Human Resource Management*, 4(1), pp. 45–65.

Warner, M. (1995) *The Management of Human Resources in Chinese Industry* (London: Macmillan; and New York: St. Martins Press).

Warner, M. (1996) 'Chinese Enterprise Reform, Human Resources and the 1994 Labour Law', *International Journal of Human Resource Management*, 7, pp. 779–96.

Warner, M. (2000), 'Introduction: Asia Pacific HRM Revisited', Special Issue on Asia Pacific HRM, *International Journal of Human Resource Management*, 11, 2, pp. 171–82.

Warner, M. and Ng, S-H. (1999) 'Collective Contracts in Chinese Enterprises: A New Brand of Collective Bargaining under "Market Socialism"', *British Journal of Industrial Relations*, 37(2), pp. 295–314.

Whittaker D. H. (1998) 'Labour Unions and Industrial Relations in Japan: Crumbling Pillar or Forging a "Third Way"', *Industrial Relations Journal*, 29(4), pp. 280–94.

Part II

Human Resource Management of Western Firms in China

10 Cross-Cultural Human Resource Strategies in China and India

Brij N. Kumar, Birgit Ensslinger
and Susanne Esslinger

INTRODUCTION

In today's global marketplace cross-cultural human resource deployment in multinational corporations (MNCs) is as important for attaining and sustaining strategic advantage as product policy or technology choice. Staffing key positions around the globe in foreign subsidiaries with the right people at the right time is perhaps a challenge greater than any other managerial job, and the strategic role of cross-cultural human intelligence deployment is now generally recognized.

It lies within the natural scope of the multinational corporation that its cross-cultural human intelligence deployment cover staffing key positions around the globe with personnel irrespective of nationality and based mainly on crucial criteria such as qualification and mobility. But on the other hand, MNC practice shows that in reality executive nationality does play an important role, especially when the choice is between host-country (local) managers and parent-country/parent-company (foreign) expatriates. In most Asian countries nationality becomes often a dominating factor within a legal and cultural frame of the host-country which usually supports assignment of local nationals. On the other hand, to the extent that Asian subsidiaries also become a part of global networks, *a priori* favouring of local managers becomes counter-productive. Two Asian countries where this practice can be observed by and large are India and China. At the outset we can assume different staffing and development practices in the MNC-subsidiaries in both countries depend on country-related differences in MNC-strategies and specific environmental influences.

The following chapter reports the results of a study on human resource deployment in joint ventures of German MNCs in India and China. The question investigated is how are key positions in the Chinese and Indian joint ventures staffed between local nationals and German expatriates? Is there any difference between China and India? What is the rationale? The comparative research will especially open perspectives on cross-cultural influences needed in designing global human resource deployment strategies in the MNCs.

LITERATURE REVIEW

An emerging literature focuses on the area of cross-cultural human resource deployment (Kumar and Wagner, 1998). Within this area two streams of research can be identified. The first is directed at policies and practices of multi-national corporations that relate to staffing 'international' positions. These are jobs in the parent-company and in foreign subsidiaries responsible for cross-border issues. Specific studies include recruitment, selection of 'international managers' and choice between local and expatriate executives (Mendenhall *et al.*, 1987; Black *et al.*, 1992; Kumar, 1993; Brewster and Pickard, 1994), training (Tung, 1981; Black and Mendenhall, 1990), expatriate compensation (Bonache and Fernandez, 1997), expatriate repatriation (Gregersen, 1992; Kumar, 1993) and expatriate support (Marlias *et al.*, 1995). This research has contributed to the insight that international human resource management must be treated as a competitive asset connected with the global strategy of MNCs (Kumar, 1993). The second stream of research focuses specifically on the individual expatriate and the issues related to successful overseas assignment. These especially include problems of expatriate motivation and loyalty (Black *et al.*, 1992; Banai and Reisel, 1993) and adaptation (Mendenhall and Odou, 1985; Stroh *et al.*, 1994; Caliguiri, 2000).

   Our research question is basically driven by two observations in connection with both streams of research. First, although the general importance of MNC corporate and global strategy for international human resource management has been established, there are few studies relating specific strategy types and strategy determinants to issues of international human resource management, for instance to the problem of choice between local managers versus expatriates. We need to put the investigation of the issue on a theoretically sound concept. The question of choice between expatriate and local managers must be guided by influencing factors which together reflect the basic strategic thrust of the MNC. After all, assisting and developing personnel and staffing key positions is instrumental for achieving strategic goals and should therefore also be analyzed within the strategic framework of the corporation. This way of looking at the issue of choice between locals and expatriates has hitherto been rather neglected, or dealt very generally.

Secondly, while studies related to international human resource practices in general do exist, there is dearth of research pertaining to specific host-country strategies, particularly in Asia. Our intention to investigate the choice between the assignments of host nationals and expatriates in India and China in comparative perspective will not only provide information on German MNCs' human resource deployment practices in the two particular Asian countries, but will also add a cross-cultural dimension to the strategic framework we intend to employ.

THEORETICAL FRAME OF REFERENCE

The Issue of Executive Nationality in Staffing Key International Positions

The global activity of MNCs gives them the possibility of recruiting staff of various nationalities for international positions: parent-company or parent-country nationality, third country nationals and host-country managers. As known from MNC-practice, key positions in the parent-company are, however, mainly staffed by parent-country nationals (Kumar, 1993). In spite of the fact that qualified foreign staff may be available, most MNCs around the world prove to be quite conservative and discriminating in this respect, although there are signs of change. On the other hand, positions in foreign subsidiaries are generally open to all three national groups, even though preference for long-term assignments is moving towards host-country nationals.

Generally speaking, several attributes have been connected with the various nationalities while selecting between parent-company nationals (expatriates) and local managers. The former have generally proven to be more suitable for positions with a strong corporate strategy orientation requiring higher coordination, parent-company loyalty and knowledge of corporate assets and know-how. On the other hand, host-country managers can evidently manage local needs and adaptability better than expatriates. Such discriminating attributes on both sides are, of course, based more on empirical observations than on theoretical reasoning, since one can assume that both groups, parent-country nationals and local managers, could acquire the opposite qualifications with adequate socialization in the host-country environment and in the parent-company respectively. But apart from such affirmative attributes, the choice between expatriates and local managers is generally also guided by a range of other factors, such as availability of qualified staff in the host-country, cost of expatriation, indigenization policies of host-countries, etc. Barriers for foreign assignments also come from the potential expatriates themselves who because of real and anticipated problems like interruption of spouse career, repatriation uncertainty, etc. (Stahl, 1998) are showing increasing unwillingness to relocate. This is especially true of assignments in countries which are considered less attractive, where scope for personal development is low, and on the other hand adaptation requirements for expatriates and their families in the foreign country are high due to substantial divergence in culture and standard of economic development.

In most Asian countries Western MNCs are confronted with host-country environments that are extremely divergent from home. Most Asian countries like China and India also follow quite strict indigenization policies so that from that point of view the nationality issue invariably boils down to favouring local managers above expatriates. On the other hand, strategy arguments play an important role where expatriate assignment can become indispensable. The following considerations explore this strategic avenue in a little more detail to form the conceptual framework for our investigation.

Strategic Considerations and Choice of Expatriates vs. Local Executives

As mentioned earlier, we take a strategy-oriented approach to investigate the choice of expatriate vs. local managers in India and China. The importance of international strategy for human resource management has been stressed often. Adler and Ghadar (1990, p. 245) state, 'the effectiveness of particular HRM approaches and practices depends directly on the firm's environment and strategy'. Whether local executives or expatriates are assigned to key positions in foreign subsidiaries will depend on what the principle strategic motives of the firm are in operating own foreign subsidiaries. Previous research on the choice between local and expatriate executives has not differentiated according to this strategic background of the company, but has looked directly at the reasons and goals of expatriation. Stahl (1998) classifies the various objectives (e.g., Edström and Galbraith, 1977; Kenter, 1989; Wirth, 1992) into three categories: (1) know-how transfer to foreign subsidiaries, (2) coordination and control of foreign subsidiaries and (3) development of local counterparts and of the expatriates themselves. In practice all three objectives together play a role in differing importance.

In this chapter we take a contingency approach by identifying different situations in which firms resort to expatriate assignment, and when they do not. We conceptualize the contextual frame according to the theory of international operations and strategy. Out of the different models known in extant literature (Dunning and Dilyard, 1999), we can summarize three different approaches which explain the firms' strategy to set up foreign operations (Culpan and Kumar, 1994).

Market-Based Perspective

Firms expect to exploit and service foreign markets much more efficiently from local operations than through exportation. The existing local market can be penetrated more intensively, and the market potential more easily tapped. Servicing local markets efficiently requires intimate knowledge of host-country marketing systems, distribution channels and customer demands. Above all, cultural empathy is necessary in marketing positions to conduct amicable negotiations with local customers, to influence them and to be sensitive to their whims and woes. Western managers in Asia often find it difficult to develop appropriate empathy towards such divergent cultural traits and expectations. For instance, one of the main reasons often cited for German companies' reluctance for intensive activities in Japan is the intuitive fear of the foreignness of its culture. Considering such problems and the attributes of executive nationality we can argue that key positions in marketing-oriented MNC subsidiaries should be rather filled in by local executives than expatriates. This leads us to the first proposition.

Proposition 1:
German MNCs with a higher market orientation in their activities in China and India will have a larger overall proportion of host-country executives in key positions in the local subsidiaries than their counterparts with a lower market-orientation (ceteris paribus).

Resource-Based Approach

Companies go in for foreign direct investment in order to avail themselves of resources in the host-country that are not so easily available at home. Local procurement of critical resources can cut down uncertainties regarding availability and can reduce dependency. For MNCs engaged in exploiting natural resources the resource-based motivation for foreign direct investment is clear, but also for others who must rely on certain imports and who have a high proportion of factor costs which are lower in foreign sites will be prompted to relocate production. China and India in particular offer attractive opportunities to Western MNCs for availing themselves of reasonably priced and fairly well qualified manpower, a resource increasingly becoming important in global competition.

As in the case of market-oriented perspective, foreign subsidiaries that are set up mainly on the resource-based rationale will generally have a greater environmental interface. Sourcing in the host-country for reliable local suppliers and maintaining long-term relationships, or even handling local employees in acquired subsidiaries, would require considerable knowledge and sensibility towards the local environment and culture on the part of key executives. Here again, therefore, subsidiary management would be better put in the hands of local managers than assigned to expatriates.

Proposition 2:
German MNCs with a higher resource-oriented motivation in their activites in China and India will have a larger overall proportion of host-country executives in key positions in the local subsidiaries than their counterparts with a lower resource-orientation (ceteris paribus).

Transaction-Cost Approach

In theory, minimizing transaction costs by building up internal markets on the basis of production abroad is an important motivation for foreign direct investment (Buckley and Casson, 1976). The rationale, however, can only be realized in practice if and when the MNCs are capable of efficiently coordinating decentralized subsidiaries' activities. Coordination and integration of international operations requires on the part of the executives good knowledge of corporate resources and policies and loyalty to central goals, characteristics attributed to expatriates rather than to local managers. The demand for the latter executive category in this case is also relatively limited because with the emphasis on global integration strategy the subsidiaries' interface with the local environment is on the other hand quite narrow and the need for local interaction correspondingly low. In view of this type of approach we can formulate the next proposition.

Proposition 3:
German MNCs with a higher transaction cost orientation in their activities in China and India will have a larger overall proportion of expatriates in key positions in the local subsidiaries than their counterparts with lower transaction cost motivation (ceteris paribus).

Ownership Strategy and Size of Subsidiary as Differentiating Variables

Ownership Strategy

German MNC investments in China and India are mostly organized in the form of joint ventures with local partners (Tables 10.1 and 10.3). In recent years host-country policies towards restricting subsidiary ownership have been liberalized and the proportion of 100 per cent ownership has risen. Nevertheless, joint ventures continue to be the favoured strategy in these countries for many reasons (Kumar and Khanna, 1999; Kumar *et al.*, 1999). Ownership strategy basically constitutes one element of the structural framework of the foreign subsidiaries which influences the achievement of the foreign invest-ment objectives. Therefore, choice of ownership strategy, whether joint venture or 100 per cent ownership, and the determinants of foreign investment are interdependent.

- *Ownership strategy and market-based approach*: Since servicing local markets and local customer perpective is the basic rationale, local partners can be a support in achieving this objective. Many local partners contribute with their own distribution channels, market share and other marketing facilities so that joint ventures appear to be more suitable for this special type of foreign investment.
- *Ownership strategy and resource-based perspective*: Foreign investments with a resource-based perspective also require good local contacts and relationships where again local partners can be of help. They can also provide own resources like trained manpower and knowledge of local suppliers to the foreign investor who otherwise would have to build up their own resource base. Joint ventures seem to be a more efficient strategy for achieving these objectives.
- *Ownership strategy and transaction-cost motivation*: Global strategy and coordination of international investments with the corporate framework is the general issue here which requires unanimous control of subsidiary activities on the part of the foreign investor. Joint ventures with local partners can be a liability for this purpose since control would have to be shared. Hundred per cent or majority ownership on the other hand can fulfil these requirements in a better way.

These brief arguments can be summed up in the following proposition.

Proposition 4:
Ownership strategy of German MNCs in India and China will have a differentiating effect on the investment rationale in those host-countries and, in relationship to that, a moderating influence on the choice of assigning expatriates versus local managers.

Size of Company

Although the size of the MNC and foreign subsidiary *per se* does not necessarily mean much, the underlying resources and task complexity do offer some arguments that will influence the foreign investment rationale of MNCs.

- *Size and market-based perspective*: Foreign investments with emphasis on building up and servicing local markets generally will require a substantial amount of resource base. Especially large host-countries like China and India are at first glance difficult to cover for small and medium-sized companies. Marketing in these countries requires foreign experience in Asian cultures, organizational competence, financial and manpower resources for frequent visits to the far-away local market, market research capabilities and the like, which are relatively more scarce in smaller companies than larger companies.

- *Size and resource-based motivation*: The statement seems plausible that smaller MNCs will prefer to pursue foreign direct investments with emphasis on availability of local resources. This holds true especially for the majority of companies which due to paucity of financial assets resort to labour-intensive production to a higher degree than large MNCs and therefore more extensively seek to invest in cheap labour countries like China and India.

- *Size and transaction-cost orientation*: It has been empirically shown that the transaction cost perspective of foreign investment falls more in the realm of larger MNCs than smaller internationalized companies (Kumar, 1988). The explanation lies in optimizing the achievable advantages of internalization and the accruable coordination costs. Only above a certain minimum level of foreign investment and number of foreign subsidiaries which basically only large MNCs can maintain, is the pay-off between the potential saving of transaction costs on internal markets and the costs incurred for coordinating them positive. Smaller companies only rarely are capable of achieving such minimum levels of investment so that their internationalization is resource-based rather than transaction-cost directed.

Following these brief arguments on the influence of company size on the internationalization process, we can formulate our next proposition.

Proposition 5:
The size of German MNCs in China and India will have a differentiating effect on the foreign investment rationale and, in relationship to that, a moderating influence on the choice of assigning expatriates versus local managers.

THE MODEL WITH REFERENCE TO CHINA AND INDIA

The arguments and propositions presented hitherto can be put together in a general model which can be used as a research design (Figure 10.1).

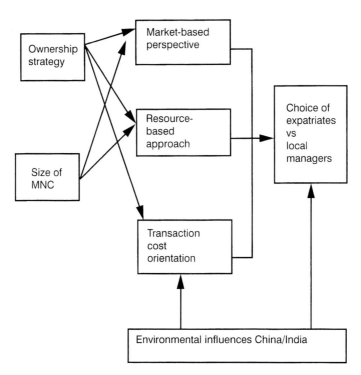

Figure 10.1   Research design

It is the objective of our chapter to compare German MNC practice and decision-making patterns in China and India. We obviously assume some differences depending on the host-country context. Generally speaking, environmental factors, of course, influence all the phases of the internationalization process, beginning with the decision to invest abroad through to the phase of managing foreign subsidiaries, which includes issues in human resource management like the choice between expatriates and local managers. Thus divergencies found between German MNC HRM-practice in China and India can be attributable to differing environmental influences, such as varying market potential, availability of resources and suppliers' industry, competition and anti-trust laws curtailing horizontal integration and formation of internal markets. Besides such dimensions which influence the choice of expatriates vs. local managers *indirectly* via the investment rationale, we can also identify factors that determine the staffing decision *directly*. These are, for instance, government policies regarding employment of foreigners, cultural divergence and adaptation requirements for expatriates and their families, cost of expatriation and living abroad, availability of infrastructure in the host-country (expatriate housing, schools for children), and other amenities. The mentioned list of 'indirect' and 'direct' host-country environmental influencing factors is by no means systematic or exhaustive. What is important is that China and India as host-countries for foreign investment of Western MNCs offer quite specific conditions depending on their differing historical past, political, economic and development systems and pattern followed, and last but not least different culture. Since opening its economy in the 1980s China has attracted a vast amount of foreign direct investment (total FDI in 1998: 261 billion US$), whereas India has been and still is quite restrictive in this respect inspite of its basic democratic and market economy structures and a substantial amount of liberalization in the past years (total FDI in India 1998: 13 billion US$). Such and other institutional and cultural elements form the divergent contextual framework in China and India on which the varying pattern of the internationalization process including the differing choice of expatriate vs. local manager assignment will depend.

Method and Measurement of Variables

The propositions are investigated on the basis of questionnaire surveys conducted in 1998. Questionnaires were submitted to German MNCs with direct investment and subsidiary operations in China and India. The company data was compiled from various sources such as German Chamber of Commerce and Industry, German-Indian Chamber of Commerce and Industry and German Embassy Peking. Our final sample includes 33 German MNCs and 36 German MNCs with production subsidiaries in India or China.

The main variables of the model were measured with the following indicators.

- *Choice of expatriates vs. local executives*: Number of German MNCs which had assigned German expatriates (vs. local executives) to the position of chief executive officer in their operations in China and India.
- *Market-based perspective*: Degree to which importance was attached by German MNCs to market potential and availability of marketing services (e.g. distribution channels, market research) in connection with their investments in China and India. Measured on a 5-point Likert scale.
- *Resource-based approach*: Degree to which German MNCs attached importance to availability of resources (capital, materials, etc.) and qualified low-cost manpower in India and China in connection with their investments there. Measured on a 5-point Likert scale.
- *Transaction cost approach*: Since reduction of transaction costs is related directly to formation of internal markets and their coordination, the most

reliable proxy is: degree of control of German parent company on Chinese and Indian operations (extent of coordination measured on a 5-point Likert scale).

RESULTS

The overall picture is that more German MNCs assign German expatriates to CEO in China (75 per cent) than in their subsidiaries in India (42 per cent).

China

Tables 10.1 and 10.2 show that neither ownership strategy nor MNC size apparently have a significant direct relationship to choice of executive nationality in the Chinese subsidiaries.

Figure 10.2 shows their differentiating affects in relationship to the importance of the internationalization factors. In both joint ventures and majority and wholly-owned subsidiaries the importance of perceived subsidiary control correlates positively to the assignment of expatriates. This is in line with proposition 3. Whereas in joint ventures the importance of availability of local resources and market potential positively correlates with assignment of local nationals (Proposition 1 and 2), in the wholly-owned operations these two factors do not seem to have any influence on nationality choice.

In large German MNCs there were no local CEOs at all, and in both small and large companies the main driving force for expatriate assignment is again the perceived need for subsidiary control (Proposition 3). In smaller companies we find a significant difference between the assignment of local nationals and expatriates depending on the felt importance of servicing the local market. The higher the market orientiation, the more likely that Chinese nationals are assigned to the position of CEO (Proposition 1). Other than

Table 10.1 Ownership strategy and choice of CEO nationality in China

Expatriate assignment	Joint ventures (N = 25)	Maj./100 per cent ownership (N = 11)
Yes (N = 27)	20	7
No (N = 9)	5	4

$Chi^2 = 1.091$; df = 1; $p \leq 0.296$.

Table 10.2   Size of MNC and choice of CEO nationality in China

Expatriate assignment	Small/medium sized (N = 32)	Large (N = 4)
Yes (N = 27)	23	4
No (N = 9)	9	–

Chi^2 = 1.563; df = 1; p ≤ 0.211.

	German MNCs in China (N = 36)							
Influencing factors on a 5-point scale 1 = very important 5 = least important (Mean values)	Ownership Strategy [1]				Size of MNC [2]			
	Joint Venture N = 25		Maj/ 100 per cent N = 11		Small/medium N = 32		Large N = 4	
	Choice EXP/LOC				Choice EXP/LOC			
	LOC N = 5	EXP N = 5	LOC N = 4	EXP N = 4	LOC N = 9	EXP N = 23	LOC N = 0	EXP N = 4
Market potential/ marketing service	1.4[+]	1.8[+]	1.5	1.57	1.4[+]	1.74[+]	–	1.25
Availability of local resources/ cheap manpower	2.6[+]	2.75[+]	3.25[+]	2.71	2.8	2.78	–	2.5
Control of subsidiary by parent comp.	2.2[+]	1.75[+]	2.75[*]	1.14[*]	2.4[+]	1.61[+]	–	1.5

Figure 10.2   Influence of ownership strategy and size of MNC on internationalization factors and choice of executive nationality in Chinese subsidiaries
Note: [1] Joint Venture = 50 per cent and less German capital; Maj./100 per cent = >50 per cent German capital
[2] Small = < 1000 employees; Large = > 1000 employees; [+] p ≤ 0,05, [*] p ≤ 0,05.

that, we find no significant differentiating effects of company size on the internationalization factors and subsequently on executive nationality in China.

India

In India we find a somewhat different picture. Tables 10.3 and 10.4 show the direct relationship between choice of executive nationality and ownership strategy and size of MNC.

In both cases we find a significant relationship indicating that ownership strategy and size of MNCs are both direct determining factors for nationality choice. According to the contingency table, obviously German expatriates are significantly less employed in joint ventures and smaller companies than in majority and wholly-owned and large subsidiaries in India.

Irrespective of ownership strategy and size of MNCs the influence of the internationalization factors on executive nationality is as hypothesized in the Propositions 1–3. Expatriate assignment rises with the felt need for reduction of transaction costs and control of the Indian subsidiary, even though the felt importance is higher in wholly-owned subsidiaries than joint ventures. On the other hand, staffing with Indian executives becomes the favoured strategy where servicing the local market and harnessing local resources are important.

Table 10.3   Ownership strategy and choice of CEO nationality in India

Expatriate assignment	Joint ventures (N = 16)	Maj./100 per cent ownership (N = 17)
Yes (N = 11)	4	10
No (N = 19)	12	7

Chi^2 = 0.26; df = 1; p ≤ 0.05.

Table 10.4   Size of MNC and choice of CEO nationality in India

Expatriate assignment	Small/medium sized (N = 28)	Large (N = 5)
Yes (N = 14)	10	4
No (N = 19)	18	1

Chi^2 = 0.65; df = 1; p ≤ 0.05.

Influencing factors on a 5-point scale 1 = very important 5 = least important (Mean values)	German MNCs in India (N = 33)							
	Ownership Strategy [1]				Size of MNC [2]			
	Joint Venture N = 16		Maj/ 100 per cent N = 17		Small/medium N = 28		Large N = 5	
	Choice EXP/LOC				Choice EXP/LOC			
	LOC N = 12	EXP N = 4	LOC N = 7	EXP N = 10	LOC N = 18	EXP N = 10	LOC N = 1	EXP N = 4
Market potential/ marketing service	1.94+	2.00+	1.93+	2.60+	2.44+	2.55+	3.0+	3.33+
Availability of local resources/ cheap manpower	2.00+	3.50+	2.78+	3.10+	2.55+	3.05+	1.0+	2.66+
Control of subsidiary by parent comp.	3.62+	2.65+	2.35*	1.6+	3.08+	1.95+	2.5+	1.87+

Figure 10.3   Influence of ownership strategy and size of MNC on internationalization factors and choice of executive nationality in Indian subsidiaries

Note: [1] Joint Venture = 50 per cent and less German capital; Maj./ 100 per cent = >50 per cent German capital
[2] Small = < 1000 employees; Large = > 1000 employees; + $p \leq 0.05$.

DISCUSSION: COMPARISON OF GERMAN MNCs IN CHINA AND INDIA

Our findings show that German MNCs in China deploy relatively more expatriates than in their subsidiaries in India (Figures 10.2, 10.3). They do this irrespective of ownership strategy and size of MNC. In contrast, expatriate assignment in India is very much dependent on ownership strategy and size. There are definitely more expatriates in wholly-owned subsidiaries and majority ventures and in larger MNCs than in joint ventures and smaller companies. In Indian joint ventures only 25 per cent of CEOs are German expatriates;

in Chinese joint ventures 80 per cent. On the other hand, in majority and wholly-owned subsidiaries the assignment of expatriates is about comparable. It is also interesting to note that in India only 35 per cent of CEOs in smaller subsidiaries are expatriates; in China over 70 per cent. In large subsidiaries expatriate assignment is again comparable.

According to our findings the main reason for more expatriate assignment in China than in India lies in the perceived need for stronger subsidiary control in the former host-country. This itself could be connected to several factors. Chinese subsidiaries of German and other Western MNCs are invariably former state-owned enterprises acquired partly or wholly by them. *De novo* ventures as in India are relatively seldom, which means that in most cases not only old and unmodern assets, equipment and materials must be taken over and put to some use, but also previous employees and organization structures. Although new labour laws in China now allow foreign investors to discharge employees and reshuffle their personnel, the core staff invariably remains, often with their old functionary culture and socialistic perceptions and mindsets. In joint ventures Chinese partners also often still represent socialistic thinking, and – what is really annoying and dysfunctional in view of many German partnering firms – still lack entrepreneurial and managerial qualities like initiative and willingness to shoulder responsibility. With such characteristics of the subsidiary, German MNCs feel a relatively high need for control in China.

In contrast, joint ventures in India are mostly founded with established local companies where Indian partners often have a long entrepreneurial background. Many subsidiaries, joint ventures and majority and wholly-owned companies are, moreover, greenfield projects with modern equipment and newly hired staff which is trained for the special needs of the collaboration. Especially in joint ventures, therefore, the need for direct involvement in management is considered low, and is then mostly left up to the discretion of the Indian partner. Naturally, this presupposes good partner relationships in the form of trust, commitment and the like which have to be built up (Kumar and Khanna, 1999).

Our findings show that even though the market-based perspective in the Chinese operations is stronger than in India, deployment of German expatriates in the former is more intensive. Apparently, even on the sales side, local Chinese staff must be supported by German executives in marketing methods not so commonly known and practised in China as in India which has a long tradition in multinational companies in the country.

On the other hand, German operations in India have a stronger resource-based orientation than the Chinese subsidiaries, which is a reason for higher local executive deployment than assignment of expatriates, as argued earlier.

Following these findings and arguments we can conclude that the higher use of German expatriates in China than in India is basically due to the lesser experience and qualification of Chinese local personnel to staff key positions in the respective host-country subsidiaries. German MNCs apparently find it (still) difficult to leave management in the hands of Chinese managers which often must be recruited from the staff of the acquired state-owned enterprises.

Indian executives and joint venture partners, on the other hand, bring along substantive experience in running a business in a market economy. Here the problem is not so much of qualification of local staff but rather of building up reliable and trustful relationships with the Indian partners and subsidiaries in order to confidently run local operations without much expatriate assignment. Considering the problems of expatriation in general, e.g. high costs, adaptation difficulties inside and outside the company, repatriation conflict, etc., and that also localization of management positions is politically desired in the host-countries, German MNCs must more and more 'resort' to deployment and training of Chinese manpower. Already German MNCs like Siemens are operating large management training centres in China where annually hundreds of young academics from local universities are qualified for the around 50 Chinese subsidiaries of the company. Several German universities collaborate with Chinese universities and professional institutions to foster management training of students for recruitment in German companies. For years to come, China more than India and in fact any other important host-country elsewhere is likely to remain a domain where German MNCs will have to continue to concentrate on development of local managers.

References

Adler, N. J. and Ghadar, F. (1990) 'Stratetic Human Resource Management: A Global Perspective', in R. Pieper (ed.), *Human Resource Management: An International Comparison* (Berlin: De Gruyter) pp. 235–60.
Banai, B. and Reisel, W. D. (1993) 'Expatriate Managers' Loyalty to the MNC. Myth or Reality? An Exploratory Study', *Journal of International Business Studies*, 24, pp. 33–49.
Black, J. S. and Mendenhall, M. E. (1990) 'Cross-Cultural Training Effectiveness: A Review and Theoretical Framework', *Academy of Management Review*, 15, pp. 113–36.
Black, J. S., Gregersen, H. B. and Mendenhall, M. E. (1992) *Global Assignments* (San Francisco: Jossey-Bass Publishers).
Bonache, J. and Fernandez, Z. (1997) 'Expatriate Compensation and its Link to the Subsidiary Strategic Role: A Theoretical Analysis', *International Journal of Human Resource Management*, 8, pp. 457–75.
Brewster, C. and Pickard, J. (1994) 'Evaluating Expatriate Training', *International Management and Organization*, 24(3), pp. 18–35.

Buckley, P. and Casson, M. (1976) *The Future of the Multinational Enterprise* (London: Macmillan).

Caliguiri, P. M. (2000) 'Selecting Expatriates for Personality Characteristics: A Moderating Effect of Personality on the Relationship between Host National Contact and Cross-Cultural Adjustment', *Management International Review*, 40, pp. 61–80.

Culpan, R. and Kumar, B. N. (1994) 'Cooperative Ventures of Western Firms in Eastern Europe: The Case of German Companies', in P. Buckley and P. Ghauri (eds), *The Economics of Change in East and Central Europe* (London: Academic Press) pp. 267–78.

Dunning, J. and Dilyard, J. (1999) 'Towards a General Paradigm of Foreign Direct and Foreign Portfolio Investment', *Transnational Corporations*, 8(1), pp. 1–45.

Edström, A. and Galbraith, J. (1977a) 'Alternative Policies for International Transfers of Managers', *Management International Review*, 17, pp. 11–22.

Gregersen, H. B. (1992) 'Commitments to a Parent-Company and a Local Work Unit during Repatriation', *Personnel Psychology*, 45, pp. 323–40.

Kenter, M. E. (1989) 'Entsendung von Stammhausdelegierten', in K. Macharzina and M. K. Welge (eds), *Handwörterbuch Export und internationale Unternehmung* (Stuttgart: Poeschel) pp. 1925–37.

Kumar, B. N. (1988) 'Investment Strategy of German Small and Medium-Sized Firms in the USA and the Theory of Direct Investment', in F. Khosrow (ed.), *International Trade and Finance* (New York) pp. 175–89.

Kumar, B. N. (1993) 'Internationale Personalpolitik bei mittelständischen Unternehmen', *Personalführung*, 26, pp. 484–6.

Kumar, B. N. and Khanna, M. (1999) 'Partner Relationships, Autonomy and Performance in International Joint Ventures', in J. Engelhard and E. Sinz (eds), *Kooperation im Wettbewerb* (Wiesbaden: Gabler) pp. 237–67.

Kumar, B. N. and Wagner, D. (eds) (1998) *Handbuch des Internationalen Personalmanagements* (München: C. H. Beck).

Kumar, B. N., Mao, Y. and Ensslinger, B. (1999) 'Deutsche Direktinvestitionen in China: Strategien und Erfolgsfaktoren', *China Industrial Economics*, 3, pp. 35–45.

Marlias, M. R., Hanson, D. P. and Hook, M. K. (1995) 'The Need for Local Agencies to Provide Expatriate Support Programs', *The International Executive* 37, pp. 81–9.

Mendenhall, M. and Odou, G. (1985) 'The Dimensions of Expatriate Acculturation', *Academy of Management Review*, 10, pp. 39–47.

Mendenhall, M., Dunbar, E. and Odou, G. (1987) 'Expatriate Selection, Training and Career-Pathing', *International Journal of Human Resource Management*, 26, pp. 331–45.

Stahl, G. (1998) *Internationaler Einsatz von Führungskräften* (München, Oldenbourg).

Stroh, L. K., Dennis, L. E. and Cramer, T. C. (1994) 'Predictors of Expatriate Adjustment', *International Journal of Organizational Analysis*, 2, 176–92.

Tung, R. L. (1981) 'Selection and Training of Personnel for Overseas Assignment', *Columbia Journal of World Business*, 16, pp. 21–5.

Wirth, E. (1992) *Mitarbeiter im Auslandseinsatz: Planung und Gestaltung* (Wiesbaden: Gabler).

11 Human Resource Development for Localization: European Multinational Corporations in China

Verner Worm, Jan Selmer
and Corinna T. de Leon

INTRODUCTION

From the Communist revolution of 1949 to 1978, China was a very isolated country whose economic growth was slower than the world average. By the early 1960s, China's annual GDP growth rate was 2.3 per cent, in sharp contrast to the average 6 per cent growth of Asian economies (Maddison, 1998). It was only after the gradual introduction of an open, market-oriented economy in 1978 that China became a front runner in economic development. The average growth in GDP since 1980 is more than 9 per cent, making China the fastest growing economy in the Asian region (Thompson, 1998).

The high growth rate over the latest 20 years is partly explained by China's great success in attracting foreign direct investments (FDIs). By the end of 1998, the PRC government had approved more than 300,000 foreign invested enterprises (FIEs), of which half operate with actually utilized FDI in excess of US$ 260 billion. With US$ 45 billion in FDIs in 1997–8, China has positioned itself as the second largest FDI receiver after the United States.

In 1998, roughly 18 million workers were employed in FIEs, comprising 18 per cent of gross industrial output and almost half of China's foreign trade of US$ 321 billion (www.tdc.org.hk, 1999). Despite the tremendous interest of Western multinationals in China investment, particularly during the 1990s, the average return of investment (ROI) was estimated to be only 1.5 per cent in 1998.

Under the planned economic system of pre-1978 China, the labour market was abandoned because it was considered a capitalist phenomenon. It was the belief then that in the state-operated enterprises (SOE), there was no need for a 'manager' in the Western sense of someone who has the ability to take initiative in overseeing operations. In a planned economy, the managerial role was confined to executing orders given by government bureau above the firm, reducing it to a mere production unit. Consequently, by the time European Multinational Corporations (EMNCs) began to enter China, the non-existence of a labour market and lack of need for managerial qualifications meant that managerial skills were non-existent among Chinese staff.

Departments of management studies were established at universities in Shanghai and Beijing in the early 1900s, but were disbanded in 1952. The specialization was reopened only in 1978 when Deng Xiaoping mandated that management is one of the fields of study that China should learn from the Western countries. However, management training did not exist until 1980, and the majority of cadres and professors at that time remained sceptical to applicability of Western management knowledge to China. Consequently, in EMNCs, human resource development (HRD) of Chinese managers has to start from the basic foundations, to enable the *gradual* replacement of positions currently held by the expensive expatriates.

Localization of management is one of the (few) issues in which the opinions of the Chinese government and EMNCs are identical, although their reasons differ. The Chinese government wants modern management techniques transferred to Chinese managers as part of its modernization programme. On the other hand, EMNCs want to reduce expenditures by employing more local staff in management positions.

The *exact* number of expatriates living in China is not available; however, in EMNCs the ratio of expatriates to locals is typically between 1:10 and 1:20. The average expatriate remuneration including allowances per year (US$ 30,000–US$ 60,000) is around ten times more than the typical salary of the local manager (20,000–40,000 yuan per month). About 60 per cent is for pensions as well as medical, unemployment, work-related injury and illness, maternity and death benefits.

Localization refers to the process by which local Chinese managers replace expatriate managers in EMNCs. Localization is a long-term process in China, which requires at least five steps. First, the EMNCs must have an intention to localize as well as a strategy for its implementation. Second, personnel with high potential have to be recruited and identified. Third, functional skills have to be learned by the locals through formal training. Fourth, on-the-job training should include direct experience on how expatriates execute the acquired skills and competencies. Fifth, the retained local managers should have the competencies to independently exercise the managerial skills necessary for a market-economy. Ultimately the Chinese managers should assume responsibility for and take initiatives towards the further development of the business without the need for expatriate expertise.

A study published by the Economist Intelligence Unit (*China Hand*, 1998) indicated that 70 per cent of the respondents considered management localization as important, but only 11 per cent felt that they were completely successful. The transfer of management capabilities was considered important for improved profitability by 62 per cent of the respondents, but success was reported only by 7 per cent. Furthermore, 67 per cent of the respondents claimed that a lack of quality managers was a restriction on profitability, a constraint cited more frequently than competition, credit difficulties and low market share. These findings demonstrate the need to focus on the localization process of FIE management.

PREVIOUS RESEARCH

In the existing literature on HRM issues in Western companies in China, most empirical studies focused on expatriate adjustment to different aspects of the peculiar Chinese environment (Worm, 1997; Sergeant and Frenkel, 1998; Selmer, 1999). Nonetheless, throughout the past decade, many articles in practitioners' magazines have pointed out the lack of qualified local managers in China; such as *Far Eastern Economic Review*, *China Business Review*, and *Business China*. In 1998 the Economist Intelligence Unit published an in-depth survey on business operations in China, which included a chapter on human resources (*China Hand*, 1998).

The vast majority of young Chinese do not have any tertiary education, since only 1.4 per cent of the Chinese population have gone to university (*China Hand*, 1998, p. 6). Furthermore, the few university graduates received a theoretical education with little practical content. It was not surprising that the expatriate respondents considered the young Chinese as very open but lacking in experience, in contrast to the generation that had undergone the Cultural Revolution. Modern Chinese history is not taught at all in the Chinese educational system; and the parents are either embarrassed about their revolutionary behaviour or reluctant to talk about their sufferings. The positive consequence is that the young Chinese are not afraid of taking responsibility or assuming challenges, are very self-confident, and believe that they are in control of almost everything. Humility is a traditional Chinese virtue that has lost its value among the contemporary Chinese, although respect toward authority is shown when seen as deserving. The disadvantage of the reticence on the Cultural Revolution is that the young Chinese have an idealized attitude towards their society, underestimating the power of the government and the party.

A few academic publications attempted to study the lack of managerial skills among the Chinese (Wagner, 1990; Bjorkman, Lasserre and Ching, 1997; Bjorkman and Lu, 1997; Zhu, 1997). The existing literature leads to the conclusion that the Chinese are underdeveloped as managers and that expatriates will continue to be needed for a long time (Child, 1991; Hoon-Halbauer, 1996; Worm, 1997). However, several research questions proposed by Warner (1992) have not received much attention; such as, the differences between generations and the time dimension of human resource development (HRD). There is a lack of a detailed and in-depth analysis of the localization process in EMNCs operating in China. Specifically the question on the internalization of modern management values among the host-country nationals (HCNs) has not yet been directly addressed. A more comprehensive understanding of the particular circumstances in China will enable FIEs to make *planned* transformations towards localization, foreseeing the limitations and necessary adaptations to HRD structures and systems.

RESEARCH OBJECTIVE AND METHOD

Research Objective

The purpose of this preliminary investigation is to explore the evolving localization process, so as to draw insights from participants' observations of actual EMNC experiences and make appropriate recommendations. Hence, the main focus is on the broader concept of localization, rather than the narrower but more common interest on the training needs of HCNs in China (Warner, 1992; Borgonjon and Vanhonacker, 1993; Verburg, 1996). However, insofar as HRD is essential to and precedes localization in EMNCs, relevant training issues are also discussed.

The presentation follows the process of localization in five steps proposed above: (1) Intention to localize and strategy of implementation, (2) Identification and recruitment of high potential personnel, (3) Functional skills learning through formal training, (4) On-the-job training, and (5) Retention of competent local managers.

Research Method

The exploratory study was conducted in seven major European MNCs with substantial operations in China; specifically, Nokia, Ericsson, Hoechst, Siemens, Asea Brown Boveri (ABB), Novo Nordisk, and Danfoss. In these EMNCs, the number of employees worldwide ranges from 13,000 to 100,000.

Augmenting a review of earlier research, in-depth semi-structured interviews with *expatriate* human resource managers or directors of training centres of the seven EMNCs were conducted in Beijing during January 1999. In each EMNC, complementary interviews were done with a local Chinese manager who was under consideration as an expatriate replacement and had received training to that effect. HR managers were selected because the HR departments in the holding companies function as a general service centre for the training in subsidiaries which typically do not establish their own HRD units.

The interview was conducted in English, Mandarin or in a Scandinavian language, following the respondent's choice. Most of the interviews were conducted by one of the authors with a research assistant, recorded on audiotape, and transcribed. The data was organized thematically for the analysis of results.

RESULTS

Step One: Intention to Localize and Strategy of Implementation

The common view in the EMNCs was that expatriates are not only expensive, but also unreliable. The estimate by one respondent was that one out of five expatriates fails (leaving China within six months), considerably higher than the average worldwide rate of 6–7 per cent (Tung, 1998). Furthermore, lack of adjustment to the environment and cross-cultural misunderstandings lead to poor performance by many expatriates. A Chinese manager suggested that 80 per cent of expatriates should never have come to China.

For locals to assume the managerial responsibilities usually held by expatriates, the long-term process of attitudinal change has to occur, which is initiated only when HCN candidates change from a passive to an active stance. Furthermore the success of localization is determined by the active participation of expatriates who contribute their experiences and abilities, as well as by the nature of the organization. The HRD process requires that the expatriates are good mentors and the organization must empower HCNs towards the 'learning curve'.

The usual procedure among EMNCs is to select personnel for overseas assignments based on functional professionalism and management skills (McEnery and DesHarnais, 1990; Laabs, 1991; Bjorkman and Gertsen, 1993). But effective localization requires additional cross-cultural skills, particularly the ability to transfer expertise to local replacements. It should be noted that since the mid-1990s, *head offices* of some EMNCs were established in China, which have taken responsibility for strategic HRM planning for their subsidiaries. One of the tasks of the holding companies in China is the coordination of HRD activities towards future localization.

All the companies included in the study stated definitely that there was a clear intention to localize their management. However, most respondents expressed the reservation that localization is an ideal, as the firms lack concrete plans for its implementation. Even the large EMNCs did not have the necessary information to make such plans, which put more constraints on their localization efforts. There was a consensus that organizations suffered an inability to forecast market developments in China. The HR managers admitted that there was also little knowledge on the requirements of an effective HRD process to instil managerial skills among the local Chinese. The demands of localization are tremendous, because HCNs have to break away from the traditions of planned-economy socialism and learn how to apply modern Western managerial practices to an undeveloped Chinese market (Child, 1991; Warner, 1993; Selmer, 1998).

It was the shared view that *mid-term* business strategies could not be envisioned, because of continuous changes in market competition. Government interference alters the conditions on which competitive advantages are built, evidently a deliberate policy of the communist state. Since foreign enterprises are permitted in China mainly to act as conduits for modernization, only technologically dynamic firms can look forward to their relatively permanent presence. A lack of long-term business strategies implies that it is impossible for the EMNCs to have comprehensive HRD plans, as described by an HR manager.

An expatriate respondent described the difficulties faced by an EMNC that is unable to have a long-term business strategy or HRD plan for China:

> We have a problem in management, because we sent twenty very capable engineers on fifteen weeks' training at our factory in the US where they could learn normal working processes. This means that we now have twenty potential middle managers. This is a problem because in the next twenty years they will monopolize company management positions, because I don't think we will grow so fast that we will need 20 more mangers in the next few years. What shall we do with them? We talk about broader job descriptions, but that does not motivate the Chinese. They want to be managers, not generalists.

This company will have an overstock of functional managers, if the business does not develop as anticipated. On the other hand, in an organization which cannot develop enough managers the localization activities are essential, if the enterprise grows as originally estimated, because such managerial candidates would not be available elsewhere from the embryonic labour market in China. However, an optimum solution to this problem was achieved by ABB, as discussed in the case shown in Exhibit 11.1.

According to the respondents, general management positions are the most difficult to localize. Traditionally the Chinese emphasized technical competence and strong functional division of labour, combined with little delegation of decision-making power in the steep hierarchy of state-owned enterprises. So as to shift focus, EMNCs stress *softer* management skills like communication abilities and people knowledge, to encourage efficient interaction among the few well-educated local employees. In addition, although the organizational structures of EMNCs in China will become more hierarchical than is common in the West, the trend is towards a more inclusive leadership style with increased horizontal communication (Worm, 1997).

Evidently most EMNCs have underestimated the length of time it takes to localize management positions, which is now deemed to be at least 10 years in a large organization. The enormous expenses of maintaining expatriate manangement in China was also unexpected. As a result, the localization policies were vague, without specifying the annual rate of expatriate positions that should be replaced by locals. When asked on definite targets, most resepondents gave general statements, as follows:

> We want to localize when the time is right, because we do not assign people jobs that they are not qualified for. We have seen too many examples of companies wanting to localize from day one. The result was that they had to bring the expatriates back, due to declining product quality.

The HR managers were very aware that qualified local candidates are essential, to avoid serious disturbances in operations. The most frequently mentioned obstacle to localization was the HCNs' lack of experience. However, a few expatriates were more reflective; and one particularly deplored the lack of appreciation for cultural diversity:

> European managers want to hand over to successors who are a bit like themselves. The Chinese employees we promote have spent a lot of effort to learn from Westerners, to the extent that they perhaps even forget how to deal with local subordinates. Some local managers even try to look like foreigners in the way they dressed.

Previous studies have seldom discussed the topic, but the present findings indicated that the Chinese learn better from other Chinese than from expatriates. For historical reasons, the Chinese are not eager to be under the tutelage of Westerners. Also, language barriers are more serious in actuality than as evident from previous research (Worm, 1997; Sergeant and Frenkel, 1998; Wang, Zhang and Goodfellow, 1998).

Exhibit 11.1 Localization in Asea Brown Boveri (ABB)

With 7,000 employees, ABB was the largest company included in the present study of European multinational corporations (EMNCs) in China. However, it has comparatively the lowest number of expatriates with a ratio of 1:100 locals: specifically, there were 55 parent-country nationals (PCNs) and 35 third country nationals (TCNs). The company has a formalized action plan for localization referred to as the 'management localization process' (MLP), which is viewed as the key strategy for the company's growth in China. The stated purpose of MLP is to develop local managers who are aware of ABB's global needs and are responsive to specific demands of the Chinese market. The HR-manager emphasized that the MLP rationale is to enhance competitiveness, because local customers normally prefer to deal with local people, provided that they have the necessary skills to satisfy customers' needs. Needless to say, local managers are much more adept in the local language, culture, business practices and politics than expatriates can ever hope to be.

Since MLP intends not only to reduce the number of expatriates but also to ensure business success, the implementation should have a positive effect on attracting and retaining local talent. MLP ensures that the expatriate-successor plan is systematically implemented with specific targets that are evaluated quarterly and annually. Success in achieving targets determines the individual monetary bonus given to expatriates. In ABB localization is a business goal, in line with profit and market share.

As business results tend to be short-term, the company's holistic approach shifts the focus to more long-term and broader interests: as stated by the HR-manager of ABB, 'localizing the business is the same as localizing the people'. It is widely recognized by management that without the bonus incentive, many TCNs will have no interest in the localization process which would ultimately render themselves superfluous. It would not be suprising that TCNs may be reluctant to go back to their home country, since the expatriate living in the Chinese metropolis is becoming increasingly more comfortable (Antoun and Leong, 1995; Ness, 1996; Parry, 1997). A similar problem had earlier occurred in Hong Kong where ABB has been totally localized. Another obstacle to localization in China could be the objective of line managers to produce good 'bottom line results' in the short term, and therefore tend to give less priority to training and development of HCNs.

ABB policy states that PCN assignments in China should only be for 2–3 years. PCNs are discouraged from spending time on learning the Chinese language, and are expected instead to concentrate on the transfer of ABB experience to the local staff. Currently 70–80 HCNs per annum are sent abroad to gain international experience. However, it was still not known at the time of the study how many Chinese would be included in the corporate plan to train 600 managers in the period 1996–2000. Although corporate leadership would prefer all managers to be local by then, this is not possible because, in late 1998, only 132 high-potential candidates and 49 local expatriate-successor candidates had been identified. Between 1995 and 1998, the company sent 70 candidates to the China-Europe International Business School (CEIBS) in Shanghai. Another 40 trainees attended the ABB/MLP School which offers a tailored MBA-programme (with modules in Foundation of Management, Finance, Sales Management, International Trade, Supply Management, Production Management, HRM, Strategic Planning, General Knowledge about China, etc.). However, ABB China had only 10 candidates nominated for the newly started Asia Pacific Advanced Management Programme. These figures indicated that developing local managers is not only a matter of finding the talented, but also of enhancing the organization's capabilities for broad international training.

Step Two: Identification and Recruitment of High Potential Personnel

Earlier studies have shown that recruiting managers was the primary problem faced by EMNCs in the mid-1990s (Bjorkman, Laserre and Ching, 1997). Recruitment is still considered by many HRM expatriates in China as the critical decision that should not be left to others. Apart from the lack of managerial talents, recruitment is more important in China than in Western countries because of the difficulties in terminating employment.

Local managers are required to know a little about everything, which takes time to acquire. Most new educated recruits have university degrees in the technical fields or have work experiences limited to SOEs. The lack of skilled Chinese managers has led many EMNCs to recruit externally, especially among Overseas Chinese or preferably mainland Chinese returnees who were educated abroad, as shown by the quotation from an expatriate manager:

In the beginning all joint-venture general managers were from Germany. Now, 3–4 years later, we use many overseas Chinese mainly from Singapore and Taiwan. After 8–10 years, the locals will take over. In some joint ventures we immediately try to find overseas Chinese or returned Chinese students with working experience in the West for 5–6 years.

If they held a foreign passport and had a few years' working experience in the West, the returnees typically requested expatriate compensation, making them as expensive as expatriates. However the returnees were seen as more efficient than expatriates or Overseas Chinese, because they share the local mentality and language (dialect). Furthermore the mainland returnees exert strong influence on other locals, as living examples of the benefits and opportunities of foreign experience.

The present study found that EMNCs preferred employing the younger Chinese than those who had experienced the Cultural Revolution who are now between 40 and 50 years of age. The older generation was considered too old for the long training required and too conservative in taking initiatives. Young Chinese were seen as more open, more adaptable and more eager to learn.

In the 1980s, many joint ventures recruited managers from their Chinese partner. However, this practice had declined in the 1990s, because the candidates often did not have the qualifications or experiences needed in a market economy. Another reason was that the recruits from local organizations were mostly socialized in the organizational culture of the SOE, and were incapable of managing a modern profit-oriented firm.

From a long-term perspective, the most attractive recruits are recent graduates from the local universities. As students choose companies recommended by their professors, large EMNCs have been able to employ top students through direct personal contacts with prestigious academics. Cultivating personal relationships may not be worthwhile for EMNCs who hire only a few management trainees per year. Recruitment is now facilitated by on-campus 'career days' hosted by some universities. In 1998, 'career education and advisory offices' (similar to European university-recruitment centres) were established in many universities, particularly to assist EMNC employers. It has been estimated that 60–70 per cent of EMNCs which hire on an annual basis have formal relationships with universities, in one form or another (*China Hand*, 1998).

Some larger EMNCs offer scholarships to well-known universities, which at the same time promotes their corporate image. It has become increasingly important for companies in China to focus on image-building, as prestige and good reputation attract top students. Nowadays, Chinese students put a priority on career possibilities rather than the salary (Bjorkman, Laserre and Ching,

1997). The advantage of university recruitment is that graduates can be directly socialized into the corporate culture of the Western firms that typically emphasize managerial effectiveness and professionalism more than the SOEs. The disadvantage is that considerable investment is needed to develop the newcomers who have no business experience whatsoever.

Foreign and Chinese executive-search firms are also used by the EMNCs, especially for recruits in finance and human resources. Headhunters are found mainly in the southern part of China, but are expanding lately in the Shanghai area. Most respondents expressed little trust in such consultants, who tend to poach as many managers from a company as they offer to it, since there is such a small pool of qualified candidates.

An alternative route for recruitment is through recommendations or personal connections. Managers found through the network of contacts have proved to be more loyal, showing a lower propensity to change employment. People recommended by government officials will also often bring along strong connections with the local government, to the benefit of the company. A respondent described the process as follows:

> We recruit through newspapers and recommendations from employees and government authorities. We base our selection on job descriptions containing qualification criteria and the principle of accountability. The HR-department interviews all for the general aspects. For the operational aspects it is the line manager, if he requested the position; and he decides ultimately. Sometimes we refuse people recommended by the authorities.

Mass media are also used for recruitment, as in the West. However advertisements bring in a flood of 'useless' resumés, the amount relative to the company's reputation and the newspaper's circulation. Apparently, many companies are shifting from countrywide publications (e.g., *China Daily*) to trade and general-interest publications, where advertisement rates are cheaper. Most of the mass media (including television) have multi-tier fee structures in which foreign companies pay more than local companies; for example, FIEs can be charged up to 60,000 yuan for a half-page advertisement.

'Talent markets' have opened in the larger cities of China, as an embryonic stage in the development of a free labour market. Several respondents said that they had used such venues, mainly to recruit rank-and-file positions. Despite the large audience, these markets fail to attract managerial talent. However, the talent markets give foreign companies a wide exposure to promote the image of the company in the general public, which eventually encourages able candidates to consider employment.

The main selection method seems to be personal interviews, as resumés and references are not yet common but are becoming more prevalent. A few companies are experimenting with psychological tests hesitantly, as the inventories may not be culture-free. A respondent summarized the selection procedure:

We are starting with psychological tests, partly for selection and partly to find out whether an employee has the capabilities to reach a certain level. We have a number of psychologists working around the country. The selection interview consists of 2–3 people; for example, the line manger, the HR manager, and maybe an external consultant. The line managers are not trained in conducting interviews, but learn little by little. After all, how many mistakes can one line manager do?

In summary, most of the larger EMNCs depend on in-house recruitment of key local managers (McEllister, 1998). In the earlier planned economy, Chinese officials determined job opportunities for young graduates who had good connections. The EMNCs have shown considerable adaptation to Chinese circumstances in the present market economy, although the recruitment and selection procedures are moving in the direction of Western practices.

Step Three: Functional Skills Learning Through Formal Training

There was a strong consensus among the respondents that comprehensive training is a precondition for localization. It was observed that the young Chinese are highly motivated to participate in management training which takes place both outside and inside China. Postgraduate-degree holders are respected in the status-oriented society much more than in the egalitarian West, leading one young manager to state bluntly: Capabilities without degrees are unsatisfactory. We Chinese respect degree holders very much. They have a high status. It is also easier to get a job with an MBA-degree. The market prefer people with an MBA degree.

Training Outside China

All the EMNCs had assigned staff abroad, but *on-the-job training* methods varied considerably. Most EMNCs conducted the training in a subsidiary outside China, if not at the headquarters of the parent company. Large EMNCS also send a few employees to Western universities, mainly top managers who are sent to business schools. The objectives for the overseas training are usually to familiarize them with Western business practices and socialize them to the corporate culture.

The medium-sized EMNCs had shorter periods (e.g., three months) for overseaas training at the headquarters, with a supplementary visit to a subsidiary in another country. In the larger companies, the predominantly young Chinese are sent abroad for 2–3 years. Typically the trainees were rotated in different functional departments, to become generalists.

In a few of the EMNCs, families accompanied some trainees; however, the general trend is that HCNs were expatriated alone, even those who are married. Several of the Chinese respondents who had been sent abroad spoke of their loneliness during expatriation. Literature on expatriate managers has extensively discussed 'the spouse problem' and concluded that the presence of the family abroad can make the expatriate more effective (Black and Stephens, 1989; Kauppinen, 1994; Selmer, Ebrahimi and Li, 2000). Apart from the cheaper cost, it is not clear *why* EMNCs prefer to send Chinese trainees alone. A surmize is that the Chinese manager is sent abroad solely for training purposes, unlike European expatriates who are expected to safeguard the performance of the organization (Edstrom and Galbraith, 1977; Torbiorn, 1982; Brewster, 1991).

According to the HCN respondents who had experienced training outside China, the main advantage was that they learned how things were done in other countries, to better understand the requirements of the PCNs. Moreover, living abroad made them more at ease in the company of foreigners. The expatriates also emphasized the motivational aspect of sending Chinese overseas, as travel is highly desired by the younger generation. The disadvantage of the foreign experience is that conditions in a Western consumerism society and those in China's undeveloped market are very different.

On the whole, HCNs were strongly aware that managerial responsibilities in China are much more cumbersome than in the West. They believed that there will be complex issues involved when they replace the expatriates and manage the firm by themselves. The long-term implication is that high-flyers may prefer to leave China or that more of the operations in China will be outsourced as the service sector develops.

Training Inside China

Off-the-job training in China is offered by many different institutions in China. The two-year MBA-course at the China-Europe International Business School (CEIBS) in Shanghai is the programme most frequently cited by the respondents. The postgraduate degree from CEIBS is considered the most prestigious (and the most expensive) in China, because it is taught exclusively by foreign teachers and includes a three-month internship in a company abroad.

Among the Chinese respondents, there was only one graduate from CEIBS. She emphasized that, due to the many topics covered during the two-year programme, she now knew something about fields other than her own. As an HR manager, she said that the general knowledge acquired from her MBA had helped her to provide better advice to subsidiary managers.

In comparison to other experimental programmes in management education operated by foreigners in China, the CEIBS programme appears comparatively successful (Warner, 1992). However, it is most relevant for people in general management or in positions where broad, but not in-depth, knowledge of different aspects of management is required. One of the HR-managers mentioned that his company temporarily had stopped sending employees to CEIBS, because the modules were too theoretical and too general.

Prestigious local universities have also started offering MBA courses recently, with or without a partnership with a foreign business school; e.g., Peking University and Qinghua University in Beijing, as well as Jiaotong University and Fudan University in Shanghai. Apparently, to control the development of foreign influence on education in China, the Ministry allows only one joint foreign programme in each Chinese university. It has been observed that most Chinese are not keen to learn about China from a foreigner (Wang, Zhang and Goodfellow, 1998). Evidently the key to the future, Western and Chinese professors as co-teachers facilitated the integration of Western theoretical and empirical knowledge with the peculiar circumstances of the China market. Although the MBA students expressed interest in learning Western management theory, they realized that most of their professional lives will be in China, which makes it important that the joint MBA programmes are recognized by the Chinese Ministry of Education.

Private companies offering management training are mushrooming in China, many of them with fancy names, like 'I Will Not Complain'. Most EMNCs engage the services of such organizations, in one way or another. The flexibility in the programmes given by these companies is considered appealing.

Currently, it is difficult to separate off-company from in-company training. Some EMNCs use management-training firms only to provide the physical facilities, while EMNC insiders teach the courses. The use of local companies by EMNCs indicates an increasing cooperation between local and foreign institutions in training programmes, in line with the joint Chinese–foreign MBA programmes.

With reference to *in-company training*, all interviewed EMNCs offered one-day courses to part-time MBA-programmes. Siemens has established a training centre that offers shorter courses also to other, smaller European firms. Ericsson is offering an MBA programme free of charge to their staff and selected customers, which is taught by foreign and Chinese co-trainers. Adapted to the telecommunications industry, the modules are taught within Ericsson premises and at Chinese or foreign universities. Foreign institutions are not allowed to run MBA programmes in China without a Chinese partner university.

The training courses in China are more basic than is typical in more developed industrial societies. The topics include people skills, decision-making skills, time management, PC skills, English, TQM and similar practical subjects. Salesmanship is a popular course because most salespeople in China are engineers who do not have previous training in negotiation techniques. As noted before, current training programmes focus on 'soft' management skills simply because the locals had not been exposed to such topics before the introduction of the market economy.

The overall trend in designing off-the-job in-company training is the use of company-specific materials, thereby making the courses more directly relevant for actual work situations. Internalization of the training programmes requires that external trainers are invited to teach, but their participation takes place in close coordination with insiders. An additional reason for adapting the training content to the specific organizations is to render the materials useless in other job contexts and hence to reduce job-hopping.

While it is possible for the larger EMNCs to internalize training design, medium-sized companies faced difficulties in the process of course adaptation. In-house training of employees in the smaller companies is of lower quality, often taught only by one trainer. Consequently the preference is to outsource off-the job training to training centres of larger EMNCs like the Siemens Management Institute (Exhibit 11.2) or to local companies, depending on the topic and level of teaching required.

Exhibit 11.2 Siemens Management Institute

Siemens Management Institute is offering management programmes for their own employees as well as for other companies. Siemens trains people who are between 25 and 40 years old. The programmes combine workshops, computer-based learning and action learning. Action learning consists of two core objectives: firstly, to bring learning back to the work-place through a student project on real-life problems; and secondly, to enable the trainees to learn from each other by working in teams. Therefore the participants improve their team-building skills and learn more about their company.

Action learning is especially appropriate for Chinese managers who generally are more practical in orientation and seldom motivated for theoretical studies. The learning cycle consists of four stages: Experience, Reflection, Generalization and Testing. The central importance of this method is the testing of recommendations, which is not usually possible in more theoretical programmes.

Siemens is internally offering two action learning programmes on a part-time basis, each of a duration of 12 months. The target participants of the first course are high-potential employees in preparation for their first managerial tasks. The other programme is for section managers being groomed for higher managerial positions. Both programmes start with an introduction to programme objectives, followed by team-building exercises. The participants are then assigned to three months of self-study, based on materials available on Siemens' intranet. Afterwards the participants meet in a workshop, to deepen knowledge and social competence. A senior manager who acts as a coach announces the project topics and members. A second workshop is held after 3–4 months, where the teams present their project results. The last quarter of the programme is spent on project completion. The final project report is published on the intra-net, to disseminate the knowledge throughout the Siemens organization.

The projects are typically either a familiar task in an unfamiliar department or the other way around. However, both task and setting may be unfamiliar to some members of a team; for example, managers from different joint ventures worked on a project on reducing inventory in a joint venture. The project must investigate a real problem, so that specific actions can be recommended. An appropriate problem for a project should not be trivial or insoluble.

The action learning projects can delve into various problems relevant to the course content; e.g., marketing issues, formalizing communications The basic requirement is that the economic result of the implementation must be measurable. According the Director of Siemens Management Institute, students' suggestions have led to cost savings from 1000 yuan to several million yuan. The best grades were awarded to the project teams whose recommended actions had the most savings for their companies.

Step Four: On-the-Job Training

On-the-job training is pervasive in all companies, but most activities are rather informal. A respondent described the trends: 'People development is a continuous process. It is like TQM – you do not expect to see short-term results. The real skills have to come out of working experience. The best training programme is their daily work.'

It was clear from the interviews that the expatriate mentors' skills in successfully imparting their expertise are crucial for developing Chinese managers. Nevertheless one manager deplored the difficulty of meeting such a requirement:

> Everybody will tell you that expatriates are sent here mostly as trainers, but in reality they are sent to do the job. Many companies do not even have a model for core competencies of expatriate managers. So when a business unit is looking for a manager they are looking for technical skills only and not communication skills, teaching skills or adaptability.

On the whole, the role of the expatriates in on-the-job training is not clear, as it was found that the majority of the mentors were local Chinese. Apparently, training and communication skills are given more priority among the Chinese managers who had been on overseas assignment at the headquarters. These managers were strongly aware that they were expected to transfer skills learned overseas to other local employees. One corporation usually assigned a mentor to each new recruit, but the practice was not formalized:

> We have a mentoring system, but only for key candidates, not for everybody. Sometimes the mentor can be your manager. Generally, after a candidate is identified as having high potential, he or she will be given projects that involve more responsibilities, so that he or she gets experiences in working with their boss.

Job-rotation is a well-known method in management development, but it is difficult to implement in the dynamic business environment in China. The following description of 'shadowing' is representative of the views common among the EMNCs:

> Job rotation is the weak area. We do not rotate people enough. Due to rapid growth of our business, we need the people to do the job; and we do

provide at least some rotating opportunities, but not enough. In general people are interested in being rotated. Job-rotation within the 'family' makes their lives and jobs more interesting. For family reasons, some agree to rotation only in the Beijing area.

An important but seldom discussed issue is the extent to which magement development in China is determined by business development. Furthermore, the types of training activities are blurred when implemented. Management training inside and outside China may take place in the same programme. Off-the-job training is often short-term and conducted at training centres, so that the participants can go back to their offices in the evening. Undisturbed participation in courses is not possible because of the comparatively high degree of centralization, whereby work grinds to a halt when the responsible manager is not available.

Despite their extended stay in a foreign country, the Chinese respondents gave the impression that they were somewhat critical of foreign ways. None-theless, a European manager noted that after 1–2 years of expatriation, the communication style of the HCNs changed substantially. It was also observed that the local Chinese who had been trained at headquarters showed more respect for their subordinates upon their return to China.

Another important issue in localization is the length of time required for a young Chinese to internalize management theories to a degree that he can apply his knowledge without supervision. An expatriate respondent recalled the following incident of a chef engineer who had been promoted to section head:

Things started deteriorating on the same day the expatriate left. The prod-uct quality became substandard, the equipment was not maintained, and the factory was not kept clean. He had not understood our message. It had really not been absorbed, although he was one of those who had received most training. Six months in Scandinavia was too short.

The aforementioned incident represents a common experience in most EMNCs: heavy investment in training is followed by an immediate promotion, resulting in unsatisfactory performance. Evidently it takes a longer time than anticipated to develop new managers. Furthermore, it is difficult to discover if and when the Chinese fully internalize managerial techniques, as they prefer indirect and implicit communication. Leaving things unsaid gives room for 'free advance and retreat', as expressed in a popular Chinese saying (Gao, Ting-Toomey and Gudykunst, 1996; Gao, 1998). Earlier studies have shown the costs of expatriate failure (Zeira and Banai, 1984; Mendenhall and Odou, 1988;

Naumann, 1992), but an incompetent local will lose face if an expatriate has to be reinstated. Such a demotivating experience could make Chinese managers reluctant to take responsibility, thereby prolonging the managerial development process.

Step Five: Retention of Competent Local Managers

Due to the high resource-allocation to HRD in China, EMNCs are obviously concerned about the retention of local managers within the company. Job-hopping is a problem often mentioned both by practitioners and academics (Bjorkman and Lu, in press; McEllister, 1998) as a natural outcome of the dearth of managerial talent. However, the turnover rate decreased from 25–30 per cent in 1994 to around 13 per cent in 1998 (Hooydonk, 1999). The trend will probably continue during the Asian crisis, due to the increase in job insecurity and the decrease of FDI (by about one-third, from US\$ 45 billion in 1998 to US\$ 30 billion in 1999) (*Business Week*, 22 February 1999). On the average, the job-hoppers have lower salaries, as compared with those who stayed with their companies (Hooydonk, 1999) and were less often promoted to higher positions. Trust in local managers running the China operations is extremely important to parent corporations (McEllister, 1998).

Salaries of HCNs went up rapidly in China during the last half of the 1990s, to the extent that a few country managers earn 40,000–50,000 yuan (US\$ 4,800–6,000) per month. However, the managers from all the seven EMNCs stated that their particular organizations were not at the top-end of executive salaries. It was commonly observed that high remuneration was not enough to retain Chinese high-flyers, because the material incentives are becoming less important to the truly talented locals. Current findings showed that, among the factors encouraging retention of managers, salary was the least important after career opportunities, training opportunities, good corporate reputation, and a good boss (Hooydonk, 1999).

In the present study, most HR managers had the opinion that job-hopping was no longer a problem for their companies. Nonetheless one EMNC required contracts which stipulated that the trainee will work for the company five years after returning from overseas training, which was endorsed by local government authorities. The HCN is required to have a guarantor who will reimburse the training costs, if he or she should resign within the period. The formality of such an arrangement suggests that job-hopping is still a central concern. On the other hand, one of the expatriate managers took the view that job-hoppers are prone to leaving the company and lag behind in salary increases, because they show poor performance:

Job-hopping is a natural process in a developing country. Job-hopping is not bad for EMNCs. Job-hopping is a great thing because it puts a lot of discipline on the management. Basically, what the employees tell us is that if we do not treat them well and provide them with a good career path, they will leave. The company has to discipline itself to have good HR policies, good ways of taking care of people. We have to do things on a fair basis, or otherwise people will leave. Some people leave, let them leave. Good people want to stay. People know whether they are on the top 100 or top 200 list. It is 20 per cent of the people that are making the difference between companies. We should not keep everyone.

Clear, specific communication about career tracks is considered essential for retaining and motivating the local managers. It was the common practice in most EMNCs that during the annual performance review each HCN was told of the specific position he or she was expected to be promoted to within a specific period. Furthermore, the HR managers meticulously kept track of candidates' profiles and development needs. The HRD plans specified the possible future jobs and the specific actions for each individual, coinciding with overall strategy of the EMNC headquarters.

CONCLUSIONS AND RECOMMENDATIONS

To conclude, a few key findings are highlighted in the following discussion. First, there has been little success in localization, despite strong awareness that external stakeholders are more efficiently and effectively handled by HCNs than by expatriates. EMNCs with long experience in China are hesitant to make specific corporate targets for expatriate–local ratios, due to lack of transparency of government policies and lack of knowledge about future business development in China. However, all EMNCS had general HRD plans for individual candidates for expatriate succession, which monitored and facilitated an individual's career progression.

Second, with the dearth of experienced managers among the locals, EMNCs have little recourse but to depend on internal promotion, which made recruitment and selection highly central to corporate development. The embryonic labour market was explored through university recruitment, newspaper ads, talent markets, executive search firms and headhunters.

Third, there was a widespread realization that the most important precondition for localization is an intensive HRD programme. Local and overseas training activities were integrated; and on-the-job training and off-the-job training were conducted at the same time. The objective was evidently to develop a new type of international manager of Chinese origin, who are up-to-date both on business practices and on the internal and external business environment. If localization succeeds, such managers will comprise a crucial competitive advantage for EMNCs in China.

Fourth, there was a trend to internalize training within the company, although joint Chinese–Western programmes for the MBA degree are popular among HCNs. Based on the organizations' familiarity with local operating conditions, EMNCs prefer to custom-design training programmes to meet their specific needs. Training activities that are conducted by and within the company also prevent trainees from privately capitalizing on the HRD investment by job-hopping.

Fifth, although increasing rapidly, high salaries were not enough to retain promising managerial trainees. Career progression and training opportunities are the two most important factors which motivate HCN managers to stay with their companies; and salary was only of fifth importance.

Sixth, most EMNCs have overestimated the speed at which localization can take place. Although the young Chinese generation were keen to learn Western management, it will take a decade or two before locals can replace expatriate managers in most China operations. The respondents were uncertain as to what extent managerial capabilities have been developed among Chinese managers. To learn Western management theory and practices as well as become an effective manager with Chinese characteristics are two separate things. The main stumbling block is that the typical Chinese are not socialized to take the initiative. It takes much time for HCNs to utilize their new knowledge within the particular conditions of the Chinese society and economy.

Based on our findings, what are the recommendations for EMNCs in China? First there are irreplaceable benefits from introducing localization in a strategic manner, since defined HRD plans prove to be more effective. A localization programme would require more information on the required improvements on modes of instruction and on the optimum time period for individual candidates to learn the necessary skills. Although the young Chinese are different from their elders, the HRD plan should be guided by an awareness of the essential characteristics of the Chinese culture; for example, an understanding of Chinese status-orientation would provide insights on the structure and design of training activities. Furthermore, strategic planning for localization has to consider up-to-date information on the Chinese market and government.

As internal promotion is predominant, the selection process can be assisted by an assessment centre. Psychometric evaluation is helpful in compiling a comprehensive profile of an individual candidate, especially if there are long-term plans for career progression. However, despite the popularity of psychological testing, the HRD programme should use only inventories that are culture-free or at least adaptable to the Chinese context.

In recent years, modern management training has spread with tremendeous speed in China. Currently there is a substantial pool of young people holding or studying for a MBA degree, but most of them are without good business experience. In this situation, action learning seems to be an appropriate method for company-sponsored management development, because it gives trainees real-life working experiences and assists team-building. Furthermore, candidates with high potential should be expatriated to the company headquarters for an extended period, to familiarize themselves with Western business practices.

For the promising candidates for expatriate replacements, training opportunities and gradual promotion based on detailed career paths are stronger motivators than remuneration. There should be more focus on the individual characteristics of the HCNs, determining to what extent the ideal local manager should resemble European expatriates. The notion of 'effective EMNC managers with Chinese characteristics' has not been developed yet into an applicable concept. There seems to be an overly strong focus on Chinese youngsters that behave like Westerners, without due regard for their abilities to manage and motivate Chinese employees.

Both the external and internal flow of communication should be improved. In most EMNCs, interdepartmental communication is weak and difficult to implement, since the Chinese are comfortable with hierarchical communication (Worm, 1997). On the one hand, expatriates should be trained in understanding indirect modes of communication. On the other, the Chinese should be trained in communicating more explicitly.

To enhance management localization and thereby reduce the number of expensive expatriates, HRD should be a critical business issue that is completely integrated with other objectives. HRD plans should coincide with the business development plans in China, in order to facilitate the successful transfer of knowledge from expatriates to locals. To motivate participation in localization efforts, expatriates' compensation could be adjusted according to their mentoring abilities and HRD results; and hereby, the selection criteria for a China assignment should be adapted accordingly.

Finally, relevant and comprehensive information on the functioning of the Chinese market and its development is crucial for any localization programme. Since the market economy in China is undeveloped, most EMNCs are not able to make even rough estimates of their China business for the next five years. Nonetheless, in the new millenium, more mid-term or, when possible, long-term strategic business planning has to be applied in China operations, so as to secure long-term success in the midst of tremendous changes.

References

Antoun, R. and Leong, E. (1995) 'Housing in China', *Benefits & Compensation International*, 25(2), pp. 20–3.

Bjorkman, I. and Gertsen, M. (1993) 'Selecting and Training Scandinavian Expatriates: Determinants of Corporate Practice', *Scandinavian Journal of Management*, 9(2), pp. 145–64.

Bjorkman, I. and Lu, Y. (1997) 'Human Resource Management Practices in Foreign Invested Enterprises in China: What Has Been Learned?', in S. Stewart (ed.), *Advances in Chinese Industrial Studies*, vol. IV, pp. 155–72.

Bjorkman, I. and Lu, Y. (1999) 'The Management of Human Resources in Chinese–Western Joint Ventures – Sino-Scandinavian Business Cooperation in Cross-Cultural Settings', *Journal of World Business*, 34(3), pp. 306–24.

Bjorkman, I., Lassere, P. and Ching, P.-S. (1997) *Developing Managerial Resources in China* (Hong Kong: Financial Times).

Black, J. S. and Stephens, G. K. (1989) 'The Influence of the Spouse on American Expatriate Adjustment and Intent to Stay in Pacific Rim Overseas Assignments', *Journal of Management*, 15(4), pp. 529–44.

Borgonjon, J. and Vanhonacker, W. (1993) 'Management Training and Education in the People's Republic of China', *Euro-Asia Centre Research Series*, 18.

Brewster, C. (1991) *The Management of Expatriates* (London: Kogan Page).

Child, J. (1991) 'A Foreign Perspective on the Management of People in China', *International Journal of Human Resource Management*, 8(5), pp. 93–107.

China Hand (July 1998) Economist Intelligence Unit Limited, Hong Kong.

Edstrom, A. and Galbraith, J. (1977) 'Transfer of Managers as a Coordination and Control Strategy', *Adminstrative Science Quarterly*, 22, pp. 248–63.

Gao, G. (1998) '"Don't Take My Word For It" – Understanding Chinese Speaking Practices', *International Journal of Intercultural Relations*, 22(2), pp. 163–86.

Gao, G., Ting-Toomey, S. and Gudykunst, W. B. (1996) 'Chinese Communication Processes', in M. H. Bond (ed.), *Handbook of Chinese Psychology* (Hong Kong: Oxford University Press) pp. 280–93.

Hanisch, A. (1998) *Acquiring Managerial Excellence through Action Learning – Management Education at Siemens Management Institute in Beijing*, Proceedings of the Sixth Conference of International Human Resource Management. University of Paderborn, June 22–25.

Hoon-Halbauer, S. K. (1996) *Management of Sino-Foreign Joint Ventures* (Lund: Lund University Press).

Hooydonk, S. (1999) Interviewed at Nokia Learning Centre in Beijing in January. Former official at CEIBS.

Kauppinen, M. (1994) *Antecedents of Expatriate Adjustment: A Study of Finnish Managers in the United States* (Helsinki: Helsinki School of Economics Press).

Laabs, J. J. (1991) 'The Global Talent Search', *Personnel Journal*, 70(8), pp. 38–44.

Lindsey, C. and Dempsey, B. (1985) 'Experiences in Training Chinese Business People to Use U.S. Management Techniques', *Journal of Applied Behavioral Science*, 21(1), pp. 65–78.

Maddison, A. (1998) *Chinese Economic Performance in the Long Run* (Paris: Development Centre OECD).

McEllister, R. (1998) 'Recruitment and Retention of Managerial Staff in China', in J. Selmer (ed.), *International Management in China: Cross-Cultural Issues* (London: Routledge), pp. 98–114.

McEnery, J. and DesHarnais, G. (1990) 'Culture Shock', *Training and Development Journal*, 44(4), pp. 43–7.

Mendenhall, M. and Oddou, G. (1988) 'The Overseas Assignment: A Practical Look', *Business Horizons*, Sept.–Oct., pp. 78–84.

Naumann, E. (1992) 'A Conceptual Model of Expatriate Turnover', *Journal of International Business Studies*, 23(1), pp. 61–80.

Ness, A. (1996) 'No Longer a Hardship Post', *China Business Review*, 23(4), pp. 40–5.

Parry, J. (1997) 'Schooling Options Open Up For Expat Kids in Town', *China STAFF*, pp. 12–16.

Selmer, J. (1998) 'Conclusions: Current Issues and Emerging Trends', in J. Selmer (ed.), *International Management in China: Cross-Cultural Issues* (London: Routledge).

Selmer, J. (1999) 'Culture Shock in China? Adjustment Pattern of Expatriate Buiness Managers', *International Business Review*, 8, pp. 515–34.

Selmer, J., Ebrahimi, B. P. and Li, M. (2000) 'Personal Characteristics and Adjustment of Chinese Mainland Business Expatriates in Hong Kong', *International Journal of Human Resource Management*, 11(2), pp. 237–50.

Sergeant, A. and Frenkel, S. (1998) 'Managing People in China: Perceptions of Expatriate Managers', *Journal of World Business*, 33(1), pp. 17–34.

Thompson, G.(ed.) (1998) *Economic Dymanism in the Asia Pacific* (London: Routledge).

Torbiorn, I. (1982) *Living Abroad: Personal Adjustment and Personnel Policy in the Overseas Setting* (New York: John Wiley).

Tung, R. (1998) 'American Expatriates Abroad: From Neophytes to Cosmopolitans', *Journal of World Business*, 33(2), pp. 125–44.

Verburg, R. (1996) 'Developing HRM in Foreign–Chinese Joint Ventures', *European Management Journal*, 14(5), pp. 518–25.

Wagner, C. (1990) 'A Survey of Sino-American Joint Ventures: Problems and Outlook for Solutions', *East Asian Executive Reports*, March.

Wang, Y., Zhang, X. and Goodfellow, R. (1998) *Business Culture in China* (Singapore: Butterworth-Heinemann Asia).

Warner, M. (1992) *How Chinese Managers Learn: Management and Industrial Training in the PRC* (London: Macmillan Press).

Warner, M. (1993) 'Human Resource Management "with Chinese Characteristics"?', *International Journal of Human Resource Management*, 4(1), pp. 45–65.

Worm V. (1997) *Vikings and Mandarins: Sino-Scandinavian Business Cooperation in Cross-Cultural Settings* (Copenhagen: Copenhagen Business School Press).

Zeira, Y. and Banai, M. (1984) 'Present and Desired Methods of Selecting Expatriate Managers for International Assignments', *Personnel Review*, 13(3), pp. 29–35.

Zhu, C. (1997) 'Human Resource development in China during the Transition to a New Economic System', *Asia Pacific Journal of Human Resources*, 35(3), pp. 19–44.

12 Management of Human Resources in Joint Ventures in China

Brigitte Charles-Pauvers

INTRODUCTION

Under the present economic reforms, management practices in Chinese companies are being greatly affected by rapid changes (socio-economic, technological and business environment). Considering their impact on the strategic human resource development in China, four main changes have been observed: structural changes in the state-owned enterprises and market economy toward decentralization and market orientation; social changes in value orientation from collectivist values to individualistic ones; organizational changes in personnel management practice from one-way assigned jobs to the two-way-choice labour market; and cultural changes in management patterns from domestic orientation to international management orientation (Wang and Mobley, 1999). The rapid development of international joint ventures has called for the strengthening of the cross-cultural and strategic functions in Chinese management. By the end of 1998, there were more than 320,000 Sino-foreign joint ventures in China.

Considering such a context, the management of human resources is becoming the main focus of the coming battle for performance and efficiency. Clark *et al.* (1999) reviewed the published human resource management research works, noticing their increasing number in the late 1970s. More precisely, the Chinese employees who belong to core positions are very difficult to keep in the companies. Nevertheless, their stability is absolutely required to develop a corporate culture and adapt their competency and ability to the company. So, we need to examine work-related attitudes and behaviours and to compare them across different types of companies (state-owned, private, collective) and nationality of joint ventures. We have a particular interest in French expatriates and Chinese employees, in French–Chinese joint ventures (JVs).

Moreover, most management concepts and work-related attitudes and behaviours have been tested mainly in Western countries, especially in North America. Yet, the cultural differences between North American, European, and, to a larger extent, Asian contexts have to be taken into account, to avoid the parochial dinosaur (Boyacigiller and Adler, 1991).

Organizational commitment has given rise to a mass of studies, mainly in North America (Allen and Meyer, 1996; Mathieu and Zajac, 1990; Morrow, 1993). It is nowadays unanimously defined as the strength of an individual's identification with a given organization (Morrow, 1993). Leaving out any managerial apology, it can serve as an essential basis for the efficiency of a company, relying more and more on the autonomy and skills of its personnel. Very few studies have examined this construct in China (cf. Charles-Pauvers and Urbain, 1999, Hui and Luk, in Berry 1997). Verburg (1996) underlines the lack of committed workforce; Campbell and Yee (1991) propose a relationship management model, requiring high levels of commitment and trust.

Since organizational commitment has been mainly studied in the USA, the related measurement scales were tested in this cultural context. Therefore, the validity of these measures needs to be assessed before research studies can be replicated elsewhere.

Related to Chinese employees' work attitudes and behaviours, the aim of this chapter is to test the cross-cultural validity of the organizational commitment scales, to examine organizational commitment profiles of Chinese employees working, on the one hand, in state-owned companies (SOEs), and on the other hand, in French–Chinese joint-ventures (JVs).

To address these issues, the concept and measurement scales of organizational commitment are reviewed, as well as the questions related to cross-cultural validation. Furthermore, this contribution is illustrated by a study carried out in French–Chinese joint-ventures (JVs) and state-owned enterprises (SOEs) allowing practical conclusions pertaining to Human Resource Management, especially in JVs.

ORGANIZATIONAL COMMITMENT: CONTENT, MEASURES AND CROSS-CULTURAL VALIDATION

The validation of measurement scales in cross-cultural contexts requires the identification of the contents of the concepts under consideration, the characteristics of the instruments used, and the questions related to cross-cultural validation. The interest of the concept depends on its links with antecedents and consequences.

Organizational Commitment

Organizational commitment has been largely studied in North America. Organizational commitment is one major commitment of a larger concept: the work commitment. For example, in the literature, Morrow (1993) discussed four main objects of commitment: job involvement (the degree of daily absorption that an individual experiences in work activity), professional/ career (the importance of one's occupation), work ethic endorsement (the importance of work itself), and organizational commitment (employee dedication to an organization).

Organizational commitment has been the most studied of these different components. Whatever the past debate about its definition, Mowday *et al.* (1979) is consensual: 'the relative strength of an individual's identification with and involvement in a particular organization' (p. 226). Meyer and Allen consider it as 'a psychological state that characterizes the employee's relationship with the organization and has implications for the decision to continue membership in the organization' (1997, p. 11). This definition reflects a two- or three-dimensional concept, as proposed by Meyer and Allen: affective, continuance, and normative components. Most researchers agree with its multidimensional conceptualization: affective, continuance, and to a lesser extent, normative. Yet, Meyer and Allen (1997) distinguish the normative component, originally created by Wiener (1982), reflecting a feeling of obligation to continue employment. For them, employees with a high level of normative commitment feel that they ought to remain in the organization. This component is the very latest arrival (Allen and Meyer, 1990) but the reliability of the measurement scale is very low. Furthermore, the correlation between the affective component and the normative one is very high, showing a large overlap. These results let Morrow (1993) conclude that 'the future of the normative component is uncertain at best' (p. 106). We follow suit and will only consider the affective and continuance components in this study. Among them, the affective component has been the most widely studied. Its conceptualization was contributed by Mowday *et al.* (1979). Three factors characterize it:

- a strong belief in and acceptance of goals and values of the organization,
- a willingness to make considerable efforts for the benefit of the organization,
- a high desire to remain a member of the organization.

Continuance commitment, as it has recently been named by Allen and Meyer (1990), known as cognitive and calculative, has been studied according to

Becker's side-bet theory (1960); Becker defines it as a 'consistent line of activity', based on the person's recognition of the 'costs' (or lost side-bets) associated with discontinuing the activity. For their part, Allen and Meyer (1996) define it as a perceived cost associated with leaving and consider it as a psychological state.

For these authors, the organizational commitment refers to an attitude toward the organization, including at least two dimensions. Some other definitions are focused on commitment-related behaviours (e.g., Staw, 1974). Allen and Meyer have asked the question related to the nature of the organizational commitment for a long time and clearly (Allen and Meyer, 1984). As noted by the authors, such commitment often encompasses an exchange relationship in which individuals attach themselves to the organization in return for certain rewards or payments from the organization. Many researchers share the attitudinal nature of commitment.

In this research, we adopt Allen and Meyer's position. Nevertheless, we think that the continuance commitment concept needs to be more clearly defined. Morrow (1993) underlines that their position includes the perceived losses associated with terminating an organization membership and the perceived ease of movement from one organization to another.

The Affective and Continuance Component of the Organizational Component: Measures

The affective component has been mainly measured using the Organizational Commitment Questionnaire (OCQ in short), proposed by Mowday *et al.* The authors mention that two forms can be used: a comprehensive one (OCQ, 15 items) and a short one (OCQP, 9 items). Curry *et al.* (1986), Reichers *et al.* (1985), Angle and Lawson (1993), McElroy *et al.* (1995), and Charles-Pauvers (1996) use the short form and confirm its high validity. The Allen and Meyer's Affective Commitment Scale (ACS) provides a good alternative to OCQ. All researchers indicate that OCQ and ACS are highly correlated (Allen and Meyer, 1996; Dunham *et al.*, 1994; Ko *et al.*, 1997). Considering OCQ's excellent psychometric properties, we assume that these two scales are equivalent and consequently prefer to choose the OCQP, in its short form (9 items).

Much controversy has emerged from the difficulties in the operationalization of the continuance component. Allen and Meyer (1996) were instrumental in reviving the interest in it, by proving that the difficulties do not lie in the conceptualization but in the measure; they have proposed the continuance commitment scale as one part of the three-component scale. But other researchers underline the fact that the original one-factor continuance commitment scale can be two-dimensional, which then entails some methodological and conceptual difficulties (Allen and Meyer, 1996; Dunham *et al.*, 1994; Meyer *et al.*, 1989; McGee and Ford, 1987; Somers, 1993). Generally speaking, the two dimensions are: the magnitude and/or the number of sidebets that an individual makes, and the lack of perceived alternatives to work. McGee and Ford (1987) suggested that the continuance measurement scale could be bi-dimensional. Since very questionable results were obtained to confirm their results, and considering the conceptual difficulties, Allen and Meyer (1993) proposed a modified scale: two reversed items were eliminated (they were found to have the weakest loadings in the confirmatory factorial analysis reported by Allen and Meyer, 1990) and a new one was added. A test in Korea (Ko *et al.*, 1997) shows a very low correlation (.11) between this new item and others. So we decided to test the shorter form (6 items), without including the new proposed item.

The antecedents, consequences and correlates of each form will somewhat be different (Allen and Meyer, 1990; McGee and Ford, 1987; Morrow, 1993). All the studies on the antecedents of commitment are based on the results of Mowday *et al.* (1979). They identify three groups of variables influencing organizational commitment according to whether they are personal, linked to work experiences and roles, or structural. Among personal variables, age, tenure, hierarchical level, income, and educational level seem to be the ones that must be taken into account. Age and tenure seem to be positively correlated with affective commitment. The educational level seems negatively correlated. Work experiences are of paramount interest to company managers, since, in fact, one can develop commitment by acting on them. There are many other variables strongly related to this construct, such as: job challenge, role clarity, esteem, equity, participation in decision-making, choice in organizing work, and management style. Affective commitment seems to be particularly influenced by role clarity as well as participation in decision-making. Among structural variables, the size of the company and the centralization of authority are the variables whose influence on commitment has not been clearly demonstrated. Allen and Meyer (1991, 1996) confirmed the correlation between the work experiences and commitment, especially affective commitment. Affective commitment is supposed to be positively related to job performance and organizational citizenship, whereas continuance commitment might be negatively related to these consequences (see Mathieu and Zajac, 1990, meta-analytic review).

To sum up, both affective and continuance components are worth measuring. Two scales are chosen: the organizational commitment questionnaire, reduced to its short form – OCQP – and the continuance commitment scale (CCS) proposed by Allen and Meyer.

But, as noted previously, organizational commitment has been measured in a North American cultural environment. Cross-cultural use of an imported concept requires some specific precaution.

Organizational Commitment and Cross-Cultural Research Works

Generally speaking, very little research has been carried out on the concept of commitment in an international perspective. The validation of measurement scales, in a different context from the original one, is further complicated by the fact that the cross-cultural aspects to be taken into account concern two well-separated cultures: Asian and Western.

Whatever the culture – considered as a set of collectively shared cognitive structures which has been built up by means of a process implemented by institutions (Grunert *et al.*, 1993) – some differences may exist because of the cultural content of the concepts. Whereas the importance of specific cultural features is widely acknowledged (Bollinger and Hofstede, 1987), Adler *et al.* (1989) and Xie (1995) stress the need to take the specific context in Asia into consideration, particularly as soon as one wants to work on commitment or attachment (Redding *et al.*, 1994).

As regards specific validation procedures related to organizational commitment, the study of the concept of organizational commitment did not enter its international phase until 1991. Thus, Randall (1993) lists, among papers in English, twenty-three studies conducted outside the United States and remarks that twelve of them concern fields of investigation located in Canada. Only a few refer to the Asian context : Japan, South Korea, Singapore, Thailand, Taiwan, and Hong-Kong. The overseas Chinese are among the most widely studied populations, sometimes without any consideration of their possible heterogeneity (Warner, 2000). Hofstede's model (Hofstede, 1987) served as the theoretical framework for a number of these papers. The meta-analysis realized by Randall (1993) underlines the weakness of results and data and thus the difficulty to generalize. However, it shows that affective commitment is considered to be lower in collective culture countries. Putti *et al.* (1989) study the correlations between work values and organizational commitment. They identify few cultural differences and confirm the validity of construct. Near (1989) compares the commitment of Japanese and American employees by means of OCQ, but in a short form consisting of only seven items. She concludes that the Japanese are perhaps more committed since their culture encourages this attitude. Yu *et al.* (1997, in Berry *et al.*) compare organizational commitment in state-owned and non-state-owned companies and note that the level is significantly lower in the former. Employees in state-owned companies are not satisfied with their jobs.

Nonetheless, it is regrettable that the author uses the behavioural model of Staw, which has been rarely used. Finally, these results do not allow us to conclude that the concept of organizational commitment is transferable; yet they do not object to testing this concept in continental China. However, they show an important gap in the papers written so far: only affective commitment has been tested. And yet it seems that the calculative dimension of commitment is all the more essential, in that the Chinese culture is stamped with collectivism, and that economic exchanges rely on the network of relations (*guanxi*).

To the best of our knowledge, only a few studies have examined Allen and Meyer's continuance scale in France (Neveu, 1993; Charles-Pauvers, 1996, 1998) and the OCQ measure in France (Thévenet, 1992; Peyrat, 1993; Commeiras, 1994; Charles-Pauvers, 1996, 1998) and in East Asia (Putti *et al.*, 1989; Randall, 1993; Ko *et al.*, 1997; Farh *et al.*, 1997; Taormina, 1999). When OCQ is tested in an Asian context, it appears that many of these studies lack methodological validation, at least judging from the papers published: sometimes, OCQ is not submitted to validation and construct tests; sometimes, tools are created by the authors, thus precluding any valid comparisons. For instance, in order to compare the commitment of Japanese and American employees, Near (1989) uses a short form of OCQ consisting in only seven items and the behavioural model of Staw (1974), which has rarely been used. Koh and Yep (2000) use the affective subset of the Organizational Commitment Scale reported in Angle and Perry (1981).

In China, although organizational commitment as a concept is still new, an attitude of belonging and being like members in a family has been long encouraged by organizations (Wang, 1991, 1994). Given the tradition of central planning economy and life employment, the concept of organizational commitment implies strong tendencies toward working for internal development and goal achievement. That is, while the Western concept of organizational commitment is more turnover-preventing oriented, the Chinese concept of organizational commitment seems more development-seeking oriented, in the sense of emphasizing internal developmental opportunities. From this perspective, we would expect that affective commitment would have a closer relationship with performance while either normative commitment or continuous commitment would have a weaker link with performance (Charles-Pauvers and Wang, 1999).

Cross-Cultural Methodological Considerations

As described before, the organizational commitment is a North American concept. Only the certainty about the cross-cultural validity of measurement scales should permit researchers to compare the concepts concerned and factorial scores obtained among Chinese populations.

Some differences may exist because of the cultural content of the concepts (Hui and Triandis, 1983). This difficulty increases when different languages are used. This can be overcome by using translation and back-procedure from English to French and to Chinese (Brislin, 1980, in Earley, 1989). Semantic differences may introduce another bias: subjects may have specific emotional and cognitive reactions: for example, Americans are known to be more spontaneous in responding to surveys, whereas Chinese employees are not used to filling in questionnaires. Smith and Wang (in Bond, 1996) emphasize that Chinese respondents may choose central categories on rating scales in order not to take up extreme positions. Near (1989) points out that the Japanese are reluctant to use declarative statements on which OCQ is based. Indeed, the validation process involves verifying that the measured concept exists in the various cultures studied, that its components are similar and that it is expressed in the same ways.

According to Grunert *et al.* (1993), the cross-cultural validation of a measurement scale consists in determining whether the comprehension and evaluation of the items on a scale are really based on comparable structures and cognitive processes. The proposed methodology to assess the degree of cultural comparability rests on the invariance of factors. Thus, a strong cultural comparability is evidenced by means of three linked conditions concerning the data collected from samples representing different cultures: the similarity of the dimensional structure; the identity of the loadings of the items; the identity of the correlations between the factors. If none of these three conditions is satisfied, there is no cultural comparability; if only the first condition is fulfilled, there is a minimum cultural comparability; if the first two conditions are fulfilled, there is a weak cultural comparability. For their part, Nyeck *et al.* (1996) retain three hypotheses to evaluate the invariance of factors which operationalize the international validity of a measurement scale: the similarity of the dimensional structure among the studied cultures; the identity of factorial parameters (at first, identity of the loadings and, subsequently, identity of each one of the parameters); the stability of the internal consistency of the scale in the different samples. These conditions allow testing the nomological validity of the scales.

Organizational Commitment and Work-Related Variables

Therefore, beyond the research actually carried out on organizational commitment, the literature helps to point out the elements to be integrated in a study conducted in China. They mainly concern cultural considerations, having in mind the pertinent distinction between culture and social system (Bond, 1996) where 'the concept of culture represents the transmitted and created values, ideas and other meaningful systems, and the term social system designates the specifically relational system of interaction among individuals and collectivity' (Kroeber and Parsons, 1958, in Bond, 1987, p. 271). For instance, Chinese people score high on collectivism (Hofstede and Bond, 1988). For individualism, the USA scored 91 and ranked no. 1, China ranked 14 (out of 40) (Cragin, 1986). The results of Bond (1996), Verburg *et al.* (1999), and Clugston *et al.* (2000) illustrate those preoccupations.

The leadership style, the satisfaction toward colleagues and superiors as well as the perceived performance are included in our research work.

The leadership style in China has been relatively studied in the last few years. Smith and Wang (in Bond, 1996) realized a synthesis of the main research works, with a large emphasis on the cultural differences. More precisely, Wang and Satow (1994) point out differences in leadership and culture. They indicate the difficulty in assessing the most relevant management style in Sino-foreign joint-ventures. Their results show significant differences in management style according to the companies' partner : differences show up between the joint-ventures and the wholly owned Japanese companies. Jiang (1994) studies the relationship between Chinese autocratic attitudes and the traditional loyal attitude toward superiors among the Chinese in Taiwan. Employees acknowledge that others wield a lot of power over others; the style of leadership seems to be a function of the size of the company. The autocratic style is the norm mainly in small companies. Bottger and Yetton (1987) study participation among Chinese managers from Hong Kong and Singapore, and Australian managers. The results show similarities among the Chinese and differences with Australians. They confirm that Chinese managers favour a certain formalization of power, keeping a hand on the decisions regarding employees. Jin (1993) tests the OCQ in six plants located in Taiwan. She shows that affective commitment decreases when participation and consultation are used. Chow (1988) compares the managerial work of Chinese leaders in the Republic of China with that of cadres in Hong Kong and the United States. She shows that for the surveyed managers, in factories located in the province of Henan, the role of the leader is considered to be very important.

The relational factor, although very high, does not appear as decisive as was assumed. The role of 'Monitor' of Chinese managers is less important than for foreign managers. High distance to power and respect for the elders probably account for the fact that the employees are more loyal and obedient. The importance of political aspects in the PRC and the role of institutions granting resources specific to China (political and personal concerns, family issues, etc.) are also stressed. The recent split between managerial and political functions is not yet a reality in every company, due to the lack of trained managers (Jin, 1993). Wang (1999) concludes that four levels of compatibility are needed to develop a high level of cross-cultural compatibility: style compatibility, competency compatibility, commitment compatibility, and performance compatibility. Li *et al.* (1997) study interactive leadership and show that in an oriental culture (Singapore), it increases the employees' trust in their leader, improves employees' motivation and enhances their commitment to their companies.

Indeed, the traditional Chinese society is highly concerned with collectivism, social interaction and team. Fisher and Yuan (1998) compare US and Chinese employees' motivation and find that Chinese employees are much more concerned with relationships and groups. Jin (1993) studies how authority functions in China and shows that the small group is similar to a small production cell or a socio-political unit: the authority relationship is of a 'boss–customer' nature; choosing team members among peers can make up for the authoritative system. Wang and Satow (1994) conclude on the importance of developing the relationship between superiors and subordinates to facilitate the participation in the decision-making process.

As a consequence, we decided to include four variables, known as influencing organizational commitment, and of paramount importance in the Chinese companies: satisfaction between colleagues, satisfaction between managers and employees, leadership style and perceived organizational performance.

A Comparative Research Work in China: Method and Results

This section reports the results of an empirical study carried out in state-owned companies and French Chinese JVs.

Two components of the organizational commitment scale were measured with Mowday *et al.* (1982) Commitment Questionnaire (OCQP) (short form) for the affective commitment dimension, and Allen and Meyer's Continuance commitment scale (CCS) for the continuance dimension. The response format of each scale is a seven-point Likert-type scale from one (*strongly disagree*) to seven (*strongly agree*). Among variables influencing organizational commitment, the following variables are retained:

- managers'/employees' relationship satisfaction
- co-workers' satisfaction
- leadership styles
- perceived organizational performance.

Leadership style is measured by means of the questionnaire of Hersey and Blanchard (1993). For each sentence, the respondents evaluate, on a four-item Likert scale, the way they perceive their superiors' leadership style. An ascending hierarchical analysis was performed, using the Ward aggregation procedure. Three leadership styles were thus obtained: laissez-faire, distant, delegative-autocratic.

The degree of satisfaction in relationship with colleagues (co-workers' satisfaction) and superiors (managers'/employers' satisfaction) was measured with the Mogenet satisfaction questionnaire (1988), which suits well a heterogeneous population, as is the case in the survey carried out. Four groups characterize the co-workers' satisfaction: very unsatisfied, unsatisfied, satisfied, very satisfied. Four groups, as well, characterize the relationship between superiors and employees: very unsatisfied, unsatisfied, satisfied, very satisfied.

The perceived organizational performance is measured by means of a seven-item scale indicating the ratings from the market share, profitability, turnover, task accomplishment, satisfaction and investment expansion in comparison with the average level from similar industrial sectors. Four distinct groups differently perceive the organizational performance as very bad, bad, good, very good.

The data were collected by means of questionnaires that were carefully translated from the English version into French and Chinese and back into English. The questionnaires were mainly self-administered and collected in face-to-face interviews. Both are convenient samples, mainly in Shanghai and Hangzhou. Two samples are available: 220 respondents in the state-owned companies and 330 in French-Chinese JVs.

The SOEs are larger in size than JVs: 85 per cent of SOEs employ more than 500 people, as compared with 65 per cent for JVs. In these SOEs, the employees are older than in JVs; they have stayed longer in the company. These two samples do not significantly differ in the level of education.

Data Analysis

The results are organized in two major sections: first, the cross-cultural validation of organizational commitment scales; second, the analyses of the influence of the four dependant variables on organizational commitment.

Cross-Cultural Scale Validation

For the whole sample (550 respondents), the analysis followed the structural equation modelling approach recommended by Anderson and Gerbing (1982) in order to verify the hypotheses about cross-cultural validity. First, in order to identify the structure of each scale to compare it to the American original, an exploratory factorial analysis was carried out (Principal Component Analysis – SPSS 9.0 – with Oblimin rotation). The structure was submitted to the confirmatory factorial analysis (Anderson and Gerbing, 1988). The factorial structure was tri-dimensional (63 per cent of explained variance): two factors clearly represented affective and continuance commitment, but the third one had no real consistent conceptual meaning, and showed a poor reliability (alpha coefficient .55). The structural equation modelling was performed. Several measurement models were compared (two or three factors), testing the elimination of items with low extracted variance. As a result, we chose a two-factor scale: affective and continuance dimensions, with respectively six and four items. For more details on the followed method, see Charles-Pauvers and Wang (2000).

Differences in Organizational Commitment

The means are, respectively for SOEs and JVs, 17.32, and 14.12 for the CCS; 25.61 and 30.63 for the OCQP. The ANOVA results show significant differences between JVs and SOEs. It appears that affective commitment is significantly higher in JVs than in SOEs, and continuance commitment, significantly lower. A cluster analysis reveals four groups, indicating four profiles of commitment.

Testing the Influence of Variables on Organizational Commitment

Multivariate analyses of variance (MANOVA) were carried out: the principal concern was to detect the multivariate joint effect of the type of company (JVs or SOEs) and every dependent variable (leadership style, satisfaction, etc.). The results do not reveal any significant interaction effect, simultaneously implying the variable JV/SOE and any of the four other variables. But they emphasize the influence of each dependent variables on organizational commitment, mainly affective commitment (see Table 12.1).

The levels of affective and calculative commitment are influenced by the level of perceived organizational performance. Only affective commitment

Table 12.1   Effect of chosen variables on commitment

	Managers' and employees' satisfaction	Co-workers' satisfaction	Leadership-style	Perceived performance
Main effect	OCQP	OCQP	OCQP	OCQP CCS

is increased by a higher satisfaction concerning the relationships with the managers and co-workers. Leadership style also influences affective commitment: when it is 'laisser-faire', affective commitment is lower.

CONCLUSIONS

Our aim was to evaluate the differences in organizational commitment between JVs and SOEs employees, to test the influence of performance, management style, relationship between employees and manager, between colleagues on organizational commitment. The necessity of cross-cultural validity was emphasized.

As a first conclusion, the generalized use of a two-component model including affective and continuance scale seems interesting from a theoretical viewpoint. It is particularly evident in the new market-oriented Chinese economy. Educated and competent Chinese employees can gain a higher salary by changing company. But the companies need to have a certain guarantee of the employee's loyalty. On the other hand, employees who are highly satisfied with their organization will avoid withdrawal behaviour and maintain continued attachment to work (Blau and Boal, 1987). The human resource managers have to evaluate whether people are interested in the losses associated with their departure from the company; they need to have affectively committed people, who will do their best for the company. Only the two-component model addresses this need. Following Meyer and Allen (1997), the organizational commitment of an employee (and larger work commitment) should be described in terms of levels of affective and continuance commitment (at least), the nature of the links being different with the different components (Becker, 1992; Mathieu and Zajac, 1990; Meyer *et al.*, 1989).

As a second conclusion, none of our scales can be adapted directly from the original American scale without any modification, whatever the studied country. But we observe that the difficulty varies. First, it depends on the tested psychological properties of the scales: every researcher concerned with the concept and measure of commitment knows that OCQP is an excellent scale. In definitive, as Ko *et al.* (1997) noted, the continued use of the OCQ (not in its long and original form) could facilitate comparisons across studies. The CCS scale is much more recent. No research result shows a fully consistent structure. Moreover, there remains a problem of conceptualization of the construct: for example, there is a debate in the USA to decide whether the factorial structure of CCS is one- or two-dimensional. Allen and Meyer (1996) and Meyer and Allen (1997) tried to solve this problem by taking off two items. There are very few published research works that include this modification. Moreover, the need for the psychometric validation of a scale, first in its country of origin, is underlined. As explained by Grunert *et al.* (1993), the cognitive categories can be comparable, but could differ when evaluated at an abstract level. This avenue seems to be worth exploring in order to make more in-depth comparisons between the different countries especially to realize cross-cultural comparisons.

On the other hand, our results indicate significant differences in the organizational commitment profiles between JVs and SOEs. More precisely, the affective commitment level is superior in the JVs, while the continuance commitment is lower. This last result is coherent with, for instance, Ding *et al.*'s findings (2000): ownership type is significantly correlated with social security and labour turnover rate. In JVs, the continuance commitment is an indicator of the employee's perception of the rather low costs associated with leaving. As noted by Tang *et al.* (2000), Chinese employees do change jobs for money; JVs propose an average level significantly higher than SOEs (Ding *et al.*, 2000). If these results are confirmed, depending on the performance, and preserving the more market-oriented approach, it could be an opportunity for HRM directors to develop rewards politics, including incentives to encourage core employees to stay in JVs. They could allow financial support to buy a house; propose any social insurance programme, which gives increasing advantages over time; ownership is also a possibility to explore. The way to introduce them should include the costs associated with leaving. Taormina (1999) emphasizes the importance of providing better training to create a desire in the employee to continue working for the organization.

The affective commitment level is significantly higher in JVs. The commitment is a process and needs to be encouraged. The positive work experiences and role-related characteristics are major antecedents (Mowday *et al.*, 1982). Generally speaking, job scope, and career development opportunities can offer perspective to develop HRM practices. Moreover, training should be integrated in a career development process, to increase the link between the core employee, and, as noted earlier, the costs associated with leaving. Further research is needed to study how to transfer the organizational justice concept (Folger and Konovsky, 1989) to the Chinese cultural context. Special attention should be paid to procedural justice included in the HRM policies.

We also concluded that the four studied variables directly influenced the affective commitment level, whatever the type of organization. The results are very consistent with previous research works and confirm the positive interaction between work experiences and organizational commitment in an American cultural context (Mathieu and Zajac, 1990; Meyer *et al.*, 1991; Meyer *et al.*, 1989; Morrow, 1993) as well a French one (Charles-Pauvers, 1996).

When examining more precisely the variables related to work experiences and organizational performance, a very low level of perceived organizational performance significantly decreases the commitment. These results confirm what could have been presumed: when employees perceive that the organization is not efficient, they do not feel committed, especially for the affective part. Their calculative commitment is altered because the probability of staying in the company can be affected by the perceived bad organizational performances. The same interaction is observed when we consider that the laisser-faire style decreases the affective commitment and, to a lesser extent, the calculative. This result shows the necessity of developing a real politics of internal communication: employees need to be informed about the performance of the company; they must be given some signals illustrative of its good health. This should be tried together with the reward and bonus payment system.

The delegative–autocratic style influences highly and positively the affective commitment, as the research work of Hersey and Blanchard emphasized. A positive style exerts a positive influence on the commitment, in accordance with Wang (1994), who underlined that participative leadership style had a positive effect on morale and motivation.

We obtained some positive influence between the co-workers' satisfaction and the affective commitment. Huy and Tan (in Bond, 1996) emphasize the importance of a harmonious work atmosphere, as well as the teamwork norms and relations. As noted by the authors, the group could become an inhibitor neutralizing the effects of individual incentives. But the importance given by the employees to group relationship should be taken into account and could be an indicator of the development and evolution of the commitment. The same influence was observed with managers'/employees' satisfaction. It seems worthwhile to develop positive interactions between employees and managers. Some situations could favour their development: informal discussions, communication on perceived feelings during formal interviews, etc. This is not new but needs to be repeated because Western managers, in particular, are more task-oriented that Chinese ones. Wang and Satow (1994) stressed the influence of cultivating positive superior–subordinate relationships.

These modest and limited results confirm Allen and Meyer (1997): 'this body of research highlights the importance of work experiences, that communicate that the organization is supportive of its employees, treats them fairly' (p. 46). All the results are very consistent with other studies. But some limits need to be underlined. The samples are not representative of the country studied. Their size can also be discussed. Furthermore, the data were collected in a definite region. Our results need to be confirmed. The Chinese society is very different from North Western contexts. Nevertheless, it is a first attempt to analyze the generalization of Allen and Meyer's model. We confirm Ko *et al.* (1997) when they write that 'additional studies conducted in Asian societies are needed to provide more information pertinent to conceptual distinctions in the West and Asia'. We need deep investigations, to understand the real meaning of similarities and convergences. But, at the end, as noted by Huy and Tan (in Bond, 1996), 'that the leader is seen to "fair by my standards" and "willing to do things that benefit me" may become the requisites for higher work motivation in China' (p. 376) seems to open the door to universal demands, but contextual and cultural expressions need to be analyzed.

Note

The questionnaire was elaborated and the data collected with the assistance of Professor Z. M. Wang, School of Management, Zheijang University, PRC. We thank him very much, and also C. Liu, his PhD student.

References

Adler, N., Campbell, N. and Laurent, A. (1989) 'In Search of Appropriate Methodology: From Outside the People's Republic of China Looking In', *Journal of International Business Studies*, 70, pp. 61–74.

Ajzen, I. (1988) *Attitudes, Personality, and Behavior* (Buckingham: Open University Press) p. 175.

Allen, N. J. and Meyer, J. P. (1984) 'Testing the "Side Bet Theory" of Organizational Commitment: Some Methodological Considerations', *Journal of Applied Psychology*, 69(3), pp. 372–8.

Allen, N. J. and Meyer, J. P. (1990) 'The Measurement and Antecedents of Affective, Continuance and Normative Commitment to the Organization', *Journal of Occupational Psychology*, 63, pp. 1–18.

Allen, N. J. and Meyer, J. P. (1991) 'A Three Component Conceptualization of Organizational Commitment', *Human Resource Management Review*, 1(1), pp. 61–89.

Allen, N. J. and Meyer, J. P. (1996) 'Affective, Continuance and Normative Commitment to the Organization: An Examination of Construct Validity', *Journal of Vocational Behavior*, 49, pp. 252–76.

Allen, N. J., Meyer, J. P. and Smith, C. (1993) 'Commitment to Organizations and Occupations: Extension and Test of a Three-Component Conceptualization', *Journal of Applied Psychology*, 78(4), pp. 538–51.

Anderson, J. C. and Gerbing, D. W. (1982) 'Some Methods for Re-Specifying Measurement Models to Obtain Unidimensional Construct', *Journal of Marketing Research*, 19 (November), pp. 453–60.

Anderson, J. C. and Gerbing, D. W. (1988) 'Structural Equation Modeling in Practice: a Review and Recommended Two-step Approach, *Psychological Bulletin*, 103(3), pp. 411–23.

Angle, H. L. and Lawson, M. B. (1993) 'Changes in Affective and Continuance Commitment in Times of Relocation', *Journal of Business Research*, 26(1), pp. 3–15.

Angle, H. L. and Perry, J. L. (1981) 'An Empirical Assessment of Organizational Commitment and Organizational Effectiveness', *Administrative Science Quarterly*, 26, pp. 1–14.

Becker, H. S. (1960) 'Notes on the Concept of Commitment', *American Journal of Sociology*, 66, pp. 32–40.

Becker, T. E. (1992) 'Foci and Bases of Commitment: Are They Distinctions Worth Making?', *Academy of Management Journal*, 35(1), pp. 232–44.

Berry, J., Segall, M. and Katicibasi, C. (1997) *Handbook of Cross-Cultural Psychology: Social Behavior and Applications (Vol. 3)* (Allyn & Bacon).

Blau, G. J. and Boal, K. B. (1987) 'Conceptualizing How Job Involvement and Organizational Commitment Affect Turnover and Absenteeism', *Academy of Management Review*, 12(2), pp. 288–300.

Bollinger, D. and Hofstede, G. (1987) *Les différences culturelles dans le management* (Paris: Editions D'Organisation).

Bond, M. H. (1987) *The Psychology of the Chinese People* (Hong Kong: Oxford University Press).

Bond, M. H. (1996) *The Handbook of Chinese Psychology* (Hong Kong: Oxford University Press).

Bond, M. H. and Smith P. B. (1996) 'Cross-Cultural Social and Organizational Psychology', *Annual Review of Psychology*, 47, pp. 205–35.

Bottger, P. C. and Yetton, P. W. (1987) 'Managerial Decision-making: Comparison of Participative Decision Methods in australian and Singaporean/Hong Kong Chinese Samples', *australian Journal of Management*, 12(2).

Boyacigiller, N. and Adler, N. (1991) 'The Parochial Dinosaur: Organizational Science in a Global Context', *Academy of Management Review*, 16(2), pp. 262–90.

Campbell, N. and Yee, C. in Campbell, N., Plasschaert, S. R. F. and Brown, D. H. (1991) 'Relationship management in equity point ventures in China: a preliminary exploration', *Advances in Chinese Industrial Studies* (Greenwich: JAI Press).

Charles-Pauvers, B. (1996) 'Implication organisationnelle et relation d'emploi flexible', Thèse de Doctorat, Université de Nantes.

Charles-Pauvers, B. (1998) 'Concilier relation d'emploi et implication organisationnelle?', in J. Allouche and B. Sire (eds), *Ressources Humaines: Une Gestion Éclatée* (Paris: Economica).

Charles-Pauvers, B. and Urbain, C. (1999) 'Examining the Cross-Cultural Validation of Scales: The Case of Organizational Commitment and Attitude Toward Money (USA, France, China)', 23rd IAREP Conference, Belgirate (Italy), pp. 1–11.

Charles-Pauvers, B. and Wang, Z. M. (1999) 'Organizational Commitment: Examining the Case of China', 16th EAMSA *Conference*, pp. 1–13.

Charles-Pauvers, B. and Wang, Z. M. (2000) 'The Organizational Commitment: A Test to Assess the Cross Cultural Validity of a Measurement Scale in France and China: Internationalization of HRM?', 20th Annual Congress, Paris.

Chow, I. H. (1998) 'The Impact of Rules and Regulations on Workforce Flexibility in Hong Kong', *International Journal of Human Resource Management*, 9(3), pp. 494–505.

Clark, T., Gospel, H. and Montgomery, J. (1999) 'Running on the Spot? A Review of Twenty Years of Research on the Management of Human Resources in Comparative and National Perspective', *International Journal of Human Resource Management*, 10(3), pp. 520–44.

Clugston, M., Howell, J. P. and Dorfman, P. W. (2000) 'Does Cultural Socialization Predict Multiple Bases and Foci of Commitment', *Journal of Management*, 26(1), pp. 5–30.

Commeiras, N. (1994) 'La mesure de l'implication organisationnelle: existe-t-il un outil adéquat?', *Annales du Management/ XXII Èmes Journées des IAE*, 1, pp. 649–73.

Cragin, J. P. in Clegg, S. R., Dunphy, D. C. and Reddington, S. G. (1986) 'Management Technology Absorption in China' in *The Enterprise and Management in East Asia* (University of Hong Kong).

Curry, J. P., Wakefield, D. S., Price, J. L. and Mueller, C. W. (1986) 'On the Causal Ordering of Job Satisfaction and Organizational Commitment', *Academy of Management Journal*, 29(4), pp. 847–58.

Ding, D. Z., Goodall, K. and Warner, M. (2000) 'The End Of The "Iron-Rice Bowl": Whither Chinese Human Resource Management?', *International Journal of Human Resource Management*, 11(2), pp. 217–36.

Dunham, R. B., Grube, J. A. and Castaneda, M. B. (1994) 'Organizational Commitment: The Utility of an Integrative Definition', *Journal of Applied Psychology*, 79(3), pp. 370–80.

Earley, P. C. (1989) 'Social Loafing and Collectivism: A Comparison of the United States and the People's Republic of China', *Administrative Science Quarterly*, 34, pp. 565–81.

Farh, J.-L., Earley, P. C. and Lin S.-C. (1997) 'Impetus for Action: A Cultural Analysis of Justice and Organizational Citizenship Behavior in Chinese Society', *Administrative Science Quarterly*, 42(3), pp. 421–44.

Fisher, C. D. and Yuan, A. X. Y. (1998) 'What Motivates Employees? A Comparison of US and Chinese Responses', *International Journal of Human Resource Management*, 9(3), pp. 516–28.

Folger, R. and Konovsky, M. A. (1989) 'Effects of Procedural and Distributive Justice on Reactions to Pay Raise Decisions', *Academy of Management Journal*, 32(1), pp. 115–30.

Fornell, C. and Larcker, D. F. (1981) 'Evaluating Structural Equation Models with Unobservable Variables and Measurement Error', *Journal of Marketing Research*, 18 (February), pp. 39–50.

Gellatly, I. R. (1995) 'Individual and Group Determinants of Employee Absenteeism: Test of a Causal Model', *Journal of Organizational Behavior*, 16, pp. 469–85.

Grunert, S. C., Grunert, K. L. and Kristensen, K. (1993) 'Une méthode d'estimation de la validité interculturelle des instruments de mesure: le cas de la mesure des valeurs des consommateurs par la liste des valeurs LOV', *Recherche et Applications en Marketing*, 8(4), pp. 5–28.

Hair, J. F., Jr, Anderson, R. E., Tatham, R. L. and Black, W. C. (1998) *Multivariate Data Analysis*, 5th edn (Englewood Cliffs, NJ: Prentice Hall).

Hersey, P. and Blanchard, K. (1993) *Management of Organizational Behaviour: Utilizing Human Resources* (Englewood Cliffs, NJ: Prentice Hall).

Hofstede, G. (1987) 'Relativité culturelle des pratiques et des théories de l'organisation', *Revue Française de Gestion*, Sept.–Oct., pp. 10–21.

Hofstede, G. and Bond, M. (1988) 'The Confucius Connection: From Cultural Roots to Economic Growth', *Organizational Dynamics*, 16 (Spring), pp. 5–21.

Hui, C. H. and Triandis, H. C. (1983) 'Multistrategy Approach to Cross-Cultural Research – the Case of Locus of Control', *Journal of Cross-Cultural Psychology*, 14(1), pp. 65–83.

Jiang (1994) in S. G. Redding, A. Norman and A. Schandler 'The Nature of Individual Attachment to the Organization: A Review of East-Asian Variations', in *Handbook of Industrial and Organization* (Palo Alto: Consulting Psychologists Press).

Jin, P. (1993) 'Work Motivation and Productivity in Voluntarily Formed Work Teams: A Field Study in China', *Organizational Behavior and Human Decision Processes*, 54(1), pp. 133–55.

Ko, J.-W., Price, J. L. and Mueller, C. W. (1997) 'Assessment of Meyer and Allen's Three-Component Model of Organizational Commitment in South Korea', *Journal of Applied Psychology*, 82(6), pp. 961–73.

Koh, W. L. and Yep, L. K. (2000) 'The Impact of the Employee–Organization Relationship on Temorary Employees' Performance and Attitude: Testing a Singaporean Example', *International Journal of Human Resource Management*, 11(2), pp. 366–87.

Lea, S. E. G., Webley, P. and Levine, R. M. (1993) 'The Economic Psychology of Consumer Debt', *Journal of Economic Psychology*, 14, pp. 85–119.

Lea, S. E. G., Webley, P. and Walker, C. M. (1995) 'Psychological Factors in Consumer Debt: Money Management, Economic Socialization, and Credit Use', *Journal of Economic Psychology*, 16(4), pp. 681–701.

Li, J., Koh, K. L. and Hia, H. S. (1997) 'The Effects Of Interactive Leadership On Human Resource Management In Singapore's Banking Industry', *International Journal of Human Resource Management*, 8(5), pp. 710–19.

Lu, Y. and Bjorkman, I. (1997) 'HRM Practices in China–Western Joint Ventures: MNC Standardization versus Localization', *International Journal of Human Resource Management*, 8(5), pp. 614–27.

Mathieu, J. E. and Zajac, D. M. (1990) 'A Review and Meta-Analysis of the Antecedents, Correlates, and Consequences of Organizational Commitment', *Psychological Bulletin*, 108(2), pp. 171–94.

McElroy, J. C., Morrow, P. C., Crum, M. R. and Dooley, F. J. (1995) 'Railroad Employee Commitment and Work-Related Attitudes and Perceptions', *Transportation Journal*, 3–34, pp. 13–24.

McGee, G. W. and Ford, R. C. (1987) 'Two (or More?) Dimensions of Organizational Commitment: Reexamination of the Affective and Continuance Commitment Scales', *Journal of Applied Psychology*, 72(4), pp. 638–42.

Meyer, J. P. and Allen, N. J. (1987) 'Organizational Commitment: Toward a Three-Component Model', *Research Bulletin*, University of Western Ontario, p. 660.

Meyer, J. P. and Allen, N. J. (1997) *Commitment in the Workplace – Theory, Research and Application* (Thousand Oaks, USA: Sage).

Meyer, J. P., Bobocel, D. and Allen, N. (1991) 'Development of Organizational Commitment during the First Year of Employment: A Longitudinal Study of Pre- and Post-Entry Influences', *Journal of Management*, 17(4), pp. 717–33.

Meyer, J. P., Paunonen, S. V., Gellatly, I. R., Goffin, R. D. and Jackson, D. N. (1989) 'Organizational Commitment and Job Performance: It's the Nature of the Commitment that Counts', *Journal of Applied Psychology*, 74(1), pp. 152–6.

Mogenet, J. L. (1988) 'Mesure de la satisfaction au travail des personnels encadrés', *Revue de Psychologie Appliquée*, 38(3), pp. 253–73.

Morrow, P. C. (1993) *The Theory and Measurement of Work Commitment* (Greenwich, Conn.: Jai Press).

Mottaz, C. J. (1988) 'Determinants of Organizational Commitment', *Human Relations*, 41(6), pp. 467–82.

Mowday, R. T., Steers, R. M. and Porter, L. W. (1979) 'The Measurement of Organizational Commitment', *Journal of Vocational Behavior*, 14, pp. 224–47.

Mowday, R. T., Steers, R. M. and Porter, L. W. (1982) *Employee–Organization Linkages: The Psychology of Commitment, Absenteeism and Turnover* (London: Academic Press).

Near, J. P. (1989) 'Organizational Commitment Among Japanese and U.S. Workers', *Organization Studies*, 10(3), pp. 281–300.

Neveu, J. P. (1991) 'Méthodologie de L'implication', *Actes du 2ème Congrès de L'AGRH*, 14–15 Nov., pp. 141–4.

Neveu, J. P. (1993) *L'intention de départ volontaire chez le cadre (Thèse)* (Toulouse: Université de Sciences Sociales).

Nyeck, S., Paradis, S., Xuereb, J. M. and Chebat, J. C. (1996) 'Standardisation ou adaptation des échelles de mesure à ravers différents contextes nationaux: l'exemple d'une échelle de mesure de l'innovativité', *Recherche et Applications en Marketing*, 11(3), pp. 57–74.

Pedhazur, E. J. and Pedhazur Schmelkin, L. (1991) *Measurement, Design, and Analysis: An Integrated Approach* (Hillsdale: Lawrence Erlbaum Associates).

Peyrat, D. (1993) 'Participation et implication des salariés: le projet d'entreprise, approche comparative', Thèse de Doctorat, Université de Poitiers.

Porter, L. W. (1963) 'Job Attitudes in Management: Perceived Importance of Needs as a Function of Job Level', *Journal of Applied Psychology*, 47(2), pp. 141–8.

Putti, J. M., Aryee, S. and Liang, T. K. (1989) 'Work Values and Organizational Commitment: A Study in the Asian Context', *Human Relations*, 42(3), pp. 275–88.

Randall, D. M. (1993) 'Cross-Cultural Research on Organizational Commitment: A Review and Application of Hofstede's Value Survey Module', *Journal of Business Review*, 26(1), pp. 91–110.

Redding, S. G., Norman, A. and Schandler, A. (1994) 'The Nature of Individual Attachment to the Organization: A Review of East-Asian Variations', in *Handbook of Industrial and Organization* (Palo Alto: Consulting Psychologists Press).

Reichers, A. E. (1985) 'Review and Reconceptualization of Organizational Commitment', *Academy of Management Review*, 10(3), pp. 465–76.

Roehrich, G. (1994) 'Innovativités hédoniste et sociale: proposition d'une mesure', *Recherche et Applications en Marketing*, 9(2), pp. 19–42.

Roussel, P. (1994) 'Méthode de validation de questionnaire en GRH: l'exemple du QSR en phase exploratoire', *Actes du 5ème congrès de l'AGRH*, pp. 638–52.

Somers, M. J. (1993) 'A Test of the Relationship between Affective and Continuance Commitment Using Non-Recursive Models', *Journal of Occupational and Organizational Psychology*, 66, pp. 185–92.

Staw, B. (1974) 'Attitudinal and Behavioral Consequences of Changing a Major Organizational Reward', *Journal of Personality and Social Psychology*, 29(6), pp. 742–51.

Tang, T. L., Luk, V. and Chiu, R. (2000) 'Pay Differentials in the People's Rebublic of China: An Examination of Internal Equity and External Competitiveness', *Compensations and Benefits Review*, April/May, pp. 45–51.

Taormina, R. J. (1999) 'Predicting Employee Commitment and Satisfaction: The Relative Effects of Socialization and Demographics', *International Journal of Human Resource Management*, 10(6), pp. 1060–76.

Thevenet, M. (1992) *Impliquer les personnes dans l'entreprise* (Paris: Ed. Liaisons).

Management of Human Resources in Joint Ventures in China

Verburg, R. (1996) 'Developing HRM in Foreign–Chinese Joint Ventures', *European Management Journal*, 14(5), pp. 518–52.

Verburg, R. M., Drenth, P. J. D., Koopman, P. L., Van Muijen, J. J. and Wang, Z. M. (1999) 'Managing Human Resources Across Cultures: A Comparative Analysis Of Practices in Industrial Enterprises in China and The Netherlands', *International Journal of Human Resource Management*, 10(3), pp. 391–410.

Wang, Z. M. (1991) 'Recent Developments in Industrial and Organizational Psychology in People's Republic of China', *International Review of Industrial and Organizational Psychology*, 6, pp. 1–16.

Wang, Z. M. (1994) 'Culture, Economic Reform, and the Role of Industrial and Organizational Psychology in China', *Handbook of Organizational Psychology* (cap. 14), pp. 689–725.

Wang, Z. M. (1999) 'Developing Joint Venture Leadership Teams', *Advances in Global Leadership*, 1, pp. 337–53.

Wang, Z. M. and Mobley, W. H. (1999) 'Strategic Human Resource Management for Twenty-First Century China', *Research in Personnel and Human Resources Management*, supplement 4, pp. 353–36.

Wang, Z. M. and Satow, T. (1994) 'The Effect of Structural and Organizational Factors on Socio-Psychological Orientation in Joint-Ventures', *Journal of Managerial Psychology*, 9(4), pp. 22–30.

Warner, M. (2000) 'Introduction: The Asia-Pasific HRM Model Revisited', *International Journal of Human Resource Management*, 11(2), pp. 171–82.

Wiener, Y. (1982) 'Commitment in Organizations: A Normative View', *Academy of Management Review*, 7(3), pp. 418–28.

Xie, J. L. (1995) 'Research on Chine Organizational Behavior and Human Resource Management: Conceptual and Methodological Considerations', *Advances in International Comparative Management*, 10, pp. 15–42.

13 Culture and *BrainStyles*®™: New Alternatives for Human Resource Strategies to Develop Chinese–Western Cooperation

Dieter Albrecht

INTRODUCTION

In Beijing, just before Christmas, a European home-furnishing company launched an advertisement for its newly arrived lamp collection 'for the dark period of the year', obviously not knowing that winter is not the dark period of the year in Northern China as it is in Northern Europe. Beijingers only smiled about this obvious mistake.

In fact, the judgment of people working in companies in China is often dominated by prejudice, unfounded expectations, or simply ignorance of the working and living conditions, both in China and the West. Many Western managers think that their newly arrived, highly qualified co-workers will certainly 'muddle through' to find their way in the new country. Half of the assignments of American companies in China fail because the foreign experts and business people are unprepared for their job abroad. The situation on the Chinese side is similar. Although the supposed 'inadequacy' of Chinese managers is changing and their entrepreneurial spirit fostered, nonetheless, future conflicts seem inevitable, with their expectation for cooperation with foreigners to understand and accept their cultural differences.

In this chapter, I compare two approaches for understanding behaviour. First, I elaborate on the cultural environment in China, *the mental software*, as Hofstede (1991) expressed it in four different cultural dimensions. Then, I complement the functioning of people within that culture by introducing a system for describing their *mental hardware*, or their *brainstyles*, developed by Miller (1997). Knowing how the genetic hardware creates four different *brainstyles*, is helpful for the formulation of a successful human resource strategy that can take advantage of cultural or corporate conditions. First, a short introduction to the Chinese *mental software*.

CONFUCIUS, LAOZI AND SUN ZI: CREATORS OF THE CHINESE WORLD-VIEW AND VALUES

The Chinese traditional world-view has been developed over thousands of years under complicated, natural and differentiated social environments, mainly with opposite results to the Western world. Throughout the process of modernization of Chinese-influenced societies and communities such as Singapore, Taiwan, Hong Kong and Korea, their situational analyses suggest that some behaviour has changed. However, most of the basic commonly shared values and traditional beliefs have been resistant to fundamental transformation up to now. According to Bond and Hwang (1995), this is because of deeply rooted moral and ethical values and beliefs, combined with a set of complicated rituals and power games. These same elements most probably function in the People's Republic of China. The following portrait of the Chinese mind-set, the mental attitude formed by experience, education, prejudice, etc., reflects the process of cultural awareness of the author himself. It originates first in Western and Chinese descriptions of the Chinese mind, then is matched with my own observations of thinking and behaviour over the last 16 years while working with the Chinese in daily life. This is followed by a short description of the foundations of Chinese thinking and behaviour.

Confucianism had and has a tremendous influence on Chinese thinking and behaviour, in spite of several recurrent movements against its traditional values. Confucius (551–478 BC), nearly a contemporary of the Western philosopher Socrates (470–399 BC), lived in a time of political turbulence with a decline of traditional values. Therefore, he was greatly concerned with building a well-governed state with harmony between the individual and the society. He did not invent a new philosophy. Instead, he merely considered himself a protector and mediator of traditional doctrines and rites. Both philosophers stressed the role of education and virtue for a moral society and developed their thoughts in discussions with their disciples. They did not put the principles of their philosophy into writing; their work was mainly compiled by their disciples, Mengzi and Plato, respectively. While Socrates' influence on statal affairs was minimal, Confucius' thinking, since the Han-Dynasty (202–220 BC), advanced to the state doctrine and exerted a powerful influence on the Chinese society for more than 2,000 years.

The fundamental Confucian assumption is that men only exist in relationship to another. Because Chinese tend to ignore or break rules and regulations, Confucius set up a meticulous system of regulations to be followed in a male-dominated society. It is considered natural that these relationships, even those between friends, are hierarchical and based upon seniority. Women are only marginal figures. In fact, the Chinese conceptual framework of behaviour shows its unique delicacy in well-developed power games between friends, colleagues and enemies. The Western concept of the omnipotence of the individual is alien to the Chinese, who define themselves in an interactive context. With benevolence as the central concept and 'loving other men' as its starting point, it embraces the spectrum of daily human virtues, valuing childlike love, courteousness, decency, honesty, fidelity, fraternity, truthfulness, and the sense of shame – the Eight Rules of civilization.

There is no direction for how to treat foreigners. In a self-centred, isolated society, this is not a problem that emerges until China's confrontation with the West during colonial times. The slogan on the entrance to Confucius' mansion in Qufu, Shandong Province, 'It is nice to receive friends from afar', implies the welcoming of friends and foreigners as well. As in ancient Greece, the foreigner equates with a friend, and is treated accordingly. This attitude survives today.

The other factor influencing Chinese thinking and behavior is the *Daoist world-view*, based on the ideas of Laozi, a legendary philosopher who probably died in 350 BC. Similarities with his thinking can be found in the West with the Greek philosopher Heraclitus (c. 540–480 BC). His influence, however, on Western thinking was only marginal compared with the Daoist influence on Asia. According to the Daoist epistemology, there is no absolute knowledge. All knowledge is relative to the perspective of the viewer and has to be proved with empirical evidence. The dialectic logic of Laozi emphasizes that every phenomenon is connected with every other according to a hierarchical order. The world is a world of motion in ceaseless change, where all things can constantly change into their opposites.

In contrast to the prevailing principle of cause and effect in Western thinking, the Daoist thinking proposes the principle of synchronicity, suggesting that correspondence exists, not related to time and space, but nevertheless producing meaningful coincidence. This is *dao* in the Daoist term, *logos* in the term of Heraclitus. Capra (1987) and Clarke (1995) point out that with the principle of synchronicity, Daoism coincides with the scientific discoveries of contemporary physics, bridging natural sciences with metaphysics.

The ancient Daoist holistic world-view has survived until today and is also helpful for explaining the clashes and synergies in intercultural cooperation.

It helps understanding the relativity of cultural values, which are neither absolute nor necessarily represented in every individual behaviour; they are Yin and Yang values, symbolized by the black and white areas in the circle:

Yang is warm, light, and masculine, associated with reductionist thinking, producing powerful results in Western natural sciences. Yin is cold, dark, and feminine, associated with holistic thinking and closely related to metaphysics. Yang is heaven, sun; Yin is earth, moon. Colegrave (1984) points out that the 'masculine' Yang and the 'feminine' Yin represent symbolic values and should not be confused with men and women as genders.

As a conclusion, Westerners, influenced by the mechanistic Industrial Revolution, represent the masculine Yang, characterized by analytical, rational, linear, and causal thinking. Westerners are direct, individualistic, and problem/solution oriented. Germans in particular have a tendency toward perfectionism, principle adherence, and inflexibility. Truth is absolute. Decisions are made based upon facts and logic. The Chinese, although formed by a strongly male-dominated society are not openly 'macho'. Rather, men present themselves in cultural terms with the feminine values of the principle Yin, characterized by holistic, integrative, and intuitive thinking in social networks. According to their Daoist tradition, Chinese are indirect, prizing the group and harmony. Contradictions are passively absorbed, solutions are always tailored to the situation and must fit into predetermined structures. Truth is relative and deceit is allowed. Decisions are made based upon the impact on relationships.

The third world-view, an indigenous illustration of quintessential Chinese thinking, is represented by the *strategist Sun Zi* and his work 'The Art of War', now included in mainstream Western management literature. Sun Zi, also of Shandong Province – dates of birth and death unknown – is an outstanding example of another characteristic of the Chinese: their ability for strategic thinking. In his work that rose to prominence in the turbulent years of the Spring and Autumn Period (770–476 BC), Sun Zi uses a simple materialistic approach and combines it with the dialectic method. By incorporating the Chinese cultural heritage, its values and ways of thinking, he starts with defining the whole, 'know the enemy and know yourself'. Stating the whole and the purpose of war, he proceeds with a comprehensive and intuitive synthesis of ideas. This holistic approach is contradictory to the Western, reductionist thinking, represented by his more modern German counterpart, strategist Carl von Clausewitz (1780–1831). Western thinking starts with a complex matter by breaking it into component parts and then dealing with them one by one by applying logical analysis.

CULTURAL DIMENSIONS: CAUSES FOR CONFLICTS

Equipped with this mental software, China is, according to Huntington (1996), one of the 'challenger cultures', questioning the supremacy of the Western economies, their values, beliefs and business strategies. Conflicts between the cultures are rooted in expectations. In the centre of all these expectations, beliefs and strategies, behaviours, attitudes, communication patterns, rules of social etiquette, and do's and don'ts that lead to conflicts are *Values*. If deeply rooted values are disregarded, conflicts show up instantly and poison relationships. Although these values are not openly visible and in general not consciously recognized as such, conflicts can be traced back to culturally defined values. The Dutch anthropologist Hofstede has investigated the attitudes, beliefs and cultural values, the *'mental software'*, of people of 53 different cultural groups. In his book *Cultures and Organizations: Software of the Mind. Intercultural Cooperation and its Importance for Survival*, he describes the discovery of four fundamental dimensions of cultural values that, despite a great degree of abstraction, show clear strengths and limitations of the respective interacting cultures. As far as the classification is concerned, it is not so much an 'either/or' situation as a 'both, as well as'. Here, we summarize the dimensions:

- *Hierarchy and Equality*: The significance of hierarchy and equality; the behaviour in regard to authority in the society, measured as the degree of power distance.
- *Individuality and Group Orientation*: The significance of the individual's role and relation to his or her social environment.
- *Masculinity and Femininity*: The significance and the handling of softness and toughness; the importance of harmony in a society.
- *Flexibility and Security*: The significance of uncertainty and ambiguity; the handling of conflict, stress and time, measured as uncertainty avoidance.

Taking the findings of Hofstede as the basis for intercultural understanding, the Chinese differ from Westerners and Asians in a very specific way, as shown in Table 13.1.

It is worth mentioning, and Hofstede (1991) stresses this point, that corporate cultures can differ remarkably from national cultures. Within a corporate environment, the culture can vary according to the hierarchical

Table 13.1   Clustering of the four cultural dimensions for selected nations

	Power distance	Individuality	Masculinity	Uncertainty avoidance
P.R. China*	+	–	–	–
Germany	–	+	+	+
France	+	+	–	+
Great Britain	–	+	+	–
The Netherlands	–	+	–	–
Spain	+	+	–	+
USA	–	+	+	–
Japan	+	+	+	+

* *Note*: The values for the P.R. China are calculated on the basis of other Confucian-influenced societies, such as Singapore, Taiwan, Korea and Hong Kong, matched with my own observations.

level. It depends on the people in power and their 'cultural layout'. This remark will help to avoid oversimplification and leads us to the core of the problem, the individual human factor, or target of human resource strategies.

THE FOUR CULTURAL DIMENSIONS: STRENGTHS AND NON-STRENGTHS

The persistence of the Chinese values, their potentials and their limitations, derive from the consistency of the Daoist world-view with the perspective of everyday village life. Daoism has, however, a limited concept of change. Change is cyclical, not evolutionary. Together with the linear thinking of Confucianism, with its highly formal, ruling-class rituals and its strong conservative traits, both world-views have a clearly static element. Following is a portrayal of the four dimensions focused on the Chinese values, their strengths and potentials, and non-strengths or limitations.

The First Dimension: Hierarchy and Equality

Summary Statement

The societal system in China is characterized by a strict hierarchy based upon a large power distance. Chinese life is dominated by the family with power structures of authoritarian, partly despotic harshness. However, within the given power set-up, Chinese have a pronounced need for harmony in a hierarchy to balance social inequalities. Connections (*guanxi*), dealing well with people, and education, can serve to bridge the power distance.

Strengths/Potentials

The social arrangement based upon hierarchy and a large power distance with a clear commanding structure enables rapid decision-making, striking power, and clear directive authority. In the past, amazing organizational feats have been accomplished with the concentration of all these powers.

Maintaining relations with people, called 'connections' (*guanxi*), is needed to ease the power distance. It is the basis for decision-making. The Chinese version of 'It's not what you know, it's whom you know', helps speed or even enables success. The skilled, flexible playing in the network of mutual connections is tantamount to survival – and enjoyable for the Chinese as well.

Curiosity and zeal for learning has been, and continues to be, an attitude transcending power distance in China. In today's world, the value of education in contributing to the modernization of the country is highly valued. Education goes hand-in-hand with upward social mobility for the individual.

Non-Strengths/Limitations

The Chinese have a distinct fear of authority, which is mirrored in the arrogance of the powerful. The power distance is, on the one hand, politically paralyzing so that decentralization and delegation of authority are difficult to accomplish. On the other hand, the absence of power structures fosters chaotic tendencies.

Individual thinking and responsibility are often discouraged. Rules and regulations are habitually and forcibly observed. If subordinates become involved, negotiations can become nerve-racking as a result of a tedious, drawn-out decision-making process.

Privileges are often based upon rank and not upon performance of the individual, so that a pronounced jealousy exists against the successful if privileges are the result of individual performance.

The Second Dimension: Individuality and Group Orientation

Summary Statement

China is still an agrarian society depending on collective structures for survival. The traditional structures were reinforced and overlaid by those of socialism. Individualization such as in Western societies has never taken place in China. When an outsider looks at the groups, all members appear to act and think similarly. This is illusory. Actually, the group fosters internal competition and egoist behaviour. It shows up as competition outside the clans, among families and the living and working unit (*danwei*). *Danwei*-egoism is an expression of this specific survival strategy.

Strengths/Potentials

The group-oriented *danwei* as a living and working unit offered, until now, protection and security, such as job security, guaranteed housing, medical insurance, and social security benefits. In this area big changes can be expected, at least in the modernized cities of the coastal area of China. *The danwei* functioned to politically and socially stabilize society. It enabled the bureaucracy to mobilize large masses of people quickly and effectively in mass campaigns. This will continue in the traditional areas and for mass compaigns for reforestation and building infrastructure.

Non-Strengths/Limitations

The *danwei*, however, also shelters, strongly conservative elements which especially affect economics. The values and actions of the individual are hampered in decision-making. People count as part of a social unit, and must always show consideration for family ties. The development of a personal profile is hindered and undesirable. Personal professional choice and individual career planning are difficult. Due to this constriction, little inclination or possibility to change employment exist, and the recruitment of workers for private enterprises is difficult.

Although the Chinese are hard workers and decidedly utilitarian, if the possibility for personal or family success is evident, they show only little initiative to work for the common good above that of their own *danwei*, clan, or family.

Snooping to discover another's personal political conviction, strong social pressure to conform, uncooperative and inconsiderate behaviour, jealousy of another's success or envy of the successful, and denunciation, are virtues and are all essential parts of the Chinese day-to-day existence. That which helps me survive is good, is the maxim.

The Third Dimension: Masculinity and Femininity

Summary Statement

China is a patriarchal, seniority-oriented society of men, in which the masculine behaviour nonetheless appears soft and avoids open confrontation. In the West, such behaviour is often interpreted as cowardly.

Strengths/Potentials

Restraint, the ability to give way, and friendliness are markedly masculine values. Physical strength is relative. Chinese have a pronounced need for harmony; conflicts are dealt with internally. Socialism has enabled the break-through for the equality of the sexes, though women in leadership positions are not highly valued and hardly promoted or supported. In the private sphere, however, equality of men and women is seriously strived after.

Negotiations and decision-making are not carried out under pressure of time; time is usually an ally not an enemy – and – time is life, not only money. The process of negotiations and decision-making is generally open. As the Chinese practise a holistic and intuitive thinking in networks, contradictions and conflicts are dealt with passively and according to the situation.

The formation of good, harmonic personal relationships is more important than subject orientation. Connection (*guanxi*) is a behavioural trait practised by men that includes women in leading positions as well.

Non-Strengths/Limitations

Chinese hardly ever employ a linear target orientation toward a single object-ive, but rather much more of an orientation toward a target area. Analytical, rational, linear, and causal thinking – typically associated with masculinity for Westerners – is little noticeable with the Chinese.

They have no open 'dispute culture'. Conflicts are not publicly dealt with, because of the importance of face preservation, and the Chinese have no love or lust for crusades.

Danwei-allegiance and *guanxi* ensure that nepotism and corruption has always had an ideally fertile soil in China.

The Fourth Dimension: Flexibility and Security – Uncertainty Avoidance

Statement

In history until today, the Chinese society has been confronted with ambiguous and vague situations. The Chinese world-view and value system, on the one hand, were formed and influenced by political despotism and bureaucratic highhandedness; on the other hand, natural disasters and famines posed a constant threat to society.

Strengths/Potentials

Chinese use several approaches to deal with uncertainties. Strategic thinking, long-term orientation and flexibility is the Chinese answer to uncertainty in order to gain security. Because of their strategic thinking, they have a distinct acceptance for approximate solutions, multiple goal orientation and flexible planning to anticipate change. They are not threatened by ambiguous situations and consequently do not react with stress to them. Their pragmatism and utilitarianism serve as survival strategies, influencing their working style and indirect approach in relationships. Chinese are decidedly pragmatic. That which is useful is also good. Deng Xiaoping with his quip, 'It is unimportant whether the cat is black or white, most important is that it catches mice', gives an outstanding example of this trait.

Non-Strengths/Limitations

The dimension of flexibility and security, measured as uncertainty avoidance, encompasses aspects of Chinese behaviour, conflicting heavily with the values of some Westerners, especially with the Germans.

For the Chinese, progress in science and daily life are achieved through trial and error, rather than logic and linear planning for the future. Orientation to the present and a tendency toward chaotic and spontaneous behaviour is not uncommon. Interruptions while working are always welcome. Chinese have little sense for precision, or quality control, and nor do they monitor progress.

The Chinese have no predilection toward fidelity of principle; but instead a definite tendency toward letting things go undone, toward sloppiness, toward impatience and the development of unrealistic expectations. Due to their pragmatism they are action-oriented, which means that only things in temporally close proximity are accomplished. These are non-strengths that contradict strengths the Germans hold dearest. Here lies the biggest potential for clashes. The concept of *BrainStyles*® can lead us to the heart of this potential problem and poses alternatives and possible resolutions.

THE BASIS FOR DECISION-MAKING: CULTURAL DIMENSIONS AND *BRAINSTYLES*®

The four cultural dimensions enable us to locate and predict possible conflicts as well as synergies in the specific cultural and corporate environments. It seems that conflicts with Germans are inevitable because Germans and Chinese, in contrast to others, differ in all four cultural dimensions, as shown in Table 13.1. Conflicts arise most strongly from inarticulated expectations of the partners involved concerning work, family, and relationships, especially when making decisions and giving judgments. Here values of the two cultures are most divided. Are there possible synergies?

Culture and brain-based abilities can play a decisive role in the success or the failure of any collaboration, not only the Chinese–German, but within and among all partnerships and groups with a common goal. In fact, people differ distinctly in their brain-processing of new situations and unfamiliar events in contrast to learned or routine behaviour. The initial reaction is largely a result of the individual *brainspeed*, i.e., how the brain 'hardware' functions to process information between the left and the right hemisphere of the brain. Miller (1997) calls this thinking ability the specific '*brainstyle*' of a person. The following compilation is based on her publication *BrainStyles*[TM]: *Change Your Life Without Changing Who You Are*[SM]. [Note: All *BrainStyles*[TM] material is used with permission of the author and *BrainStyles, Inc.* Dallas, Texas, USA. *www.brain-styles.com*.]

A *Brainstyle* describes a person's natural and most efficient way to think through information, specifically *new* information when making decisions in the cerebral cortex. The ancient Chinese differentiation between Yang and Yin applied to the human brain suggests that:

- *The left hemisphere (Yang)* is the logical side: it speaks, processes data, evaluates, analyzes differences, recognizes literal information or facts, creates structure and is aware of time and measurement. 'Left-brained' activities are talking, setting measurable goals, sequential planning, measuring and noting differences.
- *The right hemisphere (Yin)* is the intuitive side: it creates images, processes senses, symbolizes, sees similarities, is spontaneous, and has *no* time or measures. 'Right-brained' activities include our awareness of emotions, imagining or speculating, visualizing, empathizing and storing experience.

A *brainstyle* can be determined when new or unfamiliar events occur. Defining our natural, genetically determined, *brainstyle*, or *core strength*, can bring clarity and focus to self-definition and what gifts and limitations can provide in career and interactions. Because a *brainstyle* defines the most personal and comfortable way for you to think, it can serve as the foundation for self-esteem. Even though you do not choose how your brain functions, by focusing on your natural gifts you can realize unlimited achievements in areas which your brain-processing supports. A *brainstyle*, therefore, defines you at your best. Knowing what *brainstyle* you are can be your guide to manage daily encounters at home and at work.

Brainstyles show up at moments when decisions are to be made, the times of greatest stress and of real challenge, not only in China. Further, Miller (1997) observes that *brainstyle* always shows up as a pattern of strength over time. These *brainstyle* strengths and non-strengths, misnamed weaknesses, can be useful in dealing with people of differing *brainstyles*. Simply put, a non-strength is another *brainstyle*'s strength. Accepting these differences unfolds a natural process of accepting yourself and others on a neutral level. This differentiation is especially useful in an intercultural context with a parallel premise: namely that there are no good nor bad culturally-related behaviours, only cultural differences when making decisions or judgments.

A *BrainStyle Inventory*® has been designed and validated which defines an individual's *brainstyle*.

THE FOUR PATTERNS OF *BRAINSTYLES*™: THEIR STRENGTHS AND NON-STRENGTHS

The first *brainstyle* is the KNOWER™, defined as a person who accesses the upper left brain first, fastest and most easily. *The Knower's primary strength is making logical, unemotional decisions or reaching clear conclusions quickly, based on facts, usually in a very impersonal way.* Knowers are quick at being definite and staying with a decision on a new subject. This *brainstyle* is good at seeing cause–effect relationships between unrelated things. Knowers are excellent at directly addressing issues with the least amount of emotion, worry or regret. They are clear and logical communicators, do best with structure and not as well with people. Knowers are clear on their goal. They want control in order to deliver results. They appear inflexible. Knowers use information sparingly, yet are often verbal, articulate, and persuasive. They rarely express strong feelings or sentiments, and form few close personal relationships. For them, personal relationship must have a purpose, most often a network of business contacts. They excel at careers that require precision, condensation, structure, focus, and directing the action. Often having an aptitude in foresight, mature Knowers can spot trends quickly, and perform analysis at lightning speed to define a logical future.

Non-strengths for Knowers include expressing strong feelings quickly, and making relationships with many. They are rarely seen as tolerant and accepting, open-ended or nonjudgmental, diplomatic, subtle, or tactful. The act of delegation as well as collaboration, both of which require trust and release of control, a basic skill to managing people and running a project, are non-strengths for Knowers. A Knower prefers to work and decide alone. They hate ambiguity or handling vague and abstract tasks, where there is no clear structure and no one is in charge, with no rules to follow. They seldom do more than one thing at a time, nor use random or illogical associations to create new solutions. They focus. Knowers are not seen by others as optimistic. They can be intolerant and impatient when dealing with others.

The second *brainstyle* is the CONCILIATOR^{TM}, defined as a person whose *primary strength is to access the right brain first, fastest and easiest to look for harmony everywhere*. Conciliators are naturals at overcoming distrust and hostility by verbally bonding, touching, or making eye contact. Their natural strengths include spontaneity, playfulness, being imaginative, feeling deeply and showing it to others. Emotional and intuitive responses, knowledge of relationships, conviction and passion about things and ideas are their strengths. Because of this, Conciliators tend to personalize information and react quickly with feelings, often mistaking these quick responses for decisions, especially in interpersonal situations. They can 'read' people and, when using their gifts for others, are builders of consensus, drawing from their particular gift of empathy. This makes caretaking easier for them than setting limits or working through conflicts. Their conciliating is rooted in heightened sensitivities. The Conciliator brings meaning, personal dedication, and commitment to the job by staying in touch with people, making long-term company goals achievable as well as personal for themselves and their people. Conciliators are excellent at project management. It is, however, essential that the overall direction, the mission, the vision and the priorities are clear for the Conciliator to implement. If not, a Conciliator may not be very helpful. Delegation is a matter of trust for the Conciliator. Conciliators associate ideas, brainstorming or generating imaginative options rather than using the logic of cause and effect, more natural for those with faster access to the left brain. They learn by teaching and from experience and their rapid interpretations about experience. They follow the Daoist saying, that 'the way is the aim', discovering the goal along the way.

When it comes to business, by definition a breeding ground for conflict, change, and quick and logical decision-making (left-brain strengths), the *Conciliator's non-strengths* appear. These include focus, setting priorities, defining structure, getting things organized in a sequence and keeping them organized, time awareness, routine, following rules, saying no, responding coolly, objectively, or neutrally. They imagine alternatives, but strategical thinking based on logic and structure is their non-strength. Most Conciliators hate conflict, because it involves discomfort, disharmony, and new and final decisions. This is especially true when this *brainstyle* is under time pressure. Conciliators need time to 'think about it' in order to commit instead of just react. Their natural gift is people-building (inspiration, support, team-building) rather than confrontation and the creation of a new direction.

The third *brainstyle* is the CONCEPTOR^{TM}. The gift of this *brainstyle* is to invent, create and make breakthroughs in new areas. *Foresight and creating mental images that redefine reality is the dominant strength*. Information is collected, exchanged and processed by both right-brain intuition, imagination, sensitivity and passion, combined with left-brain logic and analysis. The Conceptor sees patterns, themes, or underlying concepts, associates ideas randomly and derives decisions from a blend of reasons and feelings, which often seems illogical to other *brainstyles*. The human factor is always part of the process of their decision-making, yet most develop relationships over time without the immediate comfort of the Conciliator with others. Conceptors set up strategies while considering limits, test fantasies for practicality, yet can easily redecide. For these reasons, they are most open to redirection and real change. They have clear priorities for their ideas and seek practical application for them in order to provide new, previously unseen possibilities. Achievement is most important for Conceptors. They are best with chaos, undefined and ambiguous situations. Conceptors can be, when experienced and mature, inspirational visionaries. They are best in the beginning of things, worst after the project is developed and needs maintenance or nurturing. In fact, their strengths do not predict success, because the *non-strengths of the Conceptors* are in collecting all the facts, assessing the details, acting or performing evenly, and following through the plans. They store only those details that support the concepts they see as important. Organizing a project into a step-by-step process, routine and stability are punishments for Conceptors.

The forth *brainstyle* is the DELIBERATOR™ with three major groups within this *brainstyle*. The more typical Deliberator, with the left–right brain balanced, can be called the Diplomatic or Steady One, with general analytical strength; the right-sided Deliberator, The Explorer; and the left-sided Deliberator, The Wizard. These are persons whose *primary strength is to assess things first or quickly, to be cautious, thorough or methodical in making decisions, which takes more time than with other brainstyles*. They compare A to B, seeing what is wrong, missing or incomplete. They store information in mental order. They often seek perfection in life and relationships, naturally establishing standards. Deliberators love challenges in learning, and are the original Renaissance Man, trying to be good in everything based directly on the variety of their brain access. Overall, all three types of Deliberators first look inward to their memory, or what they have learned or experienced previously. They then apply logic, reason and facts, and sort through the specifics. Depending on access to the right hemisphere, there is a delay in adding intuition or feelings to their conclusions. Deliberators fit best in situations where calm and incremental change is desired. Good at establishing effective plans, routines, and procedures to bring stability, they want to organize and improve things, plan and set up a system, resulting in high standards for the way things 'should be'. They strive for perfection. Their talent is to see the uniqueness in things, the details, the steps. They first look at the pieces, then become aware of the whole. Environment is especially important to them. All tend to perfection in the things they care most about. Deliberators tend to look and sound 'professional' because they think before they speak. They respect tradition or they take it into account in order to innovate. Quality and style are important. Under stress, they tend to get quiet and organized, and appear more in control of themselves. In decision-making, they are quick if the decision has been made previously or if it is based upon a known process. Otherwise, Deliberators delay decision-making. They are the ones most likely to make and keep commitments over the long haul. Values, which involve previous, often emotional decisions, are central in the lives of this *brainstyle*. When values clash, relationships are difficult to form or continue.

The *non-strength of the Deliberator is vision or foresight*. Deliberators do not invent; they innovate to improve solutions that already exist. In summary, focus, quick decisions or generating multiple answers to a problem, flexibility after deciding, reformulation and setting of new priorities in new situations quickly are their non-strengths, as well as confrontation, conflict and open expression of feelings.

CULTURE AND *BRAINSTYLES*™ IN A GERMAN–CHINESE CONTEXT

Because of my familiarity with the German and Chinese Cultures, the concepts of Cultural Dimensions will be synthesized with *The BrainStyles System*® within these two cultures in order to offer new options for human resource strategies by Europeans, especially Germans in China. Based upon the fact that the two cultures differ in all of the four cultural dimensions, it is postulated that they differ also fundamentally in their predominant *brainstyles*. What is generally called 'national characteristics' can now be traced back to differences in predominant or prevailing *brainstyles*. This implies that these 'national characteristics' cannot be changed in the short term, because they are developed and rooted in the genetic hardware, the brain, perhaps of the favoured majority of that population. *Miller (1997) stresses that a person can only have one brainstyle and that decision-making is the crucial fact for the differentiation of the brainstyles.* Therefore, a focus of this chapter is whether Germans and Chinese differ in decision-making, and if so, how they differ. This is not a comparison of cultures or evaluation of either, rather it is an exploration of how the strengths and non-strengths of the two highly diverse cultures might complement one another for mutual benefit and the greater good of all.

In decision-making, clashes between the two cultures are inevitable. Germans make decisions based on facts and logic; they want results, precision, and control, based on meticulous planning and timing. This is their left-brained strength. These strengths are in direct conflict with the Chinese right-brained strengths, their thinking in networks, their indirect manner of dialogue and their situational flexibility. For Germans, this Chinese behaviour exhibits an undesirable lack of logic, unaware of how these actions are based on the Chinese uncertainty avoidance. To the German, whose strong uncertainty avoidance predominates, the Chinese react with a lack of understanding and appreciation. Decision-making related to this cultural dimension leads to the most frequent and heavy clashes.

Both cultures strive for security – but in different ways. Chinese consider long-term orientation and flexibility as the appropriate means to deal with uncertainties, embedded in a solid social hierarchy, which relies on large power distance. Germans, however, find their security in meticulous planning with precise short-term results. Rules, regulations, routine, and structures are set up to guarantee equal treatment of the social partners in a flat hierarchy. For the Germans, the Chinese strength of flexibility destroys focus and leads to chaos, whereas for the Chinese, the German strengths of precision and planning inhibit change and spontaneity and lead to unnecessary formality and rigidity.

Although Germans and Chinese have a similar work ethic – each lives to work and not vice versa – their working style is very different. Because of the polychronic working style, doing many things simultaneously (flexibility), the Chinese appear to be continually and terribly busy with a slight tendency towards chaos and waste of time and energy. In contrast the Germans, Northern Europeans and Americans have a monochronic work style with a stronger focus on security. By virtue of fragmentation and compartmentalization, they like to do things sequentially. Germans in particular appear to do so with a certain stiffness and rigidity in executing plans.

Chinese criticize Germans for their directness in dealing with conflicts. Germans criticize Chinese for their lack of awareness of time constraints and efficiency, quality consciousness, and therefore quality control. Germans point out a lack of precision and reliability together with a lack of openness in dealing with conflicts of the Chinese. Above all, Germans are extremely stressed by the ambiguous situation of Chinese rules and regulations, because they cannot assess the unfathomable bureaucratic maze. Negotiations, coupled with changing partners of unclear competence in decision-making, prove irritating and lead to an assessment that the Chinese are underhanded and insincere.

Considering culture in left and right brain terms, the orientation toward short-term results and the impatience of Westerners in general reflects their left-brain strengths, which seem to destroy the Asian need for harmony, a right-brain strength. In addition, Germans do not understand the Chinese long-term strategic thinking, based upon intuition and building good personal relationships (*guanxi*) as key factors in decision-making. This is grounded in traditions of group orientation, a 'feminine' orientation and a right-brained strength, mainly ignored by Westerners, who are primarily focused on individuality, a 'masculine', left-brained value. Chinese associate this with personal coldness.

In problem solving, Chinese do not express conflict openly, whether about a task or a relationship. The smooth surface, *face*, must be outwardly maintained. Readiness and ability to compromise or to keep harmony is paramount, based on values for right-brained (feminine or Yin) strengths, whereas the Germans, according to their 'barbarian' tradition, quarrel and will 'lose face' shamelessly even in public (a Yang or masculine approach).

Applying the terminology of *BrainStyles*™, as a working hypothesis, it seems that Germans in general belong to the left-brained KNOWER *brainstyle*. Germans have the lowest tolerance for ambiguity and make decisions based on facts, not on feelings or connectedness. They take little risk in business. In projects, the common approach is to prefer all or nothing, A or B, with an action-orientation grounded in confident belief in their capabilities. In contrast are the Chinese. They would seem to fit most readily with the description of the right-brained Conciliators, with a greater reliance on situational cues, signals and gestures, drawing most on their social network, making decisions based on relationships and interconnectedness, valuing harmony, imaginative and spontaneous options. They also seem to take if not a positive outlook on life, at least an acceptance of fate, in contrast to the 'gloomy Germans'.

USING STRENGTHS AND NON-STRENGTHS IN HUMAN RESOURCE STRATEGIES

As Miller (1997) shows, the concept of *BrainStyles*™ as a philosophy of mutual respect has proved to be very helpful in maximizing the capacities within numerous companies. Further studies substantiate the premise that 'single *brainstyle*' enterprises do not realize the results that synergy produces. Given these results, applications might also be beneficial in an intercultural context. Starting with the *BrainStyle Inventory*® to assess the human resources available, the four cultural dimensions provide the background from which to choose the right partners for a project. Determining available strengths and non-strengths with the principle that you cannot change people, takes advantage of individual abilities exactly where they are. Respect is fundamental, and personal and professional complements are sought. The focus becomes one of win–win for both cultures and the individuals or teams involved when the detrimental effect of struggling with 'weaknesses' is shifted. As a consequence, no longer are left-brain jobs assigned to right-brained groups or persons.

Miller (1997) gives some tips for pairings and their possibilities. Most interesting in this context is the *Knower–Conciliator Pair*. The German Knower and the Chinese Conciliator represent a marriage of opposites, where possibilities for disasters and successes are given. Problems can be prevented with a model Miller calls a *Strengths Contract*. When opposites are involved, the relationship must be managed continuously. Conciliators' indirect tactics assume that the other should understand, but the stormy Knower can be brutally open and judgmental, then withdrawn, which is punishing to the Conciliator. Both partners should accept that Knowers are best at managing the tasks, while Conciliators manage the relationship. This right-brained gift will often go unnoticed by the Knower. Time-outs will help to settle things down. Human Resource consultation can assist both Chinese and Germans to recognize that they cannot change one another, but as collaborators they can produce remarkable synergistic outcomes. For example, using the strengths of each side in a conscious way, the German strengths in production, engineering, logistics, and linear systems, which depend upon precision, reliability and quality control, might combine with the Chinese strengths in marketing and service, flexibility, relationships, and social networking to realize holistic results.

CONSEQUENCES FOR A HUMAN RESOURCE STRATEGY

Facilitating the process of cultural and corporate productivity as well as human development are the key concerns to direct a human resource strategy. Two factors have to be taken into account. One factor is the external cultural or corporate environment, the other factor is the internal or personal strengths and non-strengths to cope with the new environment. Both factors must be considered when defining a human resource strategy.

Culturally defined behaviour is learned and commonly agreed to by the respective society. It can be traced back to the four dimensions of values for decision-making. Culture is largely a social reaction to the natural environment, developed over time. *Brainstyles* are genetically fixed, a natural product of the individual brain speed, or thinking ability. It manifests itself in four general patterns of individual behaviour, living in that defined cultural or corporate environment. Although the similarities and complements of the four cultural dimensions with the four *brainstyles* are obvious, it remains a working hypothesis that predominating *brainstyles* are the cause of cultural differences. Culture is learned, *brainstyles* cannot be learned. Therefore, the conclusion that Miller suggests is to create corporate cultures in which differences are not only appreciated but leveraged.

For selecting personnel, the four cultural dimensions along with the individual *brainstyle* can predict where the clashes and synergies will occur.

Intercultural conflicts can be minimized by knowing the underlying values; interpersonal conflicts can be minimized by knowing the underlying *brainstyle*. Both are basic approaches to family, work and relationships recognized when making decisions, and have a common denominator. They require the willingness of a person to get more aware of himself or herself. Moreover, successful intercultural management is not a one-time-event, it is a process of constant self-examination if true understanding and acceptance of the other cultural or corporate identity is the goal. Rational and emotional, left and right-brained demands must be brought into balance, which requires commitment to a goal larger than the sum of the parts.

Incorporation into the new cultural or corporate environment will be eased through an unromantic view of the job ahead, openness, the readiness to accept more than one solution for every question, stress tolerance, and self-motivation in dealing with isolation and estrangement, but equally through curiosity for the unknown. Without a sound preparation, the stay abroad can be like a voyage with a Titanic ticket, steering into the dark towards the tip of the iceberg, while the real and dangerous clashes lure under water. Awareness training and the development of communication skills can bring clarity and reduce (unrealistic) mutual expectations in order to deal with another in an intercultural and corporate environment more productively and harmoniously.

Bibliography

Bond, M. H. and Hwang, K. K. (1995) *The Social Psychology of Chinese People* (Hong Kong Oxford, New York).
Capra, F. (1987) *Das neue Denken – Die Entstehung eines ganzheitlichen Weltbildes im Spannungsfeld zwischen Naturwissenschaft und Mystik* [*Uncommon Wisdom. Conversations with Remarkable People*] (Bern, München, and Wien: Scherz Verlag).
China Spotlights Series (1984) *In the Mansion of Confucius' Descendants* – An Oral History by Kong Demao and Ke Lan (Beijing: Beijing University Press).
Chung Tsai Chih (1992) *The Sayings of Lao Zi – The Silence of the Wise* (Singapore: Asiapac).

Chung Tsai Chih (1994) *The Sayings of Confucius – The Message of the Benevolent* (Singapore: Asiapac).

Clarke, J. J. (ed.) (1995) *C. G. Jung – Jung on the East* (London: Routledge).

Colegrave, S. (1984) *Yin und Yang – Die Kräfte des Weiblichen und Männlichen* (Frankfurt am Main: Fischer).

Csikszentmihalyi, M. (1990) *Flow: The Psychology of Optimal Experience* (New York: Doubleday).

Farson, R. (1996) *Management of the Absurd* (New York: Simon & Schuster).

Fu Meirong (1999) 'Confucian Way', *China International Business*, 143 (June), p. 42.

Gazzaniga, M. (1992) *Nature's Mind: The Biological Roots of Thinking, Emotions, Sexuality, Language, and Intelligence* (New York: Basic Books).

Hall, E. T. (1983) *The Dance of Life – The other Dimension of Time* (New York: Anchor Books, Doubleday).

Hamer, D. and Copeland, P. (1998) *Living With Our Genes: Why They Matter More Than You Think* (New York: Doubleday).

Hammond, S. A. (1996) *The Thin Book of Appreciative Inquiry* (Plano: Kodiak Consulting).

Hofstede, G. (1991) *Cultures and Organizations: Software of the Mind. Intercultural Cooperation and its Importance for Survival* (New York: McGraw-Hill).

Hofstede, G. and Bond, M. H. (1984) 'Hofstede's Culture Dimensions: An Independent Validation Using Rokeach's Value System', *Journal of Cross-Cultural Psychology*, 4, pp. 417–33.

Huntington, S. P. (1996) *The Clash of Civilizations and the Remaking of World Order* (New York: Simon & Schuster).

Lin Yutang (1938) *The Wisdom of Confucius* (New York: Random House).

Lord, R. (1996) *Culture Shock – Germany* (Portland, Oregon: Graphics Arts Center Publishing Company).

Miller, M. (1997) *BrainStyles*™: *Change Your Life Without Changing Who You Are*ˢᴹ (New York: Simon & Schuster).

Pomfred, J. (1999) 'China Aides Reveal Wave of Crime and Corruption', *Herald Tribune*, Hong Kong, 11 March, pp. 1, 12.

Sun Zi (1995) *The Art of War*, with commentaries (Beijing: Youth Press).

Wang Jian Guang (1990) *Westerners Through Chinese Eyes* (Beijing: Academic Press).

Wang Xuanming, Sui Yun (1998) *Sunzi's Art of War* (Singapore: Asiapac).

Weggel, O. (1989) *Die Asiaten. Gesellschaftsordnungen, Wirtschaftssysteme, Denkformen, Glaubensweisen, Alltagsleben, Verhaltensstile* (München: C. H. Beck).

Wilhelm, R. (1948) *Laotse – Tao te king* (Düsseldorf/Köln, Ludwig) (new edition 1972).

Wilhelm, R. (1950) *Kungfutse – Gespräche, Lun Yü* (Düsseldorf/Köln: Ludwig) (new edition 1972).

Wittfogel, K. A. (1932) *Die natürlichen Ursachen der Wirtschaftsgeschichte*, Archiv für Sozialwissenschaften und Sozialpolitik, Band 67, Hefte 4,5,6 (Tübingen) (new edition 1970, Frankfurt am Main: Junius-Drucke).

Wittfogel, K. A. (1962) *Die orientalische Despotie* (Frankfurt am Main: Dunghold).

Zeidenitz, S. and Barkow, B. (1993) *The Xenophobe's Guide to the Germans* (West Sussex: Ravette Publishing).

Index